# The Moron at the End of This Book

## Short Stories from a Life, well, lived.

D0141094

Andrew Couch

ISBN: 978-1-960207-69-2 - Paperback
ISBN: 978-1-960207-70-8 - Ebook

Book Design by HMDpublishing

*This book is dedicated to the vast majority of humanity - the dead.*

*Far too much has been written about great men and not nearly enough about morons.*

**Tyrion Lannister – Game of Thrones**

# Contents

# Introduction

First off, I'll warn you – by the time you reach the end of this book, you will have encountered more than one moron. Admitting to such a thing is not as deleterious to the self as it may sound. I would submit, like the word ignorant, moron is not exclusively pejorative in nature. It's obviously not great, but when not willful, being ignorant simply means one is operating without all the facts.

Moron, from the Greek word "Moros," meaning dull or foolish, is a word whose connotation has drifted wildly over the past 100 years, sliding from a profoundly flawed medical term to a popular but mild put-down. I'm doing my bit to help it drift a little further by suggesting it simply describes the limits of human intellect in general, rather than some failing of individual human minds. It's also a lot more fun to say than idiot, dunce, and even ignoramus.

When speaking about his own atheism, Evolutionary Biologist Richard Dawkins offered the idea that *everyone* is an atheist when it comes to most gods – meaning, for a person to believe in any single God, one must choose *not* to believe in countless others. Dawkins goes on to say that he simply pushes it one God further. In my travels, I've met many people who consider themselves "intelligent" or "smart." I'd very much like to be either of those, but often I have found the problem with the self-identified intelligent set is they tend to think everyone *else* is a moron. I think identifying as a true smarty-pants works the same way as claiming atheism; everyone else *is* a moron - I simply choose to push it one moron further. Another way of thinking about it is to consider that everyone is dull to most things, yet we're at our brightest when we admit to our dullness. This, I would argue, considering we aren't even sure how consciousness works, is the wholesale case for humanity. We're morons, each of us ignorant to more than any mind could know, clinging to one another for comfort and expertise in a world on a hard lean.

Whether or not you have the self-awareness to admit you're a moron, it's worth remembering no matter how you present yourself, there is an enormous chunk of consensus reality about which you know absolutely nothing. Personally, I've found a certain level of contentment in embracing the limits of my intelligence, particularly when I remember the following mantra:

*Be wise enough to know how dumb you are and not so dumb to think you're smart.*

In 1971, Jon Stone, a brilliant creator of children's books and entertainment, penned a story of a loveable and furry creature titled, *The Monster at the End of This Book*. Michael Smollin, the illustrator of that classic, drew a sketch of a creature known as Grover - a blue-fur-covered, spindly-armed beast with a mouth so wide it had to hinge at the back. When not found within the pages of children's books, Grover was also a well-known character from the beloved Television Program - *Sesame Street*. I imagine nearly every American kid born between the late Sixties and now has heard of and possibly watched countless hours of *Sesame Street*. If this program is news to you for some reason, yet you've found this book appealing enough to read this far, I'm equally shocked and flattered.

Whether illustrated or in puppet form, Grover sports a pear-shaped belly that appears to float above a set of legs as floppy as his gangling arms. His voice, as heard on the television program, and likely in children's heads when reading his books, carries all the sing-song qualities of a neurotic grandmother and a neighbor's ringing telephone. The premise of Stone and Smollin's work is that Grover is terrified that the person turning the page is bringing them closer to a monster, waiting at the end of the book. Grover's pleading with the reader to stop turning the page becomes increasingly desperate until the monster is revealed at the end. It's worth reading again if it's been a while since you last read it. If you've never read it, you've been dealt a shitty hand, and I'm sorry about that. Fortunately for you, there's still time.

Unfortunately for you, what you're about to read is almost nothing like that beloved classic. For one, Jon Stone was an accomplished and well-educated graduate of Yale and enjoyed a life of creative success. The author of this book is absolutely neither of those things. Unless you consider that the central character in both books is furry, loveable, somewhat gangling, and for different reasons, of course, totally afraid of the ends of their respective books, the similarities are a bit more subtle.

So, why did I choose this title and bring up a book of a similar name in the introduction? *The Monster at the end of This Book* ends with Grover feeling embarrassed for behaving so crazily and for ultimately being afraid of himself; the moron at the end of *this* book is not nearly as sorry as he should be, and unlike Grover, remains a bit fearful of himself after the big reveal. Mostly, I just like the title.

The following collection of stories is something of a mixed bag. Some of what you will read, should you choose to continue, is a travelog, without any recommendations or advice. Some of it is a prayer, but not to any specific deity and not for any reason other than my taste for the poetic structure and contemplative aspects of prayer. Some of what you will encounter is pure fiction, while most of what I will present actually happened. I'm guessing you'll know the difference between the factual and the fictitious, but if you can't tell, feel free to just go ahead and believe or disbelieve every word – it will hardly make any difference.

Also, if self-deprecation is not your flavor, now would be an excellent time to stop rough handling these pages and consider a re-gift while the book still looks new.

But before I go on about *my* stories, I'd like to pause for a beat to ask you a few questions about life.

Do you ever feel like you're playing some sort of game?
If so, are you winning?
Are you losing?
Are you even keeping score?
Is anyone?
Do you know the rules of this game?
What's the difference between the meaningful and the absurd?
Is it getting harder to tell?
What would you change if you knew the answers?
In the end, aren't we all just playing?
I've noticed
Paying close attention to the odd
And the small moments
Can give us a thing or two
To laugh about
Before we die.

In the following pages, I'll be telling you these stories for a few reasons, most of them selfish, I'd guess. But somewhere in me, I hope telling them may inspire you to tell some of your own stories.

If you're into it, I'd ask that you write down how *you* feel about this weird game, test, or whatever you perceive is happening to you. Tell a story about yourself or something you love.

Take your time with the writing and try to remember the trivial and otherwise common elements of your story to see how recounting them makes you feel. Once you've got it where you want it, feel free to send it to me so I can read it and not feel like such a schmuck for putting you through what I'm about to put you through.

Into the awkward void, we leap!

# Toast for Sisyphus

Oh, I've got reasons to be ashamed. Having performed at least one bodily function on and embarrassing myself in front of a few too many family members, I could justifiably change my name and hide forever. Mercifully, I've managed to limit those bodily functions to pissing and vomiting, and I haven't vomited or pissed on anyone in over twenty years. Other embarrassments, however, have not been so restrained by type or time. While I cringe at the thought of my past behavior, I should be much more horrified and/or humiliated by myself; I'm not for some reason. Here's hoping the following story helps you feel the same liberty from your shameful past.

Since I was very young, I've been a fan of hanging around what you might call "Old People." I liked my uncles tremendously. Spending time with my Mom's Mom was delightful. I don't have any memories of my maternal grandfather, and my dad's parents were not well and not alive for long once I came around. But I do remember one meeting with my father's father, my grandfather, Ernest Cletus Couch. No shit, that was his real name - Ernest Cletus Couch. They called him "Rockin' Ern!"

The wild patriarch of my family was a babymaker. Well, to be fair, Grandma Bridget did the heavy lifting, but Rockin' Ern obviously made a substantial contribution. 16 children were born into my dad's family, with pop coming in at lucky number 13. He was fond of saying his father was a drunk Catholic and his mother was a deaf Protestant. Before bed, Ern would ask his wife, "*Hey, Bridge, wanna go to bed or what?*" My dad referred to himself as the 13th what.

Only 13 of those children survived infancy. None are expected to survive adulthood.

It was wet, cold, grey, and mucky when my folks piled my older brother, my two older sisters, and me into the back of a car and pointed the thing to the frozen north. We lived in Mississippi; my grandfather was in a nursing home in Flint, Michigan.

I can't imagine even *wanting* to pack that group of people into a car for the 11-hour drive from Nesbit, Mississippi to Flint, Michigan, much less *doing it!* I was about 4 years old. For all I know, we all got along just fine, and no one gave anyone else any shit. That seems unlikely, though. Everyone in that car was likely to fight. My mom and dad fought as bitterly and often as my brother and oldest sister. My oldest sister still fights with just about everyone.

As for me, I was an agreeable kid, but I've always been an eavesdropper of exceptional skill (at least, that's what I tell myself). Dropping my eaves in that car wasn't hard, though. I listened intently as mom and dad talked about my grandpa the way adults often speak when children are present - as if kids aren't paying attention. The consensus was that grandpa was sick and dying and wouldn't be around much longer. At that age, my concept of death was sloppily built upon seeing insects and fish dying - sudden and easily recognizable. In my eyes, death was what happened when the body of a creature stopped moving. The broader implications, such as the terrifying concept of "forever" and what exactly happens when the moving stops, weren't as prominent on my radar then as they are now.

Anyhow, I was curious about what "sick and dying" might look like and wanted to see for myself.

I got my chance - visiting my grandfather in an "old folks" home.

Grandpa was at a table in a large room with lots of other old people in wheelchairs. Almost everyone, it seemed, was wearing white. In fact, the whole place was white; bright white walls, off-white tables, drab-white clothing, dingy-white plates, and a flat-white tile floor.

The brutal smell of that building, nearly 40 years later, has stuck with me. Every time I've encountered it since, I've been reminded of that first assault upon my senses. The air floating through the hallways and clinging to the drab sweaters of the occupants was thick with it – a sickly olfactory trainwreck of urine and disinfectant, locked in endless conflict. It did something uncomfortable to the back of my throat and made me want to stick my head out a window to prevent catching whatever the people producing it must have had.

This sharp and high-pitched odor was somewhat undercut by the warm, rounded, entirely delightful, and familiar smell of toast. A plate of it was sitting in front of my grandpa.

I've always loved the way butter and jelly mix on top of a piece of hot and crispy bread - the resulting colors, a creamy butter-yellow, also a little bit white, halted mid-melt by cold strawberry-red jelly, flecked with tiny black seeds, swirled around by a knife's edge into pools and eddies of tasty goodness on top of the crunchy slice. Even the sound of a serrated knife's edge spreading across toasted bread is charming to me. It could honestly be one of my favorite instruments.

In fact, I've had fever dreams about recording an album of experimental percussion played entirely by people eating breakfast. I hear melodies and beats; my bandmates brush their fingers rhythmically on nylon jackets and work the zippers like washboards. Crazily buttering freshly toasted bread to hold down the time, egg cracking, and spoons clinking inside full coffee cups could harmonize with the wild jacket work, while the occasional dragging of a chair across the floor could create emphasis and filler between the beats. Chaos chasing hunger, hunger chasing order, breakfast in hot pursuit of the endless task of gratification. *Chip Burnt-Toast and the buttermilks* coming to a diner near you!

We approached my grandfather mid-breakfast. I don't know exactly what I was expecting from a sick and dying man, but what I saw as the adults and older kids around me were talking with Old Granddad was honestly something I experienced quite often and without cause for alarm.

He was taking bites and munching while listening to questions and answering with his cheeks still stuffed. Only partially distracted by the delightful cadence of his teeth on toast and the false teeth of his fellow inmates as they chewed and clacked in conversation, I noticed something familiar and comforting on his face. Although it was wrinkled like a bed sheet, and his eyes seemed small and barely open, in the folds of his mouth, where his lips met his cheeks, little puddles of that glorious combination of butter, jelly, and tiny toast crumbs were forming between the bites.

I thought to myself, *I ALWAYS have butter and jelly on my face when I eat toast! My mom made me wipe it off before I left the table. And while I didn't know what being sick and dying meant, I knew how I felt. I felt great! I wasn't sick, and I wasn't dying, so how could he be? In my mind, it was decided; he was fine.*

Between granddad's colorful and rhythmic munching, my struggle with the curious whiteness and the wheelchairy-ness of the big room, begging my nose to smell more toast than piss, and a powerful fascination with what dying meant, I was totally lost in thought.

I was popped out of my little world of numb-skull ponderings by my dad, who said, "Well, say hi, boy."

I looked into my grandfather's eyes, which had so far not yet locked onto my own, and reached out to shake his wrinkly and sticky hand, saying the only thing which could possibly come out of my mouth at that moment, "You sure don't look like you're gonna die to me!"

With my small and perpetually sticky hand still in his grasp, he landed his intense yet foggy gaze on me with a sideways grin. "Hmm, now who told you I was dying?" A child-like smile squeezed a little jelly-butter swirl out of socket. As it dropped to his lap, he shifted his sarcastic gaze to my father and said, "Well, at least we know *this one* ain't the milkman's!"

And that's how it started for me. I fell in love with "old people." They just didn't seem to give a fuck, and I was hooked on that notion. Be yourself, say what you want, and eat like you mean it.

My grandfather died shortly after that. I never saw him alive again.

I no longer trust toast crumbs or jelly streaks as benchmarks for good health.

# First Communion Blues

Growing up in the Deep South, between imagination and appetite, I was a handful. The only difference between then and now is the degree to which I feel guilty for indulging either. Being raised Catholic may have something to do with that. Reconditioning my relationship with guilt seems to be a lifelong effort - one marked by resisting the mirrored-twin magnetism of doctrine and debauchery while threading the needle between madness and grace. But a middle-aged recovering Catholic banging on about his guilty conscience is old hat. Let's talk about indulgence instead.

My mother and her side of the family are devoutly Catholic. At seven-years-old, I was close. My indoctrination into the faith began in earnest with a sacrament called First Communion, which, in the life of a Catholic, is a big deal. Although the child in me has since muttered the occasional prayer, my First Communion ritual would set me on a path to become almost anything but a man of faith.

For those unfamiliar with these traditions, "Communion" is the pinnacle of a Catholic worship ceremony. Over a pile of thin, flavorless crackers and a goblet of semi-sweet wine, a priest utters an ancient, quasi-spooky incantation, transmuting it from a low-calorie snack into the actual flesh and blood of Jesus Christ. The now-holy morsel and consecrated chalice are then doled out by a priest you'd better hope is celibate, to parishioners, many of whom you may find yourself hoping are not. The gathered will then eat and drink of Jesus' flesh so Catholic man-eaters may enjoy life eternal in heaven above - sacrifice and sacrament, the cornerstones of the faith. I don't mean to mock these rituals entirely. I highlight the absurdity of this ritual to make the point that, while all faith requires leaping, some faiths need a great deal of momentum before the big jump, while others take the leap early on before the thinking engine is too heavy to clear the gap. Oh, and the faithful are expected to repeat this ritual every Sunday. Some people do it daily ... lots of leaping.

As a seven-year-old, it was creepy to consider the idea of eating Jesus, even if just a tiny bit. But the story is quite compelling when you're young and already weird. Jesus was a Luke Skywalker-type figure in my mind, and the sacrament was sold to me as something powerful, like the Force, so I was into it. In other words, my thinking engine was perfectly weighted to make an Evil Knievel-level leap of faith. But it may have been my love for the season, spring, and all that comes with it, which kept me from sticking the landing.

Springtime has always felt magical, probably because I was born in it. Shortly after my birthday, the school year would end, and the delights of goofing off all summer would be mine once more. I also knew the combination of my sister's birthday (April 11), my impending birthday (May 1), and the celebration of my First Communion would bring my grandma down for a visit.

Grandma was everyone's favorite. Just being near her filled me with joy and comfort. The daughter of Polish immigrants, and a retired nurse, she was charming, a bit strange, but overall, a very calming presence. Her sister, my great Aunt Jeanie, often came with her on these visits. She made for less relaxing company. Honestly, she gave me the creeps until I was in my twenties, when I learned more of her story and how to see the person beyond the pain. My siblings and I called her, uncharitably behind her back, of course, D.O.C. – which was short for Death On A Cracker. My room was offered-up to Aunt DOC, and I was relegated to the living room to sleep on the hide-a-bed with my grandma. I was an agreeable sort, so giving up my room to my six-foot tall and spindly great-aunt's nightly haunting, while not ideal, wasn't so bad. I was just happy not to have to share the room with her. I pictured her in there, sleepless throughout the night, unblinking in the darkness, lurking around more like Nosferatu's sister than my grandma's.

But I was nervous about sharing the bed with grandma, or anyone else for that matter. I was a bed-wetter until late in the game. Sleeping alone could be embarrassing enough; sharing a bed with someone else was an anxiety-inducing proposition, to say the least.

As always, she was heroically understanding and kind, doing her bit to help me relax about the sleeping arrangement. After a good-natured lecture on bladder management, insisting I handle my water intake and bathroom visits with a touch more precision, we agreed I could make it through the night without soaking the sheets.

Adding dry powder to my explosive enthusiasm for the season, an intoxicating element of springtime in the Southern US, was the barbeque festival - a slice of bacchanalia more deeply rooted in ancient ritual than even Catholics can muster. My dad was part of a team of guys called the "Secret Squadron," who would set up a booth at various festivals throughout the spring and summer. They spent hours making slow-smoked pork, chicken, and sausages, as well as a variety of tangy, spicy, and mildly sweet sauces. A selection of these meats would then be served to judges who would award the participants with sparkling medals and trophies with ironically happy-looking pigs on top. Several of these festivals were held throughout the region, with the big one in Memphis at the end of the spring. The atmosphere was equal parts carnival, elaborate mating ritual, and animal sacrifice, but with small rides, sugary treats, games, and all manner of craziness in place of the more overtly sacrificial or ritualistic. I loved it with all my heart, and so did our dad.

As it happened, one of these festivals took place directly across the street from our church on the day of my First Communion. Although dad didn't live with us or go to our church, he and "The Secret Squadron" would be there, cooking, drinking, and hanging out all day and night. A non-stop party was in my immediate future.

Outside the church, crisp in the spring air, the white flowers pinned to the girls' dresses were like tiny halos around the purest of hearts. Every object in sight was tickled by rays of light, glinting off the new green of healthy leaves and through fresh pine needles in the trees above. Men and boys in suits chatted aimlessly and horsed around while delicately perfumed women kissed the children and laughed with their teeth to the sun. The scene was idyllic, harmless, and unsullied by sin.

Decked out in my little suit, so close to innocence and so free from the weight of moral blemish, I marched up the church aisle to take my first bite and sip from the holy corpus. It was something of a perfect display of the small and faithful. I took the cracker gingerly, sipped a quick nip of the sickly-sweet wine, and made my way back to my seat without dropping, spilling, tripping, farting, or fucking it up in any way.

Despite the heavy significance of my sanctified snack, I was just plain hungry. No matter how you view it, a razor-thin wafer and a sip of wine just don't cut it as a meal. I knew there'd be loads of food at my dad's booth. Relieved to have the ceremony behind me, I ran across the street with my sister and our friends.

We were given paper plates filled with mountains of pulled pork next to foothills of hand-cut french fries, with crispy-fried-onions on top. Mouthwatering puddles of various barbeque sauces did their bit to cut through the salty and fatty goodness of the smoked meats. Coleslaw and potato salad rounded off the fillers, and the whole greasy affair was washed down with ice-cold Coca-Cola served in red plastic cups. Eating plate after plate, I was out of my mind.

Before I go any further, it's important to remember this is a tale from the 1980s. Parenting was a shade different then. For instance, without being harshly judged, a parent could drink heavily and socialize while their children wandered around a carnival filled with town-to-town drifters violently barking out the halitosis-scented rules of rigged games or overly enthusiastic invitations to take a spin on hastily assembled rides. My genuinely good parents, divorced and remarried as they were, were both totally occupied with drinking and socializing, leaving us free to be wild.

A popular cocktail at the time was rum and Coke. Every cup in sight was red, filled with ice, and had at least enough Coke to turn the concoction a dark, fizzy brown. For a curious young man so recently snacked on the flesh and blood of a deity, sneaking a long pull from one of these cocktails was easy to do without raising the suspicion of any nearby adults. I longed for the drink for two reasons – for one, I knew I shouldn't. That alone was sufficient motivation. Second, feeling the sweet sting of a strong rum and Coke was like receiving a clue to the opaque mystery separating the harsh world of grownups from the dreamlike world of children, tickling the throat while toggling magic levers in the mind on the way down.

Being an already rambunctious child, it would have been difficult for the increasingly inebriated adults to notice the warm buzz of intoxication creeping up on my consciousness like a vampire aunt in a dark room. Day, as it tends to do, turned to night, and I turned with it. I'd been steadily taking long sips of strong cocktails, eating multiple plates of BBQ, and spinning around on jangly carnival rides for hours. A couple members of "The Secret Squadron," laughing at the crazed little guy in the dirty suit at their feet, handed me a beer and a cigar. For their amusement, I took a long pull on the beer, a short-lived drag on the cigar, then chased the whole thing down with a coughing fit rivaled in intensity only by the rollicking laughter of the adults who watched it happen.

Exhausted from the long day and quite drunk, I stumbled into the van with my family. I was likely asleep before we drove out of the church parking lot. I don't remember getting into bed with my grandma, but I do remember waking up to the unsettling sensation of the whole house spinning sickeningly, no matter how tightly I closed my eyelids.

The gentle snoring of my grandmother, usually quite comforting, filled me with panic. Even then, so recently in Communion with my redeemer, praying to Jesus never occurred to me. I turned instead to my delightful grandma, sleeping peacefully on her side with her back facing me.

I mustered the courage to wake her. Slowly, desperate not to lose my tenuous grip on the whirling house, I reached out.

I placed my hand on her shoulder, my voice slurring, "Grandma?"

I heard the low rumble of a snore cut short as she slowly came to. "Grandma, I ... "

But before I could speak another word, I lost my grip on the spiraling house. An uncontrollable torrent of hot vomit burst from my mouth like murky river water from a dam break. I filled the space between her delicately night-gowned back and the thin mattress of the hide-a-bed with a choking, steamy mix of candy, smoked pork, french fries, barbeque sauce, rum, Coca-Cola, beer, and of course, the body and blood of our lord and savior, Jesus Christ.

A whole new mystery of the adult world was forcefully revealed by the alcohol's return journey. I had chosen a path - clearly, I wasn't cut out for a life of faith.

Ever the nurse and nurturing mother, grandma helped me out of that wild moment with sweetness and poise. Sweating, vomiting, crying, and apologizing drunkenly, I was a wreck. Her only even slightly negative comment, "It smells like beer!" landed more like a playful pinch of the cheek than the smack on the head I deserved.

Before putting us to bed at night, she always insisted we wash our hands, taking them in hers as she stood behind us at the sink. With a bar of fragrant soap, her soft, wrinkled hands would massage warm water and soap into our sticky biscuit hooks as she sang us a little wash-up tune – "oh, meoh, meoh, meoh – Oh, meoh, meoh, meoh ... " She soothed me with that charming refrain as I wept mini-wino tears into the soapy bubbles.

This same woman, despite being ripped from her slumber by a booze-barfing seven-year-old with terrible vomit actively cooling on the back of her pajamas, maintained her dignity, equanimity, and overall magnificent demeanor. She cleaned me up and put me on the toilet with a wastebasket in front of me while she changed the sheets on the bed, washed herself up, and put on a clean T-shirt. She took me back to the hide-a-bed, put the wastebasket next to me, kissed my sweaty forehead, and said, "If you're going to be sick again, try to aim for the trash can."

I'm fortunate to be dually swayed by light and darkness – angelic grandmother, heathen father. Guided by impulse, my choices are my great privilege – blindly honor the holy sacrament or tumble through bacchanalia, blinded by ecstasy. I still feel these drives somewhere in my consciousness, bickering occasionally for control over the wheel. Just as my days as a Catholic were numbered, my days as a creature in search of a full plate began taking shape.

> In phases and stages
> Memory and influence
> Blow through the mind like a crazy wind
> Leaving a little madness
> And a touch of grace
> Like blades of grass
> Remembering the wind
> So briefly
> Only to forget
> Again and again

# Halloween, 1984

Halloween 1984 is carved into my brain like the grin of a jack-o-lantern. I was five years old and much the same type of character then as I am now. Like my older brother and sisters before me and my little sisters after me, I went to a small Catholic school in an economically invisible town called Walls, Mississippi - right in the heart of the Mississippi Delta.

Our classrooms were laid out in what I later learned was an atypical setup for an elementary school. The main building, reserved for 5th through 8th graders, formed a large, L- shape. It held about seven or eight classrooms and a gymnasium which also served as a theater and lunchroom. The principal's office was tucked into a hovel in-between the classrooms and the gym, two doors down from a set of spacious bathrooms with large porcelain urinals that even a five-year-old could reach.

Separate from the main building, the classrooms for the younger pupils were housed in neat rows of mobile trailers with a few smaller structures scattered around. From above, I would imagine these trailers looked like they were waiting to be loaded with anything other than children.

The kindergarten classroom, like all the rest of the trailers, did not have a bathroom. To be granted bathroom privileges, I had to raise my hand, wait for the teacher to call on me, and ask her if I could go to the toilet. She would then make some personal value judgment to determine whether I "really" needed to go. If you were deemed worthy, she would make another kid go with you, and then two five-year-old kids would go outside by themselves, walk about 50 yards to the main building down a corridor of salt-pillar-white trailers, and enter the lower wing of the main building where the smaller and less accessible of the school's two bathrooms were located.

On one particularly windy day, just a few weeks before Halloween, I found my thoughts, much as I often find them today, overshadowed by the overwhelming need to piss as soon as humanly possible. After finally getting the teacher's attention, my urinal-bound journey was approved, and I was assigned a pee partner - a kid named David. Whether fate is cruelly intentional or benignly indifferent made no difference to a little guy minding his own business and selected at random. The two of us set out for the toilets. David didn't even need to pee.

We saw a teacher ahead of us pry open the big metal door which led into the main building. The door was difficult to use, especially on such a windy day, so David ran after it as it closed -the teacher (asshole) let it slam in our faces. I'm not great at pool or anything requiring geometry, but even as a nose-picking child, I could see that the math on David's attempt to catch and stop it from closing wasn't gonna work out. The big metal door slammed violently shut with one of his fingers still in it.

David jumped back, gripping his hand in silence. With difficulty, I opened the door and saw the upper half of my classmate's finger on the floor inside the building, lying in a small but growing dollop of blood. David quickly bent down, scooped it up with his other hand, ran to the bathroom, and promptly threw it in the toilet! I ran after him, passing another unoccupied toilet on the way, barely thinking at all about how badly I wanted to piss in it, and stopped him before he could flush it. His hand was covered in bright red blood. I told him, 'Wait here, and don't flush!' He wasn't even crying; he was just staring at his finger as the water turned increasingly pink. To this day, when I see someone panic and do something rash, I think of David's severed finger resting at the bottom of a toilet bowl.

The only person in my corner to call upon for help was the terrible sadist - whose job, so far as I could tell, was to make five-year-olds feel like garbage - our teacher. I ran back to her, bursting into the room, almost gleeful with righteous disregard for hand raising or the affront of interruption. 'David's finger just got cut off, and he threw it in the toilet!' I blurted out breathlessly, at the top of my lungs.

The teacher and I ran down the corridor together, and I was relieved to watch her struggle with the big dumb door. As soon as she was with David, she told me to run to the principal's office and tell her what was happening. I did exactly that, stopping only briefly in the big kid's bathroom on the way there to enjoy one of the most potent altered states of consciousness one can achieve without meditation or drugs, the releasing of a hard-earned and indecently delayed piss.

Of course, David survived. The principal calmly called an ambulance and sent me back to class. I passed the bathroom on the way back to our trailer and told the teacher the score. She also told me to get back to class, so I did, slowly. David's finger was likely bathed in disinfectant for as long as possible before being reattached. He did not remain a classmate for much longer. I would imagine hearing that their son's finger was severed on the trek from trailer to toilet made his parents wonder if their money might be best spent elsewhere. Having already faced a bloody finger in a toilet bowl, I figured I could handle Halloween's cardboard ghouls and quaint creepiness without even a hint of fear. It doesn't take much for a guy to be wrong about a thing like that.

Thinking about such a bizarre time and place fills me with a desire to tell you entirely too much about it. I'll fight the impulse and spare you endless details about the buildings, the play gym made from giant discarded and hand-painted multi-colored tractor tires, or that time we found a mound of adult-sized man-turds in one of the bigger ones. Rather than plow through your consciousness with images of little guys and girls with southern accents and dirty uniforms, tormenting and flirting with each other while the cotton in the neighboring fields was being mechanically harvested, I'll tell you instead about the meanest girl in my class, Scary-Sherrie!

Now, obviously, that's a made-up name. I would never have called her anything like that to her face and would not have liked it if others had either. I would also like to make a note of the fact that I will and have made up some other names here as well so as not to, by some miracle of accidental book reading, offend any of my old classmates.

Sherrie was the glue-eating variety of kid. She'd make strange animalistic sounds and was unusually violent for a five-year-old. In hindsight, I can see she was in pain and likely traumatized by being treated violently at home. My sister remembers her being bullied at school as well. This breaks my heart and reminds me how crucial it is to teach your kids, or any kids you might know, the same way my sweet mom taught me, about always being kind to people, even when they're shitty - because you never know what the fuck is going on with them when you are not around.

However, you should not let the sadness of Sherrie's life get in the way of your appreciation for the grand weirdness of what I witnessed from her so many years ago. Use that big brain of yours to separate time and tragedy, then blend them together again to appreciate the comedy of madness and know that this is not a story meant to make fun of anyone at all ... except myself, of course.

My relationship with Sherrie was not nice for me. Twice a month, I was forced to be a passenger on her bus. A girl I had a huge crush on, whose real last name was Love, was also a passenger on that bus. All I ever wanted was for Miss Love to sit next to me.

Every other Friday, my sister and I went to spend the weekend with my dad. This meant that we had to ride the dreaded bus number 5. I tried to get to the front of the bus line earlier than all the other kids in my class on those days because I was worried about having to explain to the bus driver that I usually rode with that I wouldn't be taking her bus home. For some reason, I thought it might hurt her feelings that I rode to school with her but not back. The drivers would wait outside their buses, talking to the kids and smoking cigarettes as we filed in. Our regular bus driver always came out a little late, so if I got on bus 5 early, I could dodge making eye contact with her, thus dredging the channels of pointless conflict-avoidance in my character above which I lazily float today.

As one of the first kids on board, I'd have to watch and wait for other kids to find their seats. Being a stranger on that bus, I was one of the last people anyone wanted to sit next to. It was a bit different for my sister. She was cool, and people knew it. The only other person people seemed less keen on sitting next to was Scary-Sherrie. From my window, I watched Love and Sherrie stand in line as the kids waited to board the bus. Sherrie was first, and Love was behind her. When they reached the aisle, I sent out a silent petition to baby Jesus's dad and chased it with an outpouring of goodwill meant to attract both love and Love. If you guessed that the girl I was secretly calling my girlfriend would walk past my seat shortly after Sherrie plopped down in it and sit several rows behind me, you guessed correctly.

This happened more than once. Sherrie would invariably do something horrible to me as soon as she sat down, so my unease with sitting beside her was hard-earned. She would inflict rub-burns on my arms, place hard pinches with fingernails on my skin, send pointy-toed kicks to my shins, and, on one particularly violent bus ride, when I said, "Hi Sherrie," she grabbed my hair and slammed my head into the window. Having sisters, it was burned into my mind that hitting a girl for any reason was utterly unacceptable. I wanted to explain to Sherrie that we could be friends, and I didn't care if she was wild and ate glue. I never got the chance. It never occurred to me that I could have just wrestled her a little. Live and learn. As if watching a finger get lopped off by a door weren't enough, now I had meanness and violence between myself and the candy promise of Halloween.

Yep, Sherrie was mean, strange, and, like I said, not afraid to eat a little glue. But I urge you not to judge her, or anyone else, for that.

That Halloween, each of the kids in our class was given a small pumpkin to decorate. At the front of the room, a table filled with art supplies was laid out, and we took turns picking out what we wanted.

The supplies were tame; dried macaroni, little metallic stars with sticky backs, and some pre-cut pieces of felt in the shapes of spooky eyes and witches, while some, confusingly, were in the form of pumpkins. These various, artistically questionable elements were meant to be applied with a glue whose vintage I figure only Sherrie could fully appreciate.

With middling enthusiasm, I chose some shit to paste onto my small pumpkin, rushed the job honestly, and handed the finished product over to the incomparably weird lady who was our teacher so I could go to the bathroom. Request denied. When the whole class was done (which seemed like an eternity with a full bladder, once again), we were lined up and encouraged to admire our fellow classmates' pumpkins. Sherrie was in line behind me; my palms were sweating like I was on trial.

The glued-on faces adorning our linear pumpkin patch were typical of the genre. Some attempted to look scary, while others were somewhat cubist or impressionist. A few were exceedingly cute, and of course, some looked like they'd been subjected to a half-assed effort, like mine. However, as we walked down the row of about 15 pumpkins, I stopped cold when I saw one which terrified me. It was the only pumpkin on the shelf with no glue on it. There were no pieces of macaroni, no felt, and no shitty little stars. Nothing had been added; this one had been done in relief.

The thing was staring at me with a crazed yet familiar expression. Two small and horrible eyes were bewitching and taunting me from the shelf. It was wearing a maniac's grin, crookedly torn out of the lower portion of the pumpkin, almost like it was screaming and grinning simultaneously. The nose, a simple gash just below and directly between the eyes, gave the face a sense of knowing, purposeful, and relentless meanness. But by far, the most unsettling aspect of that grisly sculpture was that it had clearly been carved by human teeth!

I was in a weird trance-like state when I heard something to my left. It was Sherrie, staring at me, making a strange sound, and laughing a little. When she knew she had my attention, she beamed a grin at me, which hit me like headlights hit a deer; that is to say, it hit me twice! Her eyes - so wild, troubled, and filled with frenetic energy, peering directly into mine - were the first flash of light, blinding, confusing, and warning me of oncoming trouble. I wasn't knocked flat until her teeth finally came into focus. Through her grin, I saw orange chunks of pumpkin flesh stuck between all four of her front teeth with what looked like bits of dry macaroni and possibly some glue thrown in for the flavor!

Her follow-up cackle, while it scared me then, makes me now appreciate her as something of a comedic genius. That kid, troubled as she must have been, understood the power of the absurd at an awfully young age and knew how useful it could be to completely disquiet one's peers. She was creative in a way far beyond the rest of us - who'd simply taken what we were given as the only option for expression - and created something almost literally soulful.

After Kindergarten, I never saw Sherrie again. Some other school, possibly not made from trailers, had taken her in. Whenever I think of her, I seriously hope she was treated kindly and given space to be as resourceful, strange, and complicated as she needed to be. Knowing what I know now about the way imaginative genius can grow out of pain like mushrooms from decay, I like to imagine her as a complex and intelligent woman, now in her forties. I picture her this time of year, in October, in her kitchen, having long outgrown her taste for glue, making pasta for someone who loves her, growling subtly, and grinning to herself for having put a little pumpkin in it.

# A Note to Shelf

In my childhood home, a magical piece of furniture occupied one side of the living room - a bar. It was a period piece, complete with all the aesthetic trappings of the late Seventies and early Eighties - amber-toned glass, polished wood veneer, a plush and pleated faux leather bar rail, and of course, a matching ice bucket. That bucket was my North Star. It was squat, brown, and leather-bound, with an inset lid that featured a polished mahogany knob in the center and a hard, white plastic-coated liner. It never leaked, and melting ice never wet the bar top or the legs of anyone's polyester slacks. There was also a sturdy yet stylish pair of silver tongs for keeping one's greasy biscuit hooks out of the ice. My interest in it, however, had nothing to do with needing a cold beverage. In fact, I approached it expecting it to be mostly empty. I came for the aroma of the thing, to marvel at its symmetry and maybe roll it around a little.

At the age of four, I was told by my father, on numerous occasions, and in no uncertain terms, not to touch it. The bar itself was somewhat off-limits to the kids in general, but fooling around with the ice bucket was particularly verboten. Looking back, I get it; kids are gross, and ice buckets are meant not to be. Dad was blind in one eye and would tell me that his one good eye was particularly good and that he would be watching me. But dad wasn't around. He wouldn't be coming back for a while, I guessed, because he and mom were tired of fighting, and he got his own place in another part of town. It was just me and the bar now, and it would soon be just me and the bucket.

I liked putting things inside of it that didn't belong. G.I. Joe men, Star Wars figurines, and a small toy pistol were frequently stored there. I occasionally brought a few of my imaginary friends along. The Munsties, I called them.

The Munsties were a colony of tiny, blue beings who lived in a corner of my room. My toys were like giant moving sculptures to them, and I would leave a few around when I had to go out. They counted on me for food and adventures. Some of them would come with me from time to time. A few brave Munsties even took a trip to meet my grandfather in Michigan. They liked being in the car as much as I did. They had real-life enemies, the small red bugs living on the air conditioning unit outside my bedroom wall. On a side note, I didn't realize those little bugs were called chiggers until I was an adult living in New York City. All my life, I had been under the impression that a "chigger" was a southern placeholder word for insect bites or itching of unknown origin. In any case, the Munsties, and what I now realize were actual chiggers, were locked in a territorial feud for control over the verdant valley of my bedroom floor.

On this particular voyage to the ice bucket, there were no Munsties, G.I. Joes, or toys. It was just me and my nose. I had taken to sniffing things regularly, almost compulsively. I sniffed everything I could: the refrigerator drawers, the dirt under stones and logs, the inside of a toolbox in the garage, or where the seatbelt lives, coiled up and ready to stretch out when you're not buckled up. These aromas were curious to me, as if I had just discovered the sense in my small body and felt its power for the first time. Every cabinet in the house had its own bouquet, depending on its function. I could smell water and cypress in the small bathroom cabinet where we kept toilet paper and the plunger. Each kitchen cabinet was different. One smelled like vitamins and plastic pill containers, another smelled like dish soap and glass, while others flooded my senses with pepper, lemon, sage, and oregano, or cereal, cardboard, Pop-Tarts, and potatoes.

Approaching the bucket led me to a cornucopia of fragrance which is still romantic to me. Located behind the bar, the smell of a stain from a dropped maraschino cherry would mix with the lingering Scotch whiskey at the bottom of a bottle cap. I would tap my fingers on the empty tin box which previously housed a bottle of Chivas Regal, and I would delight and luxuriate in the tones, aromas, and sheer rule-breaking madness of being back there at all. And, of course, there was the ice bucket.

My appreciation of the bucket transitioned from simply enjoying an exciting yet off-limits container to a sophisticated fascination with its beauty - a beauty both material and aromatic. Just sitting under the bar on a shelf, the thing looked full of potential, like a Frank Lloyd Wright home, simple, stylish, beautifully functional, yet artfully crafted. The brown leather exterior was taut, textured, and almost seamless. I tried to work out how it was done, following the stitching down one side to where it met the bottom. The material seemed to be molded to the plastic shell of the bucket's interior and delicately sewn together on one side.

The lid was its own masterpiece, as I couldn't find a single stitch on the thing. The leather simply vanished after being tucked under the white plastic of the lid. A solitary stainless-steel screw joined the plastic plate to the mahogany knob on top.

While complex, my love for the contraption tended to focus on the olfactory. I would take long pulls of its woody and smoky perfume. With the lid off, the unmistakable smells of water and clean plastic sat high above the bass notes of tobacco, wood, and warm leather. I would close the top and open it again and again just to hear the profoundly satisfying leathery pop and the accompanying whoosh of air.

After a spell of sniffing and popping the lid, I would lay the bucket on its side and roll it under my hands, noting the difference in texture between my fingertips and my palms. The pair of silver tongs would rattle around inside the bucket, like loose wire under a snare drum, slapped and played back in slow motion.

On this visit, I approached the bucket, excited to take my time with it. No dad around to shut me down or catch me meddling with the precious artifact. I could even take it down from the shelf and look at it in better light and considered bringing the empty Chivas box with me to tap on a little. I rounded the corner of the bar, and there it was – squat, round, perfect. The bar smells waved at me like a siren to a sailor. My small hands grasped the sides of the bucket, lifting it from the shelf, then lowering it to the floor. I was eager to open it, to get a whiff of its dusky yet futuristic scent.

The lid came off with the expected and delightful pop, whoosh, and rush of aroma. But once inside, my eye was met with something I did not expect. The usual sparkling silver of the tongs was muted by an object quite out of place. It was a small bit of paper folded over and tucked between the two heads of the tongs. Intrigued, I plucked it from their grip, taking note of the forethought it took to fold this paper to the exact size that would allow the tongs to hold it, just so. I was verbal but not yet able to read. I knew my alphabet but not what the letters meant when combined. The creator of this note was clearly aware of that fact, as well as several other salient facts. For one, the author knew his audience. He also knew the impact the message would have on said audience and that this audience would indeed find it. As such, the note had to communicate a simple point, but without the benefit of the written word. Like a silent movie, using body language instead of speech, this note used specific imagery to communicate something words alone could not.

I gently unfolded the note, taking a brief whiff of the easily recognizable, fine card stock from my father's office and the waxy notes of red crayon, borrowed no doubt, from my sister. I knew what it was before I even got it open all the way. It was a large, simple, red face with a furious and frowning expression. One of the eyes was drawn on the comically large side, while the other was represented by a smaller yet meaningful "X." Somehow, even the "X" seemed angry to find me there. I got the message. Carefully, I refolded the paper, tucked it back into the tongs, placed them as best as I could, roughly how I found them in the bucket, enjoying one last pop of the lid as it landed perfectly back into its home, then placed the holy object back on the fragrant bar shelf.

Later that evening, the Munsties had a community-wide laugh when I told them the story.

# A Lawn Dart
# to the Soul

In the absence of optimism for the present, I bring you stories of the past. Please don't confuse my lack of optimism
for lack of hope; there is a difference. My hope is that you're
living a full and exciting life as free from anxiety for which you
have no remedy as is possible under the circumstances.

Speaking of living a full and exciting life, I'd like to tell you
about an accident featuring a profound lack of attention to
detail. I recently managed to overfill a small pond, killing all
four of my friend and benefactor's prized koi fish and an un-
countable number of tiny mosquito fish. While I do eat animals, including fish, the death of these creatures has impacted
me in a bizarre and strangely familiar way.

The contented fish living in that pond had no reason to suspect I might do anything to harm them. Twice a year, I would
get in the water with them to clean the bottom and replant the
lilies and irises. A few years ago, I put in a small pump and a
fountain to aerate their environment, they seemed to like the
change. Feeding them was like watching history unfold - the
little fish took what they could while the bigger fish took what
they wanted.

Of course, I didn't kill these fish out of malice, but that's little consolation to me and absolutely zero consolation to them
– suffocated as they were by an overabundance of poisonous

and chlorinated city water, carelessly dumped by a guy currently telling himself, *Hey buddy, you're not a monster, you're just an idiot!*

So, let's discuss dead animals and think about injustice by
considering the following emotions – guilt, anxiety, sadness,
regret, and a dash of self-loathing for good measure. The best
way for me to do that is to think back to the summer of 1985.

I was a happy little guy at the age of six, practically bursting
at the seams with an energy I can occasionally find but for
which I am almost always searching. On one of those relent-
lessly sunny and humid summer days, my dad told my big sister
and me that he had tickets for "The Muppets, On Ice" later
that evening. What could possibly have gone wrong?

I loved Kermit the Frog, Animal the drummer, and whatever the hell Gonzo is. Kermit was my guy, though, because he's
a frog, and frogs were my absolute favorite animal. I still have
a small clay frog, the very first purchase I ever made. It rides in
our van, above the steering wheel, and has been sitting next to
a small golden Buddha and a figure of Yoda for over 35 years.

An early riser, I often ran down our long driveway to fetch
the newspaper before my mom and dad were awake. After
that, on Saturdays especially, I'd watch cartoons, sprinting to
the bathroom to brush my teeth every time a toothpaste commercial interrupted the show. Once the good shows were over,
I was outside for the rest of the day.

I was fortunate to grow up in the country, with a mix of
woods, a casually landscaped yard, large open fields, and just
enough neighbors to keep things exciting and weird. It was a
tremendous privilege to live with an endless variety of options
for an imaginative guy to spend his otherwise unoccupied time.

Like many kids of my generation, we had a set of large and
heavy pointed lawn darts. If you don't know what a lawn dart
is, take a moment to Google that phrase and keep scrolling
down until you see something that looks totally unsafe; those
are the ones we had.

For some dumb reason, I was tossing one of these things
into a shrub near the house. Leaping around like some sort

of spastic Jedi, I'd throw the dart with childish flourish, do some more leaping, then collect it from under the bush. On one crazy toss, a bizarre and weighty thud replaced the sound I expected when my projectile penetrated the wiry branches. Heavy, slightly wet, terrible - precisely the sort of sound you might hear when your life changes more than just a little bit.

Pushing back a few branches, I peered into the bush, and there it was, my faded-red dart protruding from the neck of a fat frog struggling to cross the rainbow bridge into reptile Valhalla.

My heart had never experienced such an immediate pain. Something about the inevitability of it, the howling irreversibility of what I'd just done, drained me of any access to the joy I had known only a moment before. Taking that innocent life hit me in the chest like a lawn dart made of guilt, thrown by an angry giant of my own making. I didn't know what anxiety was then, but my entire core was filled with it.

I told my parents. My mom, always the practical and compassionate type, was a great consolation, telling me not to worry and encouraging me to bury the frog under the bush. My dad, through his own conditioning, had no choice but to make fun of me for being so sensitive about the whole thing.

He knew my temperament well by that point already. Earlier that year, he discovered I had no stomach for killing things. He woke me up early in the morning and told me that not only would I be skipping school, but I would also be getting my very own rifle! After an enormous and equally greasy southern breakfast, my father, our dog, my brother, and I all made our way to a nearby field to hunt for dove.

When the first bird was shot down, I still viewed "hunting" in the abstract. I was excited to retrieve an actual bird with the dog, as we had been playing fetch with a fake one for as long as I could throw it. My dad sent me out to retrieve the bird from the dog who had run out and gently collected the fallen creature from where it landed. I called that gleeful animal and told him to "heel, sit, and drop it." Deeply satisfied, the dog did all those things. At my feet was deposited a beautiful dove with a broken neck and a dozen or so small holes in its chest. Blood and saliva blended on the wings, creating terrible threads of red and silver.

An immediate and involuntary torrent of partially digested hot-southern-breakfast burst from my mouth, landing on my favorite shoes, the poor dead bird, and an elegant field spider I'd been admiring moments before. The combination of the brutalized bird, the involuntary killing of that spider, and the vomit settling into the small Velcro buckles of my new sneakers broke my heart completely. My dad's disappointment was as clear as the sky from which the bird had been blasted. He knew right then - his youngest son would not be a hunter.

Let's return to the blazing summer heat and another dead creature breaking my heart.

Later that evening, after a day of waiting for something awful to happen - fully expecting a punishment that never came - I found myself seated in a theater between my sister and my dad. We were there to witness the crazy production of "Muppets on Ice." I was too anxious and uncomfortable to enjoy the show. I couldn't take my eyes off Kermit. He was dancing, skating, singing charming tunes, and flitting about the ice with a pig, a bear, and what looked like some freaky accountant with a giant nose. There was no shaking the feeling - I didn't deserve to be serenaded by a frog after brutally murdering one earlier in the day.

As if he knew what I was thinking, my dad snapped me out of my worried state by gently flicking one of his thick fingers into my upper arm and whispering, "Hey, who's that guy down there?"

'Which guy?' I said unconvincingly.

"That one." He said, pointing at the ice. "You know, the green one. What's his name?"

My heart was starting to pound my ribs like it wanted out. 'You mean, Kermit?'

"Yeah … Kermit. What's his last name?"

'Uh … the frog?"

"Right, the frog ... " After a pause, he gave my arm another little tap, pointing again to my guy on the ice, and said in a crazy and hushed tone, " ... he knows!"

Now, you've got to understand my dad was a joker, a wise ass of Olympic prowess. He loved crafting little craziness for us to fret over for a laugh. He was known for making up wild, improbable characters and telling stories about them. Some were genuinely terrifying, mostly they were funny, but they were all ultimately harmless and encouraged liberal use of our own imaginations to fill in the blanks.

However, looking at the overly sensitive weirdo in my skin, as I sweated and worried about why the fluids in my stomach couldn't make up their minds about how much to weigh or in which direction they might exit my body, my old man could have never guessed how deeply unsettled I was by his comment.

A break in the manic production came, and my dad gave my sister and me a few bucks each for candy, popcorn, drinks, and a souvenir. For my big sister, this was no big chore. My exposure to commerce with adults was limited to the single purchase of that small clay frog many months prior, but I felt like I could handle it. A gruff middle-aged vendor, selling toys and multicolored junk from a rectangular basket slung from his sweaty neck, eyed me with what I now recognize as disgust as I approached with an extended handful of cash. Without thinking, I immediately handed him all my money up-front and picked out two little flashlights with multicolored plastic fibers attached to their ends. One for me and one for my big sister, who was further afield getting the snacks and drinks. With every penny my dad gave me in the vendor's hands, I palmed the flashlights and turned to go, thinking our transaction to be complete. I nearly pissed myself when the vendor, in what seemed like an unnecessarily harsh tone, yelled out to me, "HEY, WAIT A SECOND!"

My heart was an unevenly loaded washing machine in my chest, rattling around like it might burst free and just keep on rattling until it ran out of juice. My guilty child's mind turned to the worst-case scenario; Kermit *DID* know what I had done and sent one of his goons to collect me! I started to run for it, hoping if I found sister on the way out the front door of the theater, she might give me the snacks so I'd have something to eat while on the run.

I was almost two steps into my escape when I heard the rest of the irritated man's sentence bang into my ears like a bird crashing into a window, "DON'T FORGET YOUR CHANGE!"

With shame and guilt climbing up my spine like monkeys on a rope, I collected the money, made my way back to my seat, and tried not to cry until I was back home and out of sight.

I sit here now, a human sculpture carved by guilt. I can still see that dying frog when I feel guilty, a giant red dart deep in its neck, struggling to breathe. The little clay frog which sits above my steering wheel reminds me to take guilt and mental anguish in stride and to be creative in how I deal with it.

Flashing forward now to the tumultuous present, when I walked outside in the calm and delightful early morning air to accompany my dog on his constitutional, I contentedly sipped my coffee and looked out at the various living things in the yard which I was responsible for keeping alive; flowers, vegetables, and, of course, the lilies and fish who occupied the pond. I was looking forward to a pleasant day of gardening.

Life had other plans for me. Those old feelings of guilt, anxiety, sadness, and regret were upon me the moment I saw the first fish floating lifelessly, belly-up and glossy-eyed. I was a little boy again, burdened with a strange weight, processing the poisoned image before me. Inevitable, irreversible, a needlessly tragic betrayal of unsuspecting creatures, and of course, entirely my fault.

No amount of time spent as an adult could make a difference. None of the work I've done to craft myself into a person of strong moral character and dependability made a dent in the problem, and none of the power one imagines one has over their reactions were available to me. I was right back in the sweltering and windless humidity of my childhood, staring into the destroyed body of a creature I was meant to love. Not only had I destroyed something so beautiful, depriving my friend of fish he'd been looking after for many years, but I had also cursed those fish to an unknowable amount of suffering and anguish before dying.

One of the many blessings and curses of gardening is its simplicity. One's mind has time to drift freely or to concentrate so fully on the task at hand that almost everything else disappears. All that freedom of thought occasionally leads to a lapse in concentration. This is the first time in a long while that it resulted in the death of an animal.

In the days following the fish kill, I thought a great deal about what it means to be alive in this world. At my most cynical, life seems like a pointless exercise in organic chemistry and a game of consciousness without a rulebook. But my nihilism does not negate the need for compassion. As far as I can tell, all life on the planet is of equal value, eight-legged, flying, breathing in water, or thoughtlessly running around killing things. It gets muddy when considering predator and prey, but there is no such paradigm within our species. We are all equal in our flawed nature, flailing about on this planet, living with hope, deluded by optimism, and faced with the grim possibility that none of it has any purpose. Choosing to ignore that possible reality, being kind, seeking solidarity, and trying to live in harmony with others is what one must do if one wants others to be happy and well.

These dead fish and the memory of other creatures I have carelessly destroyed make me think of my fellow man. We are such temporary creatures, so exposed and susceptible to powers far beyond our control. In the face of this, what is preventing us from coalescing as a species?

Is "God" watching us, or perhaps aliens judging our behavior? Whether or not we are an observed species remains to be seen. Maybe the yeast in our bread or the microbes in our intestines are the observers, and someday we'll be accountable to them? Or perhaps we'll never learn the languages of the rest of the animal kingdom, and all their wisdom will remain off-limits? It seems a bold wish to desire communication between all living things when we are so poor at it within our own species. For now, our communication with other species will have to wait until we figure out how to communicate with each other, regardless of what color skin we happen to be wearing.

We are all, right now, in each other's hands, and there may well be no cosmic hand there to catch or guide us. Delicate, vulnerable, and swimming in the same waters, our ability to cooperate has taken us to the moon and could possibly take us even further. Cooperation means so much more than solving mathematical equations or complex engineering problems. Cooperation is seeing yourself in another and treating them accordingly. Cooperation is being honest about who you are and what you are willing to do. Cooperation is not something you must do but have the rare privilege of doing if you choose to. And cooperation is paying attention to what you are doing with your time and being careful not to let your mind wander too far from this moment because if you do, you might just let someone down who is counting on you.

Remember
You're not a monster
You're an idiot
And, in any case
No one of us is powerful
Without the other
And none of us is an-other
Which makes us powerful

# Fake Radio

My love for fake Radio began long before podcasting was the popular option for people who love pretending to have an audience of listeners. I've been casually talking to no one since I can remember. After recognizing the power of music and story, I recorded my first show in the summer of 1991; I was twelve.

To properly share that story with you, I think it might be helpful to discuss the obsolete technologies at the top of my personal tech heap in those days.

Let's start with the boom box. My sister and I shared a Casio radio with a tape deck capable of playing and recording over audio cassette tapes. There was a small built-in microphone on the top of the utilitarian-gray unit. Next to it was a small but sturdy telescoping antenna, a knob that would let you browse the radio waves and a rectangular window with a range of AM & FM stations along which a slim red needle would pass indicating what station you were tuned into. On the front of the radio, sandwiched between the speakers, a clear tray housed the tape you were either playing or recording over. I loved watching the mechanical gears slowly turning when it played, and more than once I tried to follow along with my eyes when I pressed the fast-forward button. I couldn't - it was blurry every time unless I blinked as fast as I could.

My favorite feature was the record function. You could tune in to a radio station and record the broadcast onto your tape deck. You typically needed blank cassettes for this purpose, but somehow (without the help of a search engine), my sister and I learned you could cover an indentation on the corner of, say, a Bon Jovi cassette with a small piece of tape, and record over the gravely wailings of an east-coast cowboy with the tunes of your choosing.

The other piece of tech which I think needs a little discussion is the landline-based telephone. If memory serves, we had four telephones in our home. One in the dining room attached to the answering machine (which recorded messages onto its own tiny cassette tape), one in the kitchen with a cord about 15 feet long for semi-private conversations, one in my parent's bedroom, and another in my sister's room (also with a long cord). I could be wrong about this, but it hardly matters. Those phones were eventually replaced with cordless ones. Then the answering machine went away with the phone company housing messages in the air somewhere. After that, I moved out, and within a few years, the whole landline operation was supplanted by cell phones, which have been going everywhere with us, riding near our genitals, for well over two decades.

The phone I remember having access to was shaped like some sort of elongated shellfish. The earpiece sat, obviously, on your ear, while the microphone which you spoke into made it all the way to your mouth; the whole design translating into a curved, mollusk-like shape which, when nestled in its cradle and its curly cable trailing like some crazy tail, gave the impression of something at rest, but with substantial action potential.

The feature on our phone that I found as remarkable then as I do now was simple: the redial button. I don't know how the phone remembered the number I had just dialed (I certainly never could), but it did, and with the press of a single button, I could immediately call the person or business I most recently dialed. Invented originally, I would guess, to ease the burden of dialing a number repeatedly when the person or business you were trying to reach greeted you with a busy signal, the redial button held a different role in my young hands: calling radio stations!

Now, if you've never listened to the radio, this may be another piece of the pre-Youtube and Spotify world which needs explanation, but I won't be the one to give it to you … just Google "All Request Hour" and you'll get the picture.

If your life experience included all these bits of technology and/or time spent listening to the radio, then please forgive me for the entirety of what I've said so far.

As I said, I used our phone's redial button to call radio stations and request songs. Later in life, I used it to make prank calls even more infuriating to my innocent victims, but that story, while funny, is not so nice.

OK, enough with the technology, I'll tell you my story.

The home where I grew up was filled with music. My older sisters and brother are musicians, my mom and stepfather met while playing instruments and singing in a church choir, and once I put the phone down and stopped pestering DJs for music or random people with dumb-ass pranks, I would eventually learn to play guitar and sing. My earliest memories are of music, specifically, my mom playing somber Catholic hymns on the piano in our home. Nearly every moment I can recall of my life is accompanied by the song or melody in my head when it happened.

When my mom and stepdad married and moved in together, I was introduced to his record collection. Until that point in my life, I had simply listened to whatever my older siblings were into; I remember lots of Rush with plenty of AC/DC and Iron Maiden tossed in for good, angry measure. On a side note, when my dad talked about the bands my sister liked, he always called them "Pontius Pilate and the Nail Drivin' Five!" I liked their music for a spell, but my stepdad's music blew it all out of the water.

He had original pressings of more than a half-dozen Beatles records, along with Jimi Hendrix, The Doors, Jefferson Airplane, Canned Heat, Simon and Garfunkel, and many other artists from the Sixties and Seventies. I learned how to work the turntable and would listen to those records over and over again. I'm now incredibly thankful to him for being so generous with those discs, and I cringe at the thought of some sticky and clumsy kid handling such delicate and rare items.

I eventually found my way to exploring the roots of that music through Robert Johnson, Muddy Waters, John Lee Hooker, Lonnie Johnson, and others. It made me appreciate the place in Mississippi where I lived for its musical heritage. Listening to the Blues eventually led me to appreciate the unequaled Soul/R&B of the Sixties and Seventies. Much of that music had also been recorded in the south, namely Memphis, where all the radio stations I liked were broadcasting. Artists like Otis Redding, Irma Thomas, Sam Cooke, Booker T, Al Green, and Willie Mitchell were at the top of my list of favorites.

I didn't have access to any Soul music, though. I hadn't been able to purchase any tapes of my own, and my stepdad's record collection was a little light on Stax, Hi, and Motown, so I had to rely on the radio. The Soul/R&B stations played a little too much modern R&B for my taste, which, in the Eighties and Nineties, tended to be a saccharine parody of the real thing. Finding the older stuff on the radio was a little tricky.

So, I had two options if I wanted to hear a specific song. 1) I could wait around and listen to tunes and advertisements until I heard what I had in mind, or 2) I could call an All-Request Hour and politely ask for it. The first option could be tedious and frustrating and often landed some terrible commercial jingle playing on repeat in my porous brain. The second option wasn't without its limitations either. It was notoriously hard to get your call answered by a DJ, with most attempts meeting with the aforementioned busy signal - hence the beauty of the redial button on our shellfish phone. The other limitation was the type of music you could request needed to be within the scope of that station's genre. For instance, you couldn't count on having a Soul/R&B song played on a country music station. And, for various reasons unknown to me, the Soul and R&B stations didn't seem to be taking requests.

This led me to always be ready to hit record when I heard a song I liked, and I found there were two stations and times of day where I could make my requests. One was a public radio station with amateur DJs but a wide variety of genres all in one place and commercial-free. The show I was most interested in featured classic R&B. It was broadcast in the middle of the week in the middle of the day. The other was a rock station that occasionally played a cool Al Green tune or something like it, if you asked nicely. That show was on late at night, so I had to keep the volume down, but since it was summer, I was free to stay up later than normal. Between these two options, I began building my first playlist.

I found myself in awe of the radio DJ's job. I recorded DJs I liked and paid attention to how they spoke about the music they were about to play or tunes and artists they had just played. I recorded sign-ins, weather, traffic reports, the sign-off for the night, and passing the mic to the next guy. I felt I could do it, and I wanted that job. Unfortunately, I had a voice better suited for singing nursery rhymes. In fact, when I managed on rare occasions to get to a ringing telephone before my sister, the person on the other end of the line often thought I *was* her … and it wasn't because my sister had an unusually deep voice. The high-pitched and childish tones emanating from my throat did not exactly recommend me for radio work.

Being unqualified has rarely stopped me from trying something new, so I decided to create my own fake radio show. I had a VERY specific vision for how I wanted it to go down. The show, lasting almost 25 minutes, would begin with a few lines of monologue, then the intro song, after which I would record a little banter (all in a fake voice), then my playlist. After a few tunes, I'd record what few facts I had about the artists at my disposal before wrapping it up with a fake-weather report and one last song after my sign-off for the next fake DJ, who, now that I think about it, having not shown up for nearly 30 years, is definitely fake-fired.

As you may have guessed, it took enormous patience and timing for a twelve-year-old. I thank my parents for never buying us video games or letting me have a television in my room. Had they done it, there's almost no chance I would have spent so much time alone, speaking in what is now likely considered a racist parody of a black man's voice in a Mississippi patois, stealing songs, and dreaming up outrageous weather patterns, all so I could have my own, personal radio experience.

Of all my convictions, I was most strongly committed to my intro song. It absolutely HAD to be a classic.

Before I learned the art of long-distance driving, inspiration often found me late at night. The inspiration for my show's intro tune came to me one evening, sometime after 10:30, the ethereal late night of a 12-year-old. I finally knew what song I wanted to have as the lead-in: "When a Man Loves a Woman" by Percy Sledge. Being impulsive and weird, I immediately started dialing in to one of my two best bets for a fulfilled request and was shocked when I heard the DJ's voice on the other end of the phone on the first try.

Mercifully, I remembered to turn down the radio, just in case I was on-air. If you don't know why this is important, feel free to Google that as well. The DJ seemed just as shocked that a small girl was calling in so long after what surely was her bedtime. After explaining that I was a boy, I told him what I wanted to hear.

'Can you please play *When a Man Loves a Woman*'?

"Sure thing, *maaannn*. Take it easy!"

I was sweating as my finger hovered over the buttons on my radio. The DJ came back after a few more songs, fading out the last one quite nicely, and started to introduce the next batch of requested tunes in the mix. I'd spent so much time practicing my pre-show intro I had to nail the timing of when I hit the record button, so I didn't get any of the real DJ in my mix. I was anxious and had not yet turned the volume on my radio quite loud enough, and I almost missed it when he said, " ... And up first, *When a Man Loves a Woman*, by Michael Bolton!"

My fingers and brain were in total conflict, and I nearly blew the whole thing by hitting record. But something deep inside me sent the proper signal, and I narrowly missed recording the beginning of that, in my humble opinion, rat-shit awful version of such a fantastic and soulful tune.

Immediately, I picked up the pale-yellow mollusk, mashed the redial button with a bit too much enthusiasm, and was once again astonished to hear the DJ on the other end.

'Um, hey, uhh, I just called a few minutes ago to request a song.'

"Huh, yeah, man. I recognize your voice. What's up?"

'So, uh, thanks for taking my request, but uh ... Michael Bolton? That's terrible, man. Could you please play the Percy Sledge version instead?'

"You're joking?"

'Nope, totally serious. Michael Bolton sucks, man. I forgot he did this song, too.'

"Wow, man ... this ... is a first for me. I'll see what I can do."

He hung up with a laugh.

When the Michael Bolton version ended, the DJ came back on the air.

"By *request*, that was *Michael Bolton*," adding emphasis to the artist's name, "with, *When a Man Loves a Woman*." After a brief, chuckling pause, he carried on, "So, when I tell you that I just got an earful from a **child** about having played that version of the song, I mean a very young child, probably like 10." I bristled slightly but felt somehow famous. He continued. "Now, I'm not the kinda guy to ever play the same song twice for pretty much any reason really, but tonight, I hope you understand, I'm gonna play you the ORIGINAL VERSION," more emphasis from the DJ, "of When a Man Loves a Woman, this time, by Percy Sledge. If you don't like it, blame the little dude somewhere in Mississippi."

And just like that, the symbols and organ of the opening lines of the song rang out. I was so rattled I completely forgot to hit the record button on cue and missed the first three seconds of the song!

Years later, bartending in Memphis, a man I recognized from freeway billboards advertising a morning show on a popular radio station walked in and sat at the far end of the bar.

I've always found images of radio DJs to be unsettling. Mostly because I thought one of the main benefits of being on the radio is that your face gets to be anonymous while your voice is famous. Also, voices and faces rarely match, except for some reason with women; their faces and voices almost always sync up to me.

Anyhow, this radio DJ was the same guy I had pestered all those years before. He'd done his time on the late-night shift, putting up with enough of the call-in requests, and had been rewarded with a primo slot on the AM show. When his voice hit my ears, ordering a cocktail, I knew it was him.

We chatted while he drank and waited for some friends to arrive. When the timing was right, I told him my side of the call-in all those years ago. His face lit up when I said *When a Man Loves a Woman*!

He laughed at the top of his lungs, "Shit, maaan ... I've been telling that story for fifteen years!" He laughed and laughed and shook my hand as his friends arrived. Without letting go of me, he turned to his buddies and said, "Hey, check this out, man ... remember me telling you about that kid who called in and gave me a bunch of shit for playing Michael Bolton instead of Percy Sledge? Well, that son of a bitch makes a mean gin and tonic!"

Fortunately, my first fake radio project was as short-lived as it was terrible. However, it sticks with me now, almost thirty years later, as a reminder to be more childlike. Thinking of those days, I can almost feel again the newness of the experience, the strangeness of interacting with adults, the joy of discovering music, and of course, the casual joke of trying to be a person. I'm also reminded of how the music I've known has changed with me. I can listen to old songs now and feel so many of the same emotions I felt as a boy, but also be reminded of experiences considerably more complex. On rare occasions, my interpretation of these tunes is tainted by self-doubt and a pointless cynical critique. However, one tune is stuck in my memory like a lead dart. After countless times around the turntable in my head, it remains, unchanged and forever, the best lead-in tune to the worst fake radio show ever produced.

# A Letter to Mom

It was your eyes, blue-green and wise for their age, which first looked into mine. What did you see in there? What does a mother see when she gazes into the eyes of a character whose role in the story has not yet been written? Your eyes, although 40 years younger then, were accomplished and clever, having looked into the eyes of the dying without fear and the newly born without judgment. Perhaps you see something familiar in both?

I sit here today, technically a man, many years removed from the infant in your arms, breathing in the invisible molecules of our atmosphere for the very first time. Although a four-decade chunk of time separates me from that moment, I am doing my best to picture your eyes. My imagination is busy but not particularly visually adept. I can't conjure the image of your eyes on my own; I need a visual aid for the finer details. Looking at a photo of you, however, I can take that image back in time. I can envisage a tiny version of myself, endlessly comforted, finally matching a face to the voice which had been singing and speaking above and around me as I grew like an angry watermelon in your belly.

I picture your eyes, filled with tears of relief from the strain and pain of childbirth and the joy of having created yet another human life, doing your part to slowly replace the ones ceaselessly floating off the field of play. Perhaps it was that first bit of eye contact, like the turning of a key in a car's ignition, which set the engine of my being into motion. The mechanism activated by your gaze was not the physical apparatus, which is now clumsily typing these words, but an ethereal device that can detect at least a little love in just about everything it can view. My siblings have their own instruments of disposition, gifted to them by your gaze, each of us boundlessly fortunate to have had our machines tuned up for the first time by such a force.

The comfort of your voice or presence in my life is hard to overstate. I can conjure and reconstruct the great consolation I took from you with memories of sadness, stomach aches, broken bones, disappointments, and fears. Even now, as a somewhat cynical adult, when I feel pain or discomfort, I think of you and your loving company ... and even though you are still living, I miss it.

As a child, when I would visit my father, I would pine for my own room and the freedom I felt there, an openness you encouraged. His home was not mine. I was nervous, carrying the sense of being a bothersome person. I often fell ill at his house and would wish you were there to help me. Your sweet voice and reassuring presence, earned by years at the bedsides of the terminally ill, were a medicine of their own. I still feel that way from time to time.

In addition to nurturing my very nature, you also gave me music. The powerful emotion I felt the first time I truly "heard" you playing piano at home has never left me. Somber church music engulfed me, underscoring my imaginary landscape with a moody soundtrack. Your singing, the first I ever experienced, born of a soft and high voice, would glide through and around the toned-down chords and melodies like a moth navigating the leaves of an oak. I still love to hear a woman singing and always associate it with you. For this, I am thankful.

Diverting attention backward in time is an endeavor that gives *and* takes. I feel like positive and loving memories outweigh the negative and cruel ones. Although, I shudder to think of my inattentiveness, moments of unthinking and unkind words or actions directed towards you. Thanks to your patience and acceptance of me, I value the fair and kind treatment of others. I hope you have felt more of this from me than any expressions of impatience, intolerance, or judgment.

Today, I caught a trace of your perfume in a crowded place; floral, calming, warm, and not too strong. I thought about when you quit smoking, when you married my stepfather, and when my little sisters were born. I heard the heartbreak in your voice when your twin brother died. I winced when I thought of the sadness dealt to you by each of your children in various ways (especially from me). I considered how you cherished your mother, caring for her until her last breath, and the countless others you have helped transition from the world of the living. And I thought about your view of death, as integral to the experience of being as birth, new teeth, and hunger. These memories serve as way-finders for me in an inland sea of self-doubt and uncertainty. When I feel lost or confused by what bits of my story I can elicit from my brain, moments in which you were the star are concrete and tangible.

Your energy and your enthusiasm are inspirational. Your encouragement, honesty, work ethic, and commitment to your vocation have been invaluable influences. Your easy expression of vulnerability gives me courage. Although somewhat perplexing to me, your ability to operate with faith in a loving God who cares for all beings is something I admire in the faithful, but particularly so in you, as you embody the message and treat others as you would have them treat you.

We are all imperfect beings, flawed and in a state of nearly constant repair. The product of our environments, shaped by forces beyond our control, our personalities, and subsequent destinies, clash with the idea of free will in ways I haven't the intelligence to understand. Mercifully, chance brought me into a home where I could be shaped by someone so capable of looking after new people.

The little man you raised with equal parts care and trust is looking back in time at the young woman who brought him here. I can see both of us. If I could speak to those younger versions of us and be heard, I would say very little. Perhaps, a simple message; one for the present, one for the past, and one for the future - "This *is really* happening, so be thankful for every yesterday, and don't hold your breath for tomorrow ... it'll be here before you know it.

With a whisper in his ear
And a kiss on a brand-new cheek
A tiny creature
And a world of strangers
Were introduced
At long last

# My Number Two Son

"When you meet a man, you look him straight in the eyes and shake his hand with a firm grip."

My father made this very clear when I was quite young. Before I saw the ritual for the pissing contest it can often be, I passed it along to one of my nephews. I watched him exercise it for the first time on a camping trip when he was about five. Every person we met that weekend, waiters, random people in shops, and other campers, were treated to his intense gaze, as a small yet solid handshake gave an earnest introduction to a sweet and curious character. He seemed to have unlocked one of the central mysteries of being a person, confidently carrying the feeling in his young chest, empowered to introduce himself to the world of adults. I felt something akin to pride for having the good sense to hang out with a guy like him.

In contrast to my nephew's first use of the strange handshake ritual, shared by confident and insecure men alike, my own introduction was a great deal less empowering. As I write this, February 23, 2022, it has been exactly twenty years since the man who taught me to make eye contact and shake a hand with a firm grip died in sedated agony with a tube down his throat in a hospital bed.

Before I move forward, I'd like to express my gratitude for everything that man gave me. Like "A Boy Named Sue," the wounds inflicted upon me by my father made me, if not tough exactly, at least capable of handling the ironic and uncomfortable in my own way. Besides, at some point, a child's job is to realize that his or her parents are just children who grew up and made more children. One's own parents deserve all the same forgiveness and understanding one might otherwise afford to the parents of strangers to whom you bear no ill will.

But It is worth considering how we got our scars, so we won't end up scarring anyone else.

My old man grew up extremely impoverished and was one of thirteen children in Flint, Michigan. His parents, with almost no money, did their best for their children. I can scarcely imagine the wounds visited upon my father by his folks as they struggled with such a debilitating and self-inflicted burden. I didn't know my dad very well, but in conversations with those who did, they told me he was eager to separate himself from that disadvantaged background at every opportunity. Presenting his children as future rich people was likely part of the deal. My brother, for example, carries the same name as my father, followed by "Jr." - an affectation and relic of a monarchy and aristocracy from which our redneck family is quite far removed. The tradition continues with my brother's son, whose name is now followed by a "III." While my brother is likely honoring tradition, it seems possible my dad was attempting to project an air of sophistication and distance from his father, incredibly named Ernest Cletus. Fair enough.

When my dad gave me the instructions for the North American handshake comedy, I was eager to try it out. I even shook my own hand, testing the strength of my grip for handshake potency. Dad was gregarious and much more prone to speaking with strangers than with me, creating many opportunities to meet new people. Gas station attendants, grocery store clerks, other shoppers, bank tellers, and pretty women of all professions frequently found a thick-chested, one-eyed ex-marine and attorney shaking their hands and introducing whichever of his four children happened to be with him.

I have no memory of when his introduction became what it was, but at some point, I realized it contained a weird disclaimer. The first time it dawned on me, we were at a golf club, a place I never liked and where I always felt like a ladle full of punch in a bowl of turds.

My father wanted me to take lessons from a golf pro who I'll call Tad; because why not? Tad was dressed in perfectly clean-pressed pants, a tucked-in Polo shirt, white golf cleats, and a white visor with a brand of golf ball printed on the front. He was probably the cleanest and most tan white person I'd ever seen. I was wearing an ill-fitting version of the same outfit, minus the visor - a ridiculous accessory I refused to accept. On our weekend visits, our dad always made me change from my skateboard or rock band-themed t-shirts and dirty jeans into khaki pants, brown loafers, and Polo shirts. Feeling like you're wearing someone else's clothes is enough to make a person anxious about meeting new people; it only got worse from there.

Dad took me over to meet Tad, and after greeting him with humor and casual charm, he pointed to me. "Tad, this is my number two son, Andrew Paul, named after not one, but **two** saints. His mother is a Catholic."

I don't know what it was like for Tad to look into the eyes of a kid whose father had just introduced him with an apology, but I can tell you, if I'd found myself in Tad's clean cleats, I might have felt odd about the whole thing. Of course, Tad politely laughed and looked into the eyes of someone's number two son, already standing weird on the back foot. If that didn't give it away, he could probably tell I wouldn't be much of a golfer by the less-than-enthusiastic grip of the hand he was shaking.

When I think of my dad now, twenty years after his death, I don't experience a sense of loss. I feel regret and hints of the pain I once knew as a boy, unsure why his father didn't like him. I understand the whole thing much better now with twenty years of experience and having met several people I also don't like. Take my oldest sister, for example. We were raised by the same people and lived in the same house. I love her, I'm sure of that. But if you were to ask me how much I like her, I could honestly say not even a little bit. Does that make me a bad person? More importantly, does it make her a bad person? The answer to both of those questions is obviously no. But to a young man, developing under the one good eye of a father who may have had deep love but also harbored genuine dislike, it was a difficult and painful concept to understand. I would like to be forgiven for disliking others, so I try to forgive those who dislike me. There is a power in forgiveness that far exceeds the flaccid entanglement of even the most super firm handshake.

That said, I do try to give a solid handshake, minus any of the bogus posturing of prior insecure eras. Whether it is that of a man, woman, or child, I squeeze a hand only as hard as it squeezes mine. I use my grip to convey warmth, not power. I also make eye contact, not as an act of domination, but to see what beauty or pain I might find in any given eye and to offer my gaze as part of the welcome. And when I have the privilege of greeting someone for the first time, I try not to approach the gift of introduction by the terms under which I first learned them, but under my own — the number two son, agnostic and sweet, named after two saints by his Catholic mother.

# Shadows on the Wall

This morning, I watched as light from an open refrigerator briefly cast a moving shadow on the wall of an adjacent room. It reminded me of a sensation I often experienced as a boy sleeping in my dad's apartment.

I wasn't afraid of my father, but I wasn't comforted by him either. He was kind but distant to me, like the reverberations of a mighty thunderclap quietly rumbling some miles away. People tell me he was special, but the space between us was too great to experience directly. Visiting him always left me feeling more like a tolerated house guest than a beloved son. My voice was too loud, my hunger was too much, and my interests were not particularly interesting.

Dad had recently moved out of our house and into the rooms above his office. The apartment had one bed at first. At night I slept in his room. Being so close to him was like being at the confluence of two rivers - one calm and tranquil, the other raging and dangerous. I wanted to tell him what I was thinking, to somehow reach him and connect like I could with literally everyone else. Instead, I let my mind wander through the dark, keeping my thoughts to myself.

His office was on a busy road, and his blinds never fully closed. Being on the second floor, the light from passing vehicles hit the window at odd angles. Always in motion and coming in from below, the room felt, at first, chaotic, with shadows constantly forming and traveling from opposite directions across the walls to the bedsheets. The hot red of retreating taillights chased the warm white glow of headlights from side to side, switching directions as vehicles passed. When the opposed beams met in the middle, a brief and terrible confusion of light and hue collided at the midway point. The stillness of the wall and the weird mountain ranges in the sheets formed an impossible landscape, as if they too were meant to be moving but somehow managed to resist the order and remain still.

Lying next to my dad, watching this strange light show, listening to the rhythm of his heartbeat, I couldn't help but compare it to mine. His heart, augmented by a mechanical valve, was much louder than a normal heart. His rhythm, three beats to my four, made a sucking sound, followed by two metallic clicks. The reverberations of the passing cars whooshing by - rubber wheels on the pavement, followed by the muffled rumble of engines - created a soft droning sound, like being near a hive of bees, or a room filled with machines, each doing a different job. His breathing, before it turned to snoring, piled onto the din of long waveform sound.

These odd stimuli pooled around my senses, like meltwater at the base of an ice cube, leading me to a peculiar state. When I closed my eyes, I could feel my body swell to a size greater than a whole building. I could be as large as I dared, feeling the bed below me like a grain of sand under my back. In an instant, I could compel my body to shrink to a size smaller than the space between my pinched thumb and forefinger. Without effort, I could travel between these states at my leisure until I finally drifted off to sleep.

In that vacillating state, between the enormous and the minuscule, motion and stillness, the beats and breaks, I became something else. As if exposed to some mystical insight I can't reassemble as a man, so fixed by time, space, and the calcified ignorance of certainty, my young mind caught a glimpse of something behind the heavy curtain of illusion. When I reach for the feeling now, that secret of existence, unlocked by a hypnotizing show of light, rhythmic clicks, and droning sounds, eludes me. When I try to focus, to remember what it was or what it might have meant, the memory moves with the effort, like fishing for shattered bits of an eggshell from the jewel it once held or squeezing that melting cube of ice firmly between my fingers and watching it fly off like a comet.

The closest I've been to remembering the boundlessness of size and perception is in the psychedelic state. In those rare moments, I could feel my old power return, the insight with me once more. But rather than up front and center in my mind, as it once was, the wisdom of this gift is behind me, possibly benevolent, possibly malicious, patiently observing, informing action, without telling me its secrets. I don't fight it but play with the sensations like a child reading her first good book, curious and dazzled by the experience of discovering other worlds in the mind.

# Barely Godmother

There's no point in writing, "I remember," is there? Memory is implied in the act of writing. Basically, everything is either a memory or the result of one. So, with that said, let's just continue with the understanding that what I'll be describing is something I remember. In this case, I'll do my best to describe a wedding I attended when I was about ten or eleven.

I realize I'm not the first to notice that Catholics have funny rituals. Baptism is one of them and includes a component that has always seemed strange to me — the naming of the child's *Godmother* and *Godfather*. If the function of a Baptism is to conscript the christened to a life of faith in the church, then the role of a *Godparent* is to ensure that the child remains in the faith in the event of the death of the child's biological parents. It was all opaque to me, but I did like my Godparents well enough and felt like they would have my best interests at heart if my parents shuffled off and left us behind. A cousin of mine was chosen to be my *Godmother,* and a friend and mentor of my dad chosen as my *Godfather.* In reality, it meant I could expect gifts, cards, and acknowledgment of milestones from people other than the folks at home.

This cousin, Carrie, was always kind to me and seemed to enjoy being my *Godmother.* I liked it, too, and felt like it made the two of us closer somehow. We saw each other about once or twice a year when my family would pack into a van and drive from Mississippi to Illinois to visit my grandmother.

Carrie is about ten or eleven years older than I am but was fewer than ten or eleven inches taller than me when I was about ten or eleven. This math is obviously as unimportant as it is confusing, but the weirdness of it makes it worth sharing. In any case, she met a man she wanted to marry, so arrangements were made, and a big, long-winded Catholic wedding was in order. My country-ass family was invited.

Dozens of people piled into a church for the ceremony - a ceremony as indecently protracted and weirdly mystical as it was painfully formal. The priest conducted a mass that included the exchange of wedding vows and a lengthy sermon on marriage. A funny concept because, for the priest, even a ten or eleven-year-old could tell you, marriage is a subject about which he knows exactly jack-shit.

Flower girls dropped petals in the aisle where people crushed them to smithereens, a ring bearer hauled up an otherwise useless pillow with a ring tied to the middle of it, and at the end, everyone tossed bags of rice at the fleeing couple. As I said, Catholics have funny rituals.

About an hour later, we saw the couple again at the reception.

In this case, the reception venue was a spacious dance hall with large, round dining tables scattered about. A bar menaced one corner of the room. It was a classic, complete with backlit and multicolored bottles under hanging stemware, a plush leather armrest spanning the horseshoe-shaped bar top, and a round brass footrest attached to the base.

A long line of steaming tables on the other side of the hall kept various Italian-American foods hot enough to prevent rapid bacterial growth. A waxed parquet dance floor separated the bar, the dining tables, and the food. Unfortunately, the small nearby stage was not occupied by a live band but rather a DJ's table, complete with a requisite black tablecloth, crates filled with vinyl records, turntables, and a way-too-hot microphone.

Before I finished eating my third plate of food, one of my cousins' boyfriends gave me a glass of rum and coke. I downed it in seconds and had to piss within minutes. The warm and gentle grip of intoxication soon wrapped its powerful yet gentle fingers around my behavior like a python on a bunny.

On the way back from the toilet, I heard a piece of advice with which I have never been able to reckon. My cousin's boyfriend told me, "Never break the seal, man. Once you take that first piss, it never stops!" That was all I needed to hear from him. Clearly, he was an idiot of the highest order. I pictured him dancing, foolishly desperate for a piss but resisting it with ridiculous movements, his judgment needlessly clouded by urinary madness. I avoided him for the rest of the night, finding my own rum and cokes from that point forward and enjoying multiple leisurely strolls to and from the urinals.

Before I could find another drink, I saw my *Godmother* on the dance floor. Just tipsy enough to feel emboldened, I walked up to her and her new husband. Reaching several feet to tap him on the shoulder, I asked, "Mind if I cut in?"

Once everyone within the vicinity stopped laughing, I boldly took my *Godmother* by the hand and danced with her to Van Morrison's regrettable "Brown Eyed Girl." My mother approached us mid-twirl, called our names, and snapped a photo of the moment.

And here it is now, on my kitchen table, a photo of a slightly buzzed young man dancing with a literally blushing bride, the happiest woman on the planet.

So sweet
My *Godmother*
Embracing her *Godson*
About ten or eleven inches
From her happy red face.

# Of Course
# I Give a Shit.

Naptime – sounds innocent enough, right? You might picture hammocks lazily stretched between palm tree shadows or a plush and cuddly sofa in a cozy space? Maybe you spare a thought for half-read paragraphs abandoned in misshapen books, rising and falling over lungs full of effortless breathing. Naptime; what a lovely, uncomplicated, and wistful sort of term.

Yet, a nap also suggests a rest that must be brief and not enjoyed for too long, giving it a sense of the precious, fleeting, and almost-already-over. One doesn't nap from night till morning. Nap is a word flirting with tension at every turn – splendid but terse, a loosened grip on something which must not be dropped, a tiny sip of sleep's big medicine chased closely by the venom of wakeful life. Enjoying a nap may be an apt allegory for one of life's essential struggles – the conundrum of "trying to relax."

*Time,* of course, beats along with its own dark pulse. To exist is to be submerged in an endless continuum of perilous yet wholly indifferent mathematics, both fictitious and cruelly material. Consider the insufferable, insistent, and incessant ticking of a mechanical clock, counting down an unknown quantity of your living moments while coldly accounting for those wasted; each tick a maniacal whisper, "minus one, minus one, minus one … "

But *time*, in the context of denoting the appropriate moment for something as potentially lovely as a nap, can lend
itself to a more relaxed and friendly interpretation - helping
one ease into a designated, temporally-off-the-hook phase of
consciousness. A phase which is (or so you've been told) just
right for the mind, body, and, if you are so inclined, spirit.

As a child, fixations like these were not yet diluted enough
to make them manageable. Too concentrated to properly di-
gest and especially persistent in moments of stillness, I was often sickened by my obsessions. (It may be unnecessary to point
out that a mind so prone to dragging simple phrases through
such neurotic sludge would not exactly look forward to taking
a nap, but to stop pointing out the unnecessary would negate
a great deal of writing.) While the phenomenon of children
being resistant to nap time is obviously not unique to me, it
does make me wonder; how many kids are wide awake while
they are meant to be napping? How many of them are cultivating what will later be recognized as a form of existential
dread? How many lucky ones are simply dreaming pleasantly
as expected?

This is a story about leaving no such ambiguity for one of
my caretakers. It is also a story about the type of person who
seeks to know the high-minded and poetic but who, in reality,
is a knuckle-dragging beast, more likely to make a mess than a
work of art.

My big sister and I were lucky kids. Our parents loved
us so deeply they hired babysitters to show us a slightly wa-
tered-down version of that love when they weren't around. We
had a variety of sitters, but only two of them ever came to our
house. This task typically fell to a woman I only ever knew
as Sis, an older African American woman, raised in the Deep
South on a farm only a short walk from our place. When this
tender and fun-loving being wasn't available to look after us, a
stand-in was called. In our case, the stand-in was also a neighbor - a pretty, teenage girl.

Even at four years old, I had an enormous crush on that
young woman, and I was sure I loved her deeply. But with

love so deep, I'm shocked not to be able to recall her name or picture her face very clearly. While the cruel passage of time has ransacked many pleasant memories from my vault, it has unfortunately not even touched my recollection of being so shamefully desperate for her approval.

When Sis watched over us, I'm sure we had to nap, but I don't remember resisting it. Perhaps we were so full of tasty, delightfully greasy breakfast foods we just drifted off to sleep without much of a fuss. Or maybe Sis just didn't care *where* we slept. In either case, the teenager with whom I was so hopelessly in love took the *when* and *where* of nap time quite seriously – after lunch and in your room.

In fact, everything about her was in stark contrast to Sis. Sis was older, strong, and somewhat rounded in figure. Her shiny black skin almost hid the deep creases on her face, earned by years of working in the sun. The young neighbor girl was maybe 16, tan-white, and many years away from her first wrinkle - a wrinkle more likely to come from relaxing in the sun than working in it. Breakfast with Sis was fresh eggs from her farm, melting butter, tender bacon, biscuits made from scratch, and a glass of milk. Meals with the teenager were cold cereal, unpopped Pop-Tarts, and orange juice. One was warm savory, the other cold syrup. One I loved like a mother, the other I pined for like a lover (in as much as a four-year-old could, anyhow).

If Sis was like family, the teenager from across the street was more like a bored tourist. Her role was perfunctory, mechanical, and something she did strictly for folding cash. Her gift was the science of on-time arrival, marching us through the day's events and prolonging our survival until our parents' inevitable return. It didn't bother me a bit, though. I was too consumed by her pretty face and could only see a girl whose attention I craved more than anything. It took many years for me to realize she was crabby, uninterested, and ill-suited to hang out with kids. For sure, I didn't prefer her supervision, but I wasn't as disappointed as I should have been when she showed up instead of Sis.

I could feel her absence in my room when nap time came around. Wide awake, I dreamt of ways to impress and prevent her from leaving me alone to suffer another sleepless nap. I made up little stories that she tolerated. I showed her our tree house in the backyard. I gave her a Christmas card given to me; her "thanks" was as flat and emotionless as a crocodile's birthday wish. I made ridiculous displays of strength and agility, lifting, sprinting, and leaping like a spaz. These trinkets and gestures had zero effect. Something much grander was in order.

I noticed she liked talking with my siblings, especially my tall and handsome older brother. They were all very creative people - musical, artistic, and capable of creating sounds and images, which still impress me. These were not my gifts. My first attempt to join the ranks of the creative set was a complete failure which landed me in a bit of trouble with her and enormous trouble with my parents. It may not have crashed the ship of our relationship, but it was blown well off-course. While I was meant to be sleeping, I emptied out a massive package of crayons, grabbed as many as I could hold in each hand, and began to draw on the biggest canvas I could find – the walls of my room.

I was a little heartbroken when I realized she was angry with me and not amazed by the scope of my work - a daring silhouette of every piece of furniture in the room, stretching from the floor to as high as I could reach in a wild and endless patchwork of multicolored swirling crayon marks.

I'm unsure how long I had to wait for her to return for another shift at our house, but I imagine I had plenty of time to prepare something nice for her between visits. I could have made her a drawing or a sculpture out of something pleasant with a lovely aroma. Of course, I did not plan, I was not prepared, and to boot, my room had been rendered somewhat art-proof. Fortunately for me, and unfortunately for her, a lack of preparation, tools, and materials would not stop me from trying.

As I sit here now, many decades removed, having ingested numerous substances which doctors insist will wreck the memory, I can still clearly picture that room of mine. A strange and subtle magic of mid-day naptime semi-darkness made imaginary things seem a bit more real and impossible things a touch more achievable. The bed frame was fashioned from ornamental iron and painted an unfortunate faux brass. The ends of all the uprights were adorned with gnarled little clam-like figures. I would stare at them in that muted light and imagine the clams morphing into monkey fists, iron acorns, or golden turds. Checkered wallpaper had been deployed to cover my previous masterpiece, limiting the scope of the magic in the way only checkered surfaces can. My favorite statue, an unlicensed figurine of E.T., cast in plaster and painted by what I assume were toilet-wine-addled prison inmates, sat on a stool near the bed so I could see it before the lights went out at night and when I woke up in the morning. There was a large chest with rickety drawers for my clothes, a heavy and dark-stained wooden rocking chair decorated by a weird-painted floral theme, a bedside table with a lamp, a tall skinny trash can (taken away after I used it as a toilet in the night), and a closet filled with cherished toys. I was a lucky kid, privileged but not totally spoiled, grateful but not yet wise enough to express it in words.

The teenager returned to see the walls of my room in a state of repair she clearly preferred - my offensive masterwork hidden under a layer of soulless, blue and white crosshatch patterned wallpaper. She looked it over with self-assured detachment, believing all was right and proper in the world and that I had learned my lesson. With my room now wholly emptied of anything which might permanently deface the walls, she closed the blinds and shut the door to my room with a confidence in the outcome no one should reasonably expect, especially when dealing with a four-year-old smitten-kitten like me.

While some details and emotions remain clear to me, the logic and reasoning I was working with are sometimes a bit more opaque. For instance, I can clearly tell you how, while I was meant to be napping, I got up, made a workable paste to act as a sort of Plaster of Paris, and then smeared it across a small section of the wall about as high as I could reach. Using the plaster as an adhesive, I created a scene with various small toys, including a tiny tractor and some action figures acting as a clean-up crew. My hope was to create a landscape that conveyed how sorry I was for the mess I made with the crayons and just how delightfully creative and resourceful I could be - even without any ready materials at hand. At this point, you may be asking yourself, "Without ready materials? Then where did the plaster come from?" I can assure you, if you are asking this, you may wish you hadn't.

Without anything in the room to help me adhere the toys to the wall, all I needed to do was drop my drawers and make a shit into my underpants. Then, using them like a very stinky painter's palette, I mashed the poo into a workable paste and smeared it on the recently papered wall, placing the toys into the quarter-inch-thick scree-field of excrement. What I cannot tell you exactly is why I chose this medium for expression or why I chose to locate my work so close to the light switch.

My heart raced as she opened the door and reached for the light. 'Would she even notice? Would she get what I was trying to say with the piece?'

Her fingers, which never did run through my hair or gently touch my cheeks, were aimed a little low, just missing the light switch on the first try. A couple of her knuckles brushed up against my homemade plaster, knocking one of the action figures to the floor. After a short-lived pause, when a horrible calculus and reckoning with what she was encountering must have been taking place, her follow-up scream and rapidly retreating commentary simultaneously punctuated our relationship and knocked me flat. I heard her voice as she ran down the hallway, yelling in disgust on her way to the nearest sink, "EWWWW, THAT'S DISGUSTING ... SO GROSS!"

Perhaps, against the ticking clock of nap time, with my limited materials and unorthodox creative choices, I was desperate to make an impression? Maybe I think shit is art? Or maybe art is shit? Was I just a little monster? Am I still? Who knows? Everybody's a critic, I guess – it's good to learn that early.

To my knowledge, that was the last time she stood in for sweet Sis. If I ever did see her again, I don't remember it. If she remembers me, the memory is not so nice. If our paths never cross again, I think it will be alright, although never is a heavy weight I'm not eager to lift.

In the mirror, I can still see the little man - a hapless fool, a libertine, a dreamer, a romantic, and an artist who ain't no artist - just a dirty little creep, really; the kind of creature who pines for art, poetry, and meaning but might just smear shit on the wall for a bit of attention, metaphorically speaking.

Where are you now, my muse? One day you're in my atmosphere, not a transient goddess, but an ice-cold hornet, stinging my heart without a touch. As I reach for you, you leave me alone to face the elastic expanse of anxiety; a nether phase where my gnashing teeth grind down in sleepless torment and my wheels spin in hot pursuit of an ungrateful later.

Because somewhere
Between the sheets
lies a child
Dying to impress
Uncomplicated
Absurd
Hoping
In the dull teeth of hopelessness itself
For a quiet piece of sky
Where shitty little toys
Stick to the wall
And
At least one pretty girl
Might not find it so gross

# Driving Sis Crazy

Sis and Doc, our babysitter and her husband, had been our neighbors my whole life. When Sis came to watch us, she could walk from her house through the fields and arrive at our back door in about five minutes. When I was about five or six, they sold their farm and moved to a neighborhood a few miles down the road. Sis had never learned to drive and had never needed to, as Doc did all the driving, and I think she probably liked it that way.

As their routines settled in, Doc would drive Sis to our house and pick her up after work. One day, however, Doc committed to helping a friend harvest his corn, a project which would last until nightfall, which meant he wouldn't be able to drive her home. Rather than asking our mom to give her a ride, Doc felt confident that a single driving lesson en route to our place in the morning would be sufficient for the few short miles back home. Nervously, she drove Doc's old blue pickup to our house with Doc in the front seat beside her. Sis arrived sweaty and anxious but unharmed.

She was on edge all day, restlessly shooting glances at the big blue truck lurking in the driveway. When our mom came home, she offered to give her a ride, but Sis couldn't be persuaded to deviate from the plan. We watched her narrowly missing our mailbox as she negotiated the dance of breaks, steering wheel, and gas pedal. Our dad said she was using "both hands, both feet, and no brains." Funny but not exactly charitable.

After too many minutes of standing around in the yard, pointlessly staring at the empty road in front of us, mom hus-

71

tled us into the car and drove toward Doc and Sis's new home. Before we took off, we thought we heard the faint sound of something breaking in the distance.

A few hundred yards later, we turned from the straightaway of our small street and joined with the considerably more winding and curvy road which led to the highway. We noticed something literally out of place - a mailbox lying on its side in the middle of a well-manicured yard, the outgoing mail indicator flag pointing straight up like a possum's foot convincingly playing dead. From that point forward, it was a hound dog's trail of vehicular misadventure. Deep tire tracks in the lawn on the opposite side of the road lead to another downed mailbox, more tire tracks in the middle of the road, and then a gouge in the yard back on our side. This pattern repeated for several houses and ended with deep skid marks a few yards before the stop sign that managed the highway traffic.

Picking up a little speed, we saw the pattern repeat once again, thankfully contained to our side of the road, with the unfortunate yards and mailboxes in the appropriate lane suffering the same fate as the previous. Even a child could envision what was happening in that truck. The tired old vehicle veers to the right on a misaligned suspension, causing the frightened and inexperienced driver to dramatically over-correct to the left. Nervously mashing the gas with the right foot, then the breaks with the left foot as the smashing blue beast careens through yet another yard, taking another mailbox to the ground and gouging the yard while over-correcting to the right with too much speed, then slamming the breaks again, painting tire marks in the road, before tearing another gouge of turf from the yard and connecting with yet another mailbox.

We followed this trail of disaster a few short miles, stopping briefly to collect a side view mirror nestled among a shoal of unopened letters and colorful advertisements as it glistened like a trout belly in the evening sun. As you might expect, the path led directly to Sis and Doc's house, where we saw a beleaguered and considerably less-blue truck parked at a haunting angle in the front yard. The final injury of the journey ensured they would also not be expecting mail in their box any time soon.

# Babysitter Divinorum

S alvia Divinorum, a psychoactive member of the mint family, was saddled with its scientific name in 1962 thanks to the work of intrepid researchers whose tireless curiosity continues to benefit our kind long after their deaths. One of those gentlemen, the curious and daring Albert Hoffman, the first chemist to synthesize the compound known as LSD, was particularly instrumental in bringing Salvia Divinorum to the attention of North American weirdos like me.

I find it difficult to consider Salvia's connection to something as benign and harmless as mint. Similarly, I'm puzzled to have the following questions in my mind. Did Albert Hoffman have a babysitter, and if so, what was *she* like? These thoughts may seem to be unlikely relatives, but much like the curious relationship between flavorful-but-harmless mint to the maniacal moments of a lungful of salvia smoke, I will forever link one of my babysitters to the latter experience.

My sister and I had the pleasure (and occasional displeasure) of spending time with several babysitters. There was my favorite, Sis, a black cherub of infinite hilarity we all cherished deeply. When she wasn't available, a teenager who lived across the street, with whom I was quite possibly in love, would hang around the house and keep an eye on us. If those two were out, we had two more options. One of them, a horrible toad of a woman called Mrs. Brownley, whose insistence on our silence was surely pathological, would host us in her scary, owl-themed living room (all other rooms were off-limits). Our fourth option was my second favorite to Sis. Her name was Ida.

Sis occupies the kitchen of my memory, singing to us, cooking excellent yet simple breakfasts, teaching us how to scramble eggs in a skillet, and laughing out loud at our craziness with a mighty and slightly wild cackle. Sweet, maternal, and coyly mercurial, I can hardly think of her without feeling a powerful sense of aching for things long-gone.

Sis was part of our family, a funny, dark-skinned aunt who knew the magic of delicious food, telling its story with turns of phrase from a bygone era of North Mississippi. She also knew how to make almost anything fun, even the highly ordinary. Like when she brought over a big brown grocery bag filled with freshly harvested corn from the fields she and her husband, Doc, were looking after. She told us we'd be having a corn party and showed us how to prepare it in every way she knew – boiled, grilled, sweet, and cooked in bacon grease. Fun, delicious, and memorable. I can sometimes hear her white shoes squeaking on the floor of the kitchen, hot butter sizzling in a cast iron pan, eggs cracking on the side of a glass bowl, and a strong arm clacking the whisk as she laughs and hums along to the endless songs playing in her head.

The other two babysitters, the slender teenager who gave me fits and the not-so-slender meanie who scared us to death, were only stand-ins. Ida and Sis did the lion's share of keeping our heads out of the oven and food in our bellies while our folks were at work. I have not seen Sis since I was a boy, but the last time I saw Ida, I had just inhaled the aforementioned lungful of Salvia smoke.

If Sis lives in the kitchen of my memory, sweet-Ida lives in the TV room. Ida had been my parents' neighbor before we moved to the country. She and her husband, Jaime (we pronounced it, Hi-Me), were from Colombia, a rare and exotic ethnic origin for North Mississippi in the 70s and 80s. She was a professional babysitter and ran an off-the-books daycare with multiple clients whose older children were in the same classes as my older siblings. I was often joined by kids with whom I would eventually go to school.

Ida and Jaime's place was pure 1970s charm. I can still picture the plastic on the sofa, the brown depth of carpet, the orange and burnt umber of the decorations, the boxy television on a rolling stand, the colorful plasticine of the kitchen table cover, the giant yellow refrigerator, and the layout of the small but cozy home.

Ida was not interested in sharing the culinary delights of Colombian culture. For her, boiled macaroni and cheese with chunks of hotdog would suffice to feed the little rednecks in her care – and she was correct. We all loved it! And care, she did. With every phrase, Ida's sweet Latin voice filled her home with loving arias of tolerance and understanding. Even when correcting one of us, though stern, it was like she was singing. I'm unsure how the other kids felt about her, but I held my behavior together, mostly because I hated the idea of disappointing such a lovely woman.

Jaime did his best to contribute to our experience in her kitchen by bringing home treats from his work. He operated a large box truck filled with a brand of sweets crafted by Tom's, a snack company out of business for nearly twenty years now. They seemed to be doing fine in the 80s, though, selling a knock-off version of every popular chip or snack cake ever made. We were allowed one each, with two broad but tasty categories to choose from – sweet or savory. These ranged from squishy or powdery to the downright crunchy and buttery; either option was reliably delicious.

Even though I have fond memories of Ida's efforts in the kitchen, her true genius was in the TV room. Her television was always on. She watched "The Price is Right," "CHiPs," "The Incredible Hulk," and "Days of Our Lives." We watched her programs, not ours. Some kids didn't like it, but Ida wasn't interested in hearing those complaints. She put forth a simple and persuasive argument for anyone bold enough to criticize her watchlist. We had plenty of toys to play with and were free to go outside in the backyard, provided the lawn passed a dryness test. All she wanted out of the deal was control of the TV. It seemed fair to me.

When she made lunch, there was a power vacuum at the dial, and we could change the channel. But little else was on in those pre-cable days, so it was more of an exercise in control dynamics than it was to find something more entertaining. Her shows never bothered me, though, and I spent plenty of time in front of her TV with my attention fully committed to the fates of gameshow contestants as multicolored madness was heaped upon their awkward attempts to win cash and prizes. The absurdity of the whole thing was mesmerizing. Many decades later, I still see existence as one big farcical and gaudy production. This worldview may have been gently nudged in that direction by Bob Barker's long, skinny microphone as it hovered in front of his brilliant white teeth.

Jaime and Ida's children were older and in school with the big kids while we spent time with her. I had permission to look at her son's collection of Star Wars toys but not to take them out and play with them. He kept them well organized and in clean states of repair. The ones I had at home were missing limbs, scorched by matches, or cracked from being frozen in our icebox. Cleanliness and discipline in a child were new concepts to me.

Jaime and Ida spoke lovely and formal Colombian Spanish in the house. We also heard plenty of English commands, but the Spanish was ever-present and exciting as it danced in my country ears like colorful bugs on dry leaves. Thanks to that early exposure to the language, I've had a somewhat easier time learning basic Spanish as an adult.

Despite my poor pronunciation and limited vocabulary, I seem to comprehend more of what people are saying to me than I can express in return. Mostly, it is a contextual understanding, but somewhere in my subconscious mind, I must remember some of that old jitterbug Español taught to me by Jamie and Ida.

As I mentioned, the last time I encountered Ida was in a dream state induced by smoking Salvia Divinorum. If you were hoping to make it to the end of this missive without reading about a psychedelic journey, now would be the perfect time to stop reading. If you wish to join me, read on.

A few years ago, I visited a small apothecary in San Francisco. I was looking for mugwort, an herb I use to help induce more memorable, visually stimulating, and altogether weirder dreams. I did not find any mugwort, but I did find something else guaranteed to make things memorable, visually stimulating, and decidedly peculiar. I noticed a package behind the counter which read, "Captain Salvia." As it happens, in California, it is entirely legal to sell, possess, and ingest this mystical plant.

In the culture of the Mazatec people of Oaxaca, Salvia Divinorum has roots in shamanic rituals meant to invoke some sort of congress with the Virgin Mary. Confused and somewhat muddled theologies aside, I'd been interested in trying this plant for many years, so I purchased the package without hesitation. I also bought a small colorful glass pipe solely dedicated to smoking it when the time was right.

I took my small bag of Salvia home, opened it, filled the little pipe with the greenish-brown leaves, put the whole operation in a drawer, and tried not to think about it for nearly six months. Occasionally I would ask my wife, "Hey, you wanna smoke that shit with me today?" Reliably, she would say, "No."

My little pipe filled with Salvia sat in the drawer, unmolested and largely forgotten until we returned from a trip to Baja Sur for Christmas that same year. After the trip, I found myself listening to a record by Dean Martin almost every morning.

On one of those "Dino" mornings, at about 7AM, completely out of the blue, I decided I would "smoke that shit." I laid out a meditation pillow, brought the pipe and a lighter over to a low table, restarted the record from the top, and prepared myself to be introduced to the Virgin Mary.

I had researched Salvia before this and knew two things were essential. First, never smoke Salvia alone. Second, be sure to take a very deep inhale of the smoke, or the effects may not be as profound as you might hope.

Of course, I was alone, as my wife was at work already (she left before 6AM). But at least I remembered to take a deep hit.

Actually, I almost forgot the second part as well. I took a hit and held it in when I remembered a large hit was necessary, so I fired up the lighter again and inhaled as deeply as I could, filling every little bit of my lungs to capacity.

As I inhaled, Dino's voice reminded me, "I DON'T KNOW WHAT I'M DOING MORE THAN HALF OF THE TIME!"

I was sitting up when I took the hit, but after a lapse of awareness, I realized I was lying on my back. I remember stretching my arms, legs, and spine as if waking from a deep sleep. Slowly, I opened my eyes. Looking down at me, in a vibrant, nearly Sesame-Street-toned series of colors, was my sweet and lovely babysitter, Ida.

"Gooood mooorning, sleepyhead." Her voice sang to me in her beautiful Colombian accent. Seeing her there, my heart was afloat in a river of nearly impossible memory. We were in her home, the television was on, and cartoons were playing on the screen. I blinked, and it felt like it took an hour for my lids to reopen. When they finally opened again, I was sitting up, looking around at a scene I had not experienced since I was a small boy.

'How did I get here?' I said, looking deeply into her large brown eyes for the first time in decades.

She was the same Ida I knew from my childhood. She may have been close to 40 then. Her skin was light brown and firm, yet somehow swirling with Technicolor patterns and peculiar geometry. In fact, every surface in the intensely familiar home was doing the same thing. The carpet, the sofa, the characters on the screen, the plastic and floral print cover on the kitchen table, and the side of her large refrigerator were all shimmering with the same irregular sparkle.

"You were sleeping, silly boy. It's time for lunch!" Her voice was unmistakable. Ida was in front of me! Young Ida, no less! No gray hair, no wrinkles, the same stern yet forgiving face smiling at me with all the love and sweetness I remember so well.

'Where's my wife?' I asked her. A powerful sense of dread and a growing discomfort were piling up like wind-blown snow in the corners of my consciousness.

"Your wife?" She said in a surprised and joking tone. "Ha! You were sleeping pretty hard, Andrew (pronounced Ahhn-drü). That must have been some dream!" She started to laugh. It wasn't malicious, just the sort of laugh one couldn't help but make when a four-year-old wakes up from a nap and demands to know where his wife might be.

'No, no, no, I was just at home … California. My wife, she was just here. My house, my things, where's all my stuff?" I was on the wrong edge of sanity. A cruel and desperate fear gripped the bottom bit of my heart and the edges of my stomach. It wasn't simply terrifying. It was painful like it might never let go.

"Andrew," she said in the warmest and most delicate tone she had yet spoken to me, "you're in my house. Your mom brought you here this morning on her way to work. You took a little nap, and now it's time for lunch. Are you hungry?"

I could hear a song coming from the television. The singer crooned, "I come from just the other side of Nowhere … " The price was not exactly right.

My eyes darted around the familiar old room where I'd spent so many hours of my childhood. I got up, walked over to the couch, stood in front of the hallway leading to the bathrooms and bedrooms, then made my way to the front door.

I had a wife, I thought to myself. I had to get back to her. She would come home, and I wouldn't be there. She wouldn't know what happened to me and would never know. I headed towards the front door of Ida's house. Where would I go?

"Andrew," Ida said to me, still dripping with sweetness but with a sterner undertone, "you have been asleep and dreaming. Whatever you thought was happening … it was a dream. You are a little boy, I am looking after you while your mom is at work, and it is time for lunch. *Your wife, your home, your things,* it's all a dream, Andrew. You must wake up from your dreams once they're over."

" ... Just the other side of Nowhere, goin' home," Dino continued.

I couldn't accept it. I remembered something ... yes, I remembered I had taken something, and I woke up. I had to get back to that dream. I didn't want to be a little boy again. This world was too strange and moving too much. I suddenly missed my world, my dream! I missed it so intensely I found myself ready to move a mountain one stone at a time to get back to it. How do you get back to a dream ... and a dream of the future, no less? I pushed open the front door.

What greeted me on the other side was just short of mind-dissolving horror. The swirling-Technicolor aspects, which had danced in a measured way across the objects in Ida's home and played so delicately on her lovely face, were now writhing in a chaotic and violent fandango on every imaginable surface. Trees seemed to be singing to me in Dean Martin's voice, morphing the lyrics "You've walked out the front door of your life ... Ain't no goin' back once that drink is empty."

The earth below my extended foot rose and crashed in violent and filthy waves of wooden decking. Below my outstretched foot, a green and vicious insect with many needle-point arms pulsated, waiting to impale my tender four-year-old foot. The very air I was breathing was a tapestry of swirling eddies of nearly infinitesimally small creatures, each singing an impossible harmony and repeating the chorus, "I come from just the other side of Nowhere."

I somehow managed, from the other side of nowhere, to pull myself back into the house with what felt like a monumental effort. Ida was seated at her kitchen table, no longer looking in my direction. The house was vibrating crazily. I closed my eyes, crouched to the floor, put my hands behind my head, and thought of Tiffany.

Yes, Tiffany, that was her name. My wife. I could remember her name. I could see her face. Eyes, beautiful, like the azure waters under the surface of one of Saturn's moons. I could picture them. I remembered our little house. It was an RV. I had a car. She had one, too, and a job, and we had friends, and our dog had died, and I missed my dad. He was dead, too. Time swirled through me, and Ida's voice faded, and the singer's voice stopped scaring me.

I opened my eyes, and I was back in my RV. Back in California. A man in his thirties with thinning hair and weird pain in one knee. I was home, standing in the kitchen of our little place, leaning my weight on the counter by the sink. I installed this sink. I fixed that shower over there. I needed a shower.

The last lines of the song rang out, "Just the other side of nowhere, goin' home." It was over.

Throughout that episode of outrageous psychedelic floundering, I wandered around my little house, picturing myself in Ida's home. Somehow, I dropped a flip-flop outside but managed not to step on the incredibly sharp agave just to the right of the open door (a green and vicious insect with many needle-point arms).

So, perhaps I did see "The Virgin Mary." She visited me in a form my mind thought I could handle, although I couldn't. I can't imagine a softer landing for someone seeking to explore the depths of their psyche. I was gently greeted by one of the most comforting and lovely people I've ever known and was welcome to ask any question, wander anywhere I chose, or explore so long as I stayed inside that home.

Instead, I retreated to my attachments, pining for the comfort and security of my home and wife. I surely missed an opportunity to learn something. When I return to this plant, I will not miss an opportunity like that again. I will seek a guide. I will not be alone. I will not run from my fear. And I will absolutely not listen to Dean Martin.

Now, several years removed from that wild moment, I still feel as if I'm traveling through an extension of that metaphysical journey. I'm seeking and meeting guides along the way. The path has been replete with surrogate Virgin Marys, Sancho Panzas, and even a Don Quixote or two. I've seen old friends dressed up in new forms, dancing with painful memories in their beautiful masks, and I tiptoe along terrifying cliffs, wondering if those are rocks and alligators below or harmless fields of marshmallow.

Until then, I wish you all the very best in your waking life and in your dreams. I also hope you have no trouble knowing which one is which.

# Impulse is my Shepherd

Christmas Eve, 1985. Nesbit, Mississippi. Our family gathers in the car for the short trip to the church where my sister and I had spent the last month rehearsing our roles in the annual Christmas Pageant. My dad was making a rare appearance at an essentially religious function. He was an unlikely visitor to any church in those days, especially the Catholic ones, of which Mom was so fond. He had some choice words to share as we approached the parking lot. "If you both do a good job, maybe you can open one of your presents tonight … and Andrew, no goofing around." I thought it a strange comment; I wasn't the "goofing" type.

What was the part around which I was not meant to be goofing? I was playing a shepherd with a long, brown, hooded robe, a fake beard, carrying a crooked staff, and sporting some sort of non-sneaker type of footwear … flip-flops, most likely. I had an appropriately, if not insultingly, simple role: guide a bunch of other kids dressed like barn animals down the center aisle, find my mark on the stage, sing along, or at least pretend to, with as much of the songs as I could remember, then shepherd the animals off stage at the end of the show.

The pageant itself was the typical story of the birth of Jesus. There were songs about the manger, the three wise men, and the guiding star over Bethlehem. A nativity scene had been constructed in front of the altar in our small church, complete with hay and the humble furnishings of a money-grubbing ho-telier with the audacity to charge a couple for a night's stay in a barn after overbooking the joint on Christmas Eve. Obviously, that wasn't exactly the story we were telling, but if you're will-ing to believe a "virgin" was about to give birth to God's very own Bronze-age baby, then how much of a stretch is it to ac-cept the idea of an opportunistic, ancient, and characteristical-ly misleading Airbnb host? All of that aside, I think you get the gist, bigger kids sang the songs and played the roles of Joseph and Mary, while the ten and under crowd were dressed up like animals, shepherds, and other hard-to-fuckup characters with zero lines and few expectations.

My friend Andy was one such character. Far more rambunc-tious and prone to overt mischief than I was, Andy was given the role of a sheep. He was keen on wandering off, talking through the songs, and even taking his act beyond the script by crawling around on all fours, behaving more like a dog than a sheep. In fact, it was Andy who I was meant to be leading down the aisle during the opening song. The other animals would follow him, then the three wise men, and so on. We'd been rehearsing these simple maneuvers for over a month.

The whole cast of idiots and creatures stood in the foyer, waiting for the big reveal behind the double doors which led to the aisle. Mary and Joseph were already on stage, and the sing-ers, dressed in oversized red and green sweaters with stiff dress clothes underneath, were staggered on a choir bench stage left. We heard them launch into the opening number. It sounded great!

I thought about the heavy atmosphere around their parts of the rehearsals. A great deal more expectation had been heaped upon them by the director, showrunner, producer, and con-ductor. That poor, bedraggled woman had her hands full with rambunctious children, horny teens, and kids who clearly ei-ther liked performing a little too much or not at all. The songs would have to carry the show while the rest of us stood around looking cute, like moving props.

For my part, I was a low-maintenance guy. I showed up on time, did my bit, kept my head down, and made little to no trouble for a woman whose whole demeanor worried me a little. I didn't really have a working definition of stress at that age, but if pressed about it, I could have pointed to her as an example of the havoc it was capable of wreaking on a person. She joined us in the foyer just before the opening number for a pep talk. She was heavily perfumed, doused in a potent aroma more industrial than recreational. Her dress was long, green, form-fitting, and suede with large, puffy shoulders, appropriate for Christmas in the eighties. Her makeup hid the deep, dark circles and worry lines that usually gave her face character. Piled on top of a powdery white base, the ruby rouge of her cheeks and the dark blue of her eyeshadow made me wonder if she planned on taking up a surprise role in the production.

I was, and still am, prone to thinking up improbable scenarios and alternate realities. That evening, in the foyer with the director, I had a notion. At best, Christmas is a thematically confused holiday, with Jesus and Santa locked in a tug-of-war for top-billing. I thought, *why not carry that confusion all the way through, like one of the soap operas my babysitters loved?* Even though our pageant featured an absence of jolly old Saint Nick, it would nicely spice up our little show if a character appeared out of nowhere, like the crazy and tired director starring as Santa's ex-girlfriend, Rita?

Anyhow, the big kids were hitting all the notes. The director joined them after our brief pep talk. It was more of a bullet-point list of the perfectly manageable nature of our roles and less of a rally, but it was nice all the same. She was just off stage, flapping her arms like an aspiring but misguided symphony conductor, high on her own perfume.

In all that time, I never considered what it would mean to be the first character out of the gate. Of course, when we were rehearsing, there was no audience or any of the palpable energy such a gathering can bring to bear. Faced with the dimly lit, incense-scented, and cozy church, filled beyond capacity with several faces I recognized and many more I did not, something else within me, something profound, rare, and hitherto unknown, took the wheel.

I heard our cue, and the doors started to swing. I honestly cannot tell you why, but a mighty urge overtook me the moment those doors were fully open. I froze for a beat. Taking in the faces of the expectant crowd was like staring into a pool from a high dive. The excitement was practically overwhelming. If it was the Christmas Spirit, then Christmas has some serious questions to answer. Simply walking up the aisle, like some sort of dolt, seemed a waste and somehow out of character. My artistic choice, for whatever reason, seemed much more fitting.

I whispered, "follow me," to Andy, my sheep buddy. I turned to face him, already violating the only direction I needed to respect, grabbed one of his hands, placed my other hand on the small of his back, drew him close, and began to dance.

We found the rhythm, hidden deep within the sorrowful Christmas tune, and I herded my sheep like no shepherd before me. We twirled, dipped, stomped, and swung from the foyer all the way to our marks on stage. The crowd of faces, at first, thinking it part of the production, giggled sheepishly, but once the singing began to fall apart, as the big kids saw what we were doing and both Joseph and Mary doubled over and covered their cackling faces, the crowd caught on, and raucous laughter filled the room. The song sputtered along as kids dropped out of the chorus, unable to sing through their snickering. Andy and I never lost our cadence. We took our time getting to our marks.

Just shy of the stage, I saw the conductor's face. Wild with rage, her angry eyes blackened above a plastered smile that looked as if it had hardened over like wet concrete in the sun, desperately resisting the animal urge to bear her fangs at the cretins currently ruining her production. Sweating through the armpits of her dark green gown and waving her arms furiously at the struggling choir, I almost felt bad ... almost.

The electric surge of laughter's reward kept me afloat on a lightning-filled cloud of dreamy joy. I spun my sheep of a friend at the top of the stairs and dipped him like Fred Astaire handling Ginger Rogers. His costumed head got a lovely, upside-down view of the hysterical audience.

Breathless, we took our spot and realized that none of the other animals had followed. I pitied them - how *can* you follow something like that? This lull in the action was the director's chance to spike the punch with "Santa's ex," but I would guess it never occurred to her. She chose instead to hiss from the front of the church at the shell-shocked donkeys, horses, and remaining sheep. The poor creatures lurched into a sad shamble, trudging up the aisle with blank expressions, looking utterly lost. Excellent, I thought. They had embodied their characters flawlessly, as their shepherd had just abandoned them, just as he had abandoned all hopes of an early Christmas gift. A small sacrifice, well worth it, for the intoxicating and inexplicable thrill of the big laugh.

# Wobbly Compass

Can we take a moment to think about how the inner experience of self-loathing and doubt tends to spill out into the world around us? When kindness and good intentions fall apart, crumbling under the clumsy hands that would wield them, leaving a grinning fool with no good excuses to explain the damage. For me, it begins with an insistent feeling lingering in the psyche, like the specter of death haunting the halls of a nursing home, insisting I acknowledge that I've never known what to do. Awkward tendrils of shame and regret creep up my spine and settle around my neck like a strangler, bored by the task. This sensation has been with me, on and off, for most of my life. I don't remember when I began feeling this way, but I do remember when I noticed its impact on my choices. As with many of life's less gracious moments, it came at a time when, instead of doing something useful, I did something pointless.

It was early on a Saturday morning when I heard my mom speaking to a woman in the hallway of our house. She was pulling out the vacuum cleaner and giving cleaning instructions to someone. I found it strange because we did not have a house cleaner. By all rights, the two freeloading, able-bodied children - my older sister and I sleeping peacefully in our private rooms at that very moment - should have been pushing around the vacuum and scrubbing the toilets. Ten and twelve-year-olds are just the right height for deep cleaning. Instead, our kind, generous, and hard-working Mom and stepdad decided to combine big-heartedness with action and hired a woman in desperate need of income to come over and clean. I'll call this woman Jean.

I stayed put between my sheets, listening intently, hopeful that the sanctity of my room would not be violated. I could hear Jean answering my mom. She spoke with the unmistakable accent of a black woman raised in rural Mississippi. While some vowels were often elongated, other words and phrases were sped up and clipped short at the ends. Relative to the slow dirge of the accents in our house, Jean's was a toe-tapping staccato, musical, yet haunted by something opaque to the soft-handed likes of me.

I heard Jean ask, "Ain't I gonna clean them rooms in the back?"

Charitably, and with little expectation of it truly happening, my mom answered, "No, the kids have to clean their own rooms."

I was unaware that one of Jean's kids was with her, a boy my age. I'd seen the house where he lived. My mom brought me with her one day, our van filled with food and clothing donated by the church.

Jean had four school-aged children, three of them with different fathers. A single mom with little time for work and not much work on offer, in any case. Her house was a drafty, old, poorly remodeled sharecropper's shack. It suffered from intermittent utilities, often shut off by the power company for missed payments. Even when she found the money to pay the bills, there was no air-conditioning to chisel away at summer's crushing heat and humidity and no central heat to break the freezing wet cold of winter. I never went inside the house, but from the outside, I wondered where everyone slept. As Jean and my mom talked in the front yard, standing next to an old dog house with no dog and a frayed tire dangling by a ragged rope from a tree limb, I felt spoiled and soft in the front seat of the cozy minivan. As soon as Jean's kids could get jobs, they were expected to chip in and help cover expenses. The cost of my sneakers was about the same as her utility bill.

My mom made sure I understood some basic facts. Going to bed either uncomfortably hot or cold was a regular occurrence for Jean and her kids, often accompanied by an empty stomach. The kids shared a single bed. With only a long clothesline for drying and a bathtub for washing, clean clothes were limited. And, to be sure, none of the occupants had a private room with a door. What she couldn't help me with was how to handle the strange, guilty pit growing in my stomach.

The hardship of their home didn't change the fact that I envied its solitude. Situated on a country road with a large forest extending for miles in all directions, there were no obnoxious neighbors within a country mile. Obnoxious guests were forced to come by van.

My first lesson in empathy was closing my left eye to experience the half-blindness of my father. An easy tutorial further enriched by dad telling us to imagine trying to see out of our ears. But, for the first time in my remarkably privileged life, I saw the face of poverty as it gnawed on the bones of someone I knew. I realize now that piercing sadness isn't the same as empathy. Empathy, in this case, would take much more imagination than I could give to something so raw.

Before visiting Jean's home, poverty was a faraway and abstract concept; Sally Struthers on television was its avatar. Pretty blonde hair helmeting her face as she pleaded for people to send money to starving children in Ethiopia. Such sad and earnest cries made me want to go there personally and swat the flies away from the eyes of the poor children with distended bellies and spindly arms. Secretly and selfishly, I wanted Sally Struthers to cradle me in her arms like a big-haired and plump-cheeked aunt. In-person, however, the poverty of my Mississippi neighbors was of a much more painful variety. I couldn't grasp the injustice, the deprivation of nourishment and comfort to people who were essentially my neighbors. How had I never seen this before? Why did I not know this existed so close to home? What could I possibly do about it? I still don't have a good answer to these questions.

Back in our home on Jean's first day as a house cleaner, lying awkwardly awake in my second favorite pair of pajamas, with my head propped on one of the two pillows in my comfortable bed, I listened. Behind the closed door of my private bedroom, filled with luxuriantly dirty clothing, toys that were mine and mine alone, and a window affording me a view of a nearly identical house across the street, I could hear a young boy's voice in the hallway. He was right outside my door, speaking to his mother as she cleaned the bathroom. His mother's voice echoed off the tub's porcelain as she answered, "Naw, baby, they sleepin'. Leave 'em be."

He sounded bored and possibly bewildered by the sleeping kids behind the closed doors. "Why they sleepin'? Sun's up, momma!" His voice rattled my doorknob with the same pre-adolescent timbre as mine.

"Shush, boy!" Jean's normally docile and understated voice had a nice bark to it I'd not heard before.

From a strong field of uncomfortable sentences, I'll soon present a few that describe a memory so awkward I feel the need to tack on yet another disclaimer. I'll also add that I'm not writing them to excuse myself or to exorcise a guilty conscience. Whatever color you choose to shade it, my guilt is my problem, not anyone else's. I'm also not here to deal with white guilt or the privilege of being born a white male in the middle class of North America - although those conditions surely exist and have impacted everything in my life in largely positive ways. I'm more interested in calibrating my moral compass against the pull of something more meaningful than such superficial characteristics as skin color, genitals, or income.

Personally, I find it gross when a person admits to having done something wrong in hopes that someone else will forgive them for it, saying something like, "Oh, it's OK. You were young and didn't know any better." That's not where I'm coming from here. If anything, I mean to describe the following nervy moment, not to determine my guilt or to absolve myself from sin, but to get a better look at the thing. Reanimating such hard-to-explain and shameful behavior is not fun. Still, it feels necessary to reconstruct it as faithfully to the original as possible to see it with clearer eyes. Shining a light on awful shit is the best way to illuminate the ugly sheen slicking the surface of any given persona. It's good to see it from time to time, lest I start believing it when my wife says, "Don't be so hard on yourself. You're a good person."

But first, before I expose myself, I'd like to talk about toys. I had lots of them, not as many as some, but more than most. My favorites were action figures. G.I. Joe men, Star Wars figurines, and a few off-brand characters filled the ranks of my small toy army. A serviceable fleet of ships and vehicles made up the Navy and Air Force, while inherited vintage toys handled space travel. But the main thing, the true locus of joy, was the character-driven, inner experience of the individual soldiers - a place where all my powers of empathy tended to be spent. I built a world for each of them. My closet, and the toys within, represent a totem for how I've treated my creative efforts since - one of the first singularly private aspects of my life. Self-consciousness set in early.

When my friends came over, we spent our time outside. Never did I invite them into the strange world of my toys to see the bizarre and evolving universe of characters. If a kid came over and took an interest in what was happening in the closet, I would pretend not to know each figure by name or nature. I'd learned many years earlier to be ashamed of how I expressed myself creatively, and rightly so, having made disgusting use of feces to make art.

When I visited my friends' houses, they were proud of their toys and would show me relatively well-maintained and complete collections. In contrast, my toys were a bit more random and displayed a great variety of battle scars from braving blizzards in the freezer, buried in mudslides, or burned by exploding fireworks. But as action-packed as their physical lives were, the running narratives surrounding their intertwined journeys were of much greater interest to me. Although I couldn't have said as much then, the action was a theatrical device to help move the story along. I found it impossible to share the episodic and ever-changing saga I'd created for such a hodge-podge collection of inanimate objects, so I avoided it entirely.

The background anxiety of sharing the weirdness of my toys hummed its familiar tune as Jean's son languished in the hallway. A kid, by the way, whose name I do not remember because I never asked him what it was. He was right outside my door. I could practically feel how bored he was and heard him whispering to himself as his fingers traced the carpet like he was drawing pictures in the two-toned shade of the pile.

I wish I could tell you I didn't invite him in simply because I was shy about sharing the inner world of my toy universe. It would be great if I could tell you that I *wanted* to open the door at all, but that would be a lie. It wasn't just because I didn't know him. And it wasn't because he was poor or black. A fucked up web of interconnected emotions kept that door closed, physically and metaphorically. It was partly a matter of shame for my good fortune – partly a lack of understanding that human connection is all we've got and one of the few things that can hack away at the roots of the twisted, guilty tree growing in my belly. It also represented a severe lack of imagination's best product, empathy, for which I continue to carry regret.

My room suddenly seemed gross, a literal embarrassment of riches. So, instead of opening the door, introducing myself, or making a meaningful connection with the kid outside, I got up from my bed, picked out two action figures (relatively new ones with minimal battle scars), and passed them under the door. He noticed right away, pulling on them gently. I watched with curious delight as the figure was sluggishly dragged through the shallow swamp of mauve carpet fibers, scraping dramatically against the underside of the hollow core door like a hard-plastic abductee in a sci-fi flick. This created a special effect I would have otherwise loved to employ but never had the second pair of hands needed to help me do it - another in a string of opportunities missed. The exchange was wordless, leaving me wondering if maybe he didn't know what to say to me either. I hopped back into my bed and listened.

This weird "gift" did not make me feel good about anything, much less myself. Since hearing the voices in the hallway, I'd traveled from sleep, where I experienced strange, embarrassment-filled dreams, to a waking moment of instant and compiling feelings of uselessness and something similar to survivor's guilt. Fucking exhausting, really. Shame covered me like dust on old furniture. The conversant plastic click of two toys on a quest was no comfort. Like me, the kid had no problems puppeteering alone.

Jean finished up, and my mom took her home. Of course, her son and I exchanged as much goodbye as hello. When I opened my door, I was surprised to be greeted by two action figures. One was seated on its haunches, sitting upright and facing the door. His left arm outstretched, resting on the back of his fallen comrade (or victim), lying face down in the muck (carpet). It was touching, even if unintentional, reminding me of a black and white photo I'd seen in a book about the war in Vietnam.

I truly don't know why I didn't handle it better. For sure, I can't blame a lack of good examples. My mom wasn't just handing over "gifts" to a poor or underprivileged person; she was connecting with another human being in need as a friend. There is no charity in friendship, and being a good friend might be the least useless thing one can do for another.

A penny in the mouth has a flavor, and I don't like it. No matter what it's like, you're getting a taste of both sides of the coin. Selflessness and selfishness are similar in this way. Put that penny in your mouth for a moment and consider what motivates your generosity or self-regard. Is there some kind of saint in you? Are you sick of other people's demands on your attention? Are you doing this thing, plowing through the ever-changing, indifferent beauty of existence with a clear mind? Do you know why you horde one thing yet give another? Are you learning lessons, taking notes, and sharing in the wisdom of others? Have you squandered talent, advantage, or opportunity? To what extent is your guilt someone else's problem? Considering the implications of sour moments, like the brief one I just shared with you, brings me no real answers, but it does help me ask those questions honestly, at least.

A compass has no concern for where you need to go. It dispassionately shows you North – the rest is up to you. I sometimes forget that a compass does more to help you decide where not to go than guide you in the right direction. A nice feature, no?

I'd like to tell you I learned an immediate lesson from Jean's son. I'd also like to say that I've got an enviably low percentage of body fat and an abnormally high IQ, but surely you would know I was lying. It would take years to understand that weird morning, and even now, I'm not convinced I truly "get it." I suppose I'm grateful for the weight of the memory, though - Thankful for its persistent tug upon my perception of others and its capacity to remind me to not let self-loathing guide the ship. While the weak magnetism of doubt continues to confuse the needle of my moral compass, causing me to bounce between the lonely and selfish South and the communal and generous North, more often than not, I tend to land somewhere in the morally ambiguous West-Northwest. As the compass wobbles, I'll try and remember to keep the river on my right, sharing more than toys and silent wishes. And who knows, next time around, I might even get your name.

# Hang on, Diagnosis!

It should come as no surprise, the day I nearly committed suicide, it was raining. Suicide is the wrong word, of course, as I had no intention of ending my own life, but you can count on the accuracy of that weather report. This story, however, is not about self-harm or weather and certainly isn't about accuracy. No, this is a story about the power of misunderstanding and the value of knowing one's limits. Setting the mood by hanging a distraction or two in the first paragraph just feels like the right move.

After our parents divorced for the second and final time, my big sister and I spent every other weekend with our dad. We'd hang around his office after school for about an hour before he closed for the weekend.

One of my favorite things to do while waiting around for dad, when I wasn't looking at dog-eared Playboy magazines in the upstairs bathroom, was to listen to him on the phone. It didn't matter if I understood very little of what an attorney was meant to do; his phone calls were the best. Dad was a charmer with an agile mind, hilariously embracing irony, grave sincerity, and a sense of the absurd, often in the same sentence. I could hear people on the other end of his calls laughing loudly. Clients, other attorneys, judges, employees, you name it - my dad could make them laugh or piss them off entirely, and often on the same call.

I also liked his phone calls because I disliked it when he spoke to me directly. I never knew what to say in return, and he didn't seem to know what to say to me either. Hearing him speak so fluidly and comfortably with someone else was like watching a movie; I could observe without the worry of remembering my lines. In other words, it was ideal.

One of those Friday afternoons, I listened as dad spoke with an elderly female client. Her voice ambled from the speaker with a crackling and ancient southern drawl - sounding to me like a primeval sea creature had crawled from the shores of Biloxi to find another pack of smokes. She was calling to revise her "last will and testament." The concept of a "will" was new to me, so I listened carefully.

The old woman had concerns about who exactly would be getting what after her death. Dad listened patiently as she explained, "My sons are about as similar as shit and ice cream. I don't know about givin' 'em both the same amount of cash. And my daughters, well, only one of 'em knows how to clean, so she should probably keep the house, but what about her filthy little sister?" I was fascinated with the notion of designating specific gifts to just the right people without giving *anything* until it was no longer useful to the giver.

Dad was unusually serious, redirecting the sarcastic and playful tendencies of his regular phone persona to a series of silent facial expressions and hand motions. Employing eyerolls, pretending to jab a pencil into his ear, or puffing up his cheeks to look like a monkey, his physicality filled the void created by the gravity of the conversation. Besides, the lady on the phone was doing most of the heavy lifting in the comedy department. Despite his silent silliness and her carefree tone, I gathered the business of giving things away after death was worth thinking about. I decided I would write my own will, and I got to it as soon as I got home from the weekend with dad.

Being of a reasonably sound mind and kinda-small body, I bequeathed all my toys to my friend Frank. My big sister would benefit from my bedroom and any cash I had on hand. My bicycle and collection of squirt guns would go to my friend Andy – you get the idea. The meager possessions of a ten-year-old may have been doled out in short order, but what the document lacked in scope and scale, it compensated for with significance and concision.

I was almost proud of myself for being so thoughtful with my choices. I showed it to my Mom, I showed it to my sister, and I showed it to my friends. Not surprisingly, I never showed it to my dad.

There was something nice about being generous without actually parting with anything. Two of my friends wrote their own wills, possibly sensing the same. As far as I know, theirs would cause them considerably less trouble than mine would end up causing me.

Within a few days of writing this "will" of mine, the relative buzz of consequence-free altruism faded, and I pretty much forgot about it. I moved on, as I tend to do, and busied my mind with the madness of being a relatively new person.

We lived with my Mom and stepdad in a neighborhood filled with families. Lots of kids our age lived nearby, and several tall, strong, and wild teenagers were living closer still. The kids we spent the most time with, the Bavier brothers, a couple of blonde-headed and adventurous kids who improbably ended up in Mississippi via Australia, lived two houses down and one street over. Our backyards were connected by an unbroken expanse of unfenced land. It was a fantastic situation for energy-filled weirdos to burn off some sugar.

I don't know if your experience with the weather was anything like mine, but as a child, it generally came as a surprise. I must have had access to forecasts, and surely I could have asked an adult, but I couldn't be bothered. I remember occasionally being handed a raincoat or told to grab my jacket, but that was about the extent of my preparations. So, when my sister, our friends, and I found ourselves suddenly doused by heavy rain while goofing around in the climbing tree behind the Bavier's house, everyone scampered off in the direction of the nearest living room.

I stayed inside for just long enough to learn that the card game "Uno" was on deck for entertainment. I never did learn how to play that game. In fact, I still find card-based amusement to be one of the least amusing ways to spend my time. I headed back outside to face the weather and finish what I'd been working on in the climbing tree, preferring the indifferent chill of driving rain to the exasperating heat of consecutive losing hands.

The Bavier brothers had been taking karate, and two of their super long, no-longer-needed white belts had been repurposed as a rope swing. Intelligent and industrious, the brothers had lashed the two sashes together, and we were preparing to tie them around a sturdy branch when the rain sent us away. Fortunately, heavy and sudden rain in the south often lasts only a few minutes, leaving everything wet but manageable. I climbed the slippery tree and set myself upon the task of making a rope swing *without* the overbearing guidance of several kids who were older and wiser than I was.

Tying a sturdy knot around the branch was easy enough, accomplished by shimmying out on my belly and making fast the knot at the point closest to the branch below. This would allow some brave and/or foolish kid to grab it, swing out, and hopefully swing back close enough to reach the spot from which he or she had just launched.

Once my knot was secured, all I needed to do was climb back down to the "launch site" and tie a few fat knots along the length of the belt. But *that* would have been too easy, as it did not require any bravery and/or stupidity. Instead, I opted for a much more complex and exciting method of getting back down; for what is the point of playing if not to taste a little danger?

From the upper branch, I fashioned a large slipknot in the belt. This created a nice big loop with a flat bit where I could stand. With my feet securely resting in the loop, I could then drop down in the first and possibly most-epic use of the newly installed swing. Everything depended on my feet remaining in the flat bit, so it was crucial my grip was solid to prevent the knot from cinching around my feet. If all went well, I would gracefully swing myself back and reach out with a free hand to pull myself onto the "launch site." I pictured Indiana Jones doing something similar with a whip, a hat, and a soundtrack. Although I had no hat and a couple of wet karate belts were standing in for the whip, I *could* hear a song from "Outlandos d'Amour" by "The Police" drifting from where my sister and the brothers were playing cards. At least my soundscape was on the upswing.

I scooted myself over to where the knot was fastened to the branch, rested my feet on the flat bit of the belt, positioned myself to face the "launch site," gripped the business end of the slipknot, and prepared to drop over the back of the branch and swing.

Looking backward into one's past with seasoned, if still foolish eyes, one can occasionally identify moments when life offered two distinct possibilities, depending on one's choice at that bifurcation of reality. We often find ourselves speculating on the wildly different outcomes one might have faced if, say, a left turn had been made instead of a right, or a no had replaced a yes, but these are merely stories - desperate gasps of air to survive the otherwise brutal weight of life's unfolding moments. With each passing second, "possibility" becomes fiction, and "actuality" paves over any forks in the road.

With limited mechanical skills and no mind for geometry, I had no clue what sort of road I had foolishly chosen when I slid my feet into what would later look less like a misadventure in knot-tying and more like the work of a hangman.

As you've probably guessed, my plan was garbage. The moment the belt accepted my weight, the combination of worn-out shoes and plenty of forward momentum caused me to slip through the wet fabric. My small hands couldn't keep the knot from being pulled tight, and I suddenly stopped mid-fall as the belt violently tightened under my ribs. The impact knocked the wind out of my lungs, and my weight began strangling me as the knot grew tighter.

Doing my best to keep calm, I tried to swing my legs back and forth to reach the "launch site." Each movement of my legs made the knot burrow further into my rib cage. I tried to reach out with one hand for the lower branch, but when

I released my grip, I could feel the knot tighten even further. I tried to climb back up the belt, but it was too wet, and my hands and arms weren't up for the task. In short, I was fucked. Dangling straight down from an uncharacteristically perfect knot, panic began working its way into my mind.

For the first time in my life, I was afraid I might die. I was struggling to breathe. I worried if I screamed out for help, I might not be able to refill my lungs with air. I thought of what I had been told about crucifixion and how it killed a man by causing him to suffocate. The Romans spared old Jesus from death-by-suffocation by stabbing him in the ribs from the ground with a long spear so he could bleed to death instead. I would later find myself thinking a great deal about the two others to his left and right who were not so fortunate, left to slowly die from a painful and terrifying lack of oxygen. A new empathy for the sinner would find a welcome home in my chest. In either case, I didn't want to die at the end of a spear, and I especially did not want to die at the end of a karate belt.

Panic won the day. I risked it all by screaming for help, keeping the small muscles of my stomach as tight as possible to take the pressure off my lungs, gripping the belt with all my strength. I shouted out a pathetic and somewhat muted cry for help over and over again. It was like trying to run in a dream; the volume of my voice caught up in bedsheets of asphyxiation.

My sister and the Bavier Brothers could not hear me over the loud music, which must have been doing wonders to make their endless card game seem tolerable. It had never occurred to me that Indiana Jones wasn't aware of his soundtrack. I wish I had been so fortunate, as no one should have to face suffocation with "Sting" singing about a prostitute he's rather presumptuously trying to rescue.

My Mom later said she heard yelling but thought it was us just playing around.

After what felt like an eternity of raw and frantic horror, I saw the figure of a teenager leaping over a fence, then running across the uninterrupted expanse of Mississippi mud and weeds which connected the neighboring yards. When he reached me, he placed my feet in his hands and told me to stand up. I did exactly that, releasing the tension from the knot and slipping it over my body. I would have hit the ground hard if he hadn't caught me on the way down.

Exhausted yet buzzing with the chemical reaction of near-death racing through my veins, I dropped to my knees, shaking and coughing, unable to hide the tears and snot streaming from my face as I desperately sucked in as much air as I could with each breath. I wanted to thank him but couldn't manage any words. Gratitude outweighed shame. The joy of breathing, a simple act whose absence I had never considered, overwhelmed me.

Once my breathing slowed from panicked gulps to mildly crazed wheezing, the young man gently helped me to my feet. Noticing that I was wincing from the pain in my chest, he asked if I was OK. I said I was, but I obviously didn't mean it. I looked him in the eyes and thanked him for saving me. He patted my shoulder, saying, "you'll be alright." With an undignified and lumbering hobble, like a wounded animal seeking its den, I shambled back to the safety of my home. To this day, my xiphoid process, the little bone at the bottom of my rib cage, is crooked from being broken by that drop.

I never saw that young man again. Within a few months of rescuing me, he lost his own life in a tragic car crash. I was told he died with a portion of the car's engine resting in his lap as the vehicle slowly burned, killing one of his friends as well. It happened less than a mile from where he plucked me from that tree. When I got the news, my heart was broken, and I felt a strange guilt. I had nightmares for weeks. I can only hope he died instantly and was not made to suffer the additional pain of having his cries for help go unanswered; he deserved that, at least.

When I told my Mom what had just happened, she read something between the lines to find a story I had no intention of writing. Mom, shell-shocked by a runaway daughter's fragile mental condition, and deeply hurt by another child's cold shoulder, saw reality through a lens I still cannot imagine. To those loving, compassionate, and perhaps traumatized eyes, my childish "last will and testament" read like a suicide note. A sensitive kid who would rather play in the rain outside than consistently lose card games inside was seen as isolated and depressed at being left out. And, of course, I would imagine the most alarming feature to her eyes was the comically botched rope swing that wore the violent garb of a noose. Within a month, I would find myself under the care of a psychiatrist.

My dad, a guy who barely knew me, and my stepmother, a woman who had zero interest in getting to know me, got involved and insisted that I be institutionalized. Incredibly, even though she was convinced I had tried to end my own life, my Mom put forth a persuasive argument and kept me from landing in the modern equivalent of an asylum. For that, I am truly grateful.

I'm not sure what hurt more: the people I trusted thought I was suicidal or how dumb they must have thought I was for so badly botching a hanging. I hadn't the vocabulary nor sufficient command over my native tongue to convince any adult of the scope of misunderstanding we were all facing. Like suffocation, the feeling of my words falling on deaf ears was hopeless and panic-inducing. The shrink prodded and examined me like a germ under a microscope, interrogating every aspect of my life for signs of virulence, weakness, or illness.

Where before, I had been happily oblivious to any hidden meanings behind my own motivations, I became decidedly suspicious of them. A distrust in myself was crafted, amplified, then dwarfed by my suspicion of adults. A deep desire to avoid being misunderstood became the very thing that made being understood properly much less likely. Ultimately, I felt like mine was a damaged personality. It was implied that my only hope for remedy was to subject myself to the whims and diagnoses of people I did not like or trust.

The effects were felt by more than just me. At one point, the psychiatrist became fixated on a story I told him about my older brother. My memory was of my brother putting me in the large, round, black case used for his bass drum, closing it around me, and rolling me down a flight of stairs. My brother had, in fact, put me in that base drum case at the top of the stairs, but walked next to it as it went safely down to the landing, rolling it with just enough speed to make it exciting, but not so fast I might be injured. The distinction seems subtle, but the ramifications of getting that one detail of the story wrong was disastrous, particularly for my brother.

He felt like a monster, adding to his resentment of and detachment from our mother, his suspicion of me, and who knows what other forms of mental anguish. I felt like a science experiment, tested, diagnosed, and observed for changes and possible tendencies toward self-harm. I also saw myself as a terrible brother. I was, again, slipping my feet into the wet belt and leaping from the wrong branch, only verbally this time.

I cannot overstate the impact this had on my development as a person. While I was profoundly changed by the terrifying act of accidentally hanging myself, and not just because near-death tends to hit the fast-forward button on one's perspective, it was the ensuing period of diagnosis and analysis that was most impactful. I found myself, for the first time, feeling self-conscious.

Simone de Beauvoir said, "Self-consciousness is not knowledge, but a story one tells about oneself." I believe that to be true, but I now know the difference between self-consciousness and self-awareness. When I think of those desperate moments in that tree, I'm reminded of this lesson in a powerful way. While being self-conscious requires tacking on a story to explain ourselves, self-awareness demands a great and sometimes brutal honesty.

The honesty here is simple - foolishness comes as naturally to me as breathing. I've learned that to counter potentially life-threatening lapses in concentration, I need to pay more attention to what I'm doing. The tricky bit has been deciding what deserves special attention and what doesn't; sometimes, I choose wisely, and often I don't.

Of course, regardless of our choices, fate has its own cold and indifferent say. Sometimes the sun shines, and all is well. Other times you nearly hang to death in a tree you climbed for fun. One day you are saving a life, and another, you die horribly in a tragic and pointless accident. And just when you think you've written something incorruptible and generous like a last will and testament, innocence gives way to ignorance, and you land in inescapably deep shit. In any case, hoping for the best, you live, you choose, and you react to the consequences, knowing folly or glory are subject to an interconnected web of choices, good, bad, and not always yours.

It is also worth remembering no matter how we present ourselves, the odds of being terribly misunderstood are not small because the number of things each of us does not understand about the other is great. In fact, being misunderstood may be one of the few things any of us can truly count on in life.

So, I'll take a breath now,
A deep one, in fact.
To see if I can taste
A little gratitude in the air.
Eyes peeled for the next misstep.
Stumbling over the wild moments.
Savoring the myth of the possible,
Because it reads like good fiction.
Only keeping score
Of the actual,
Because it reads like cold history.
And when all else fails,
I hope I'll Know
When to belt out,
With all I've got,
One last cry
For help.

# Old Friends

Friday night, dinner for six - three guests are over 80, one is 70, and the other two, myself and my wife, in our 40s. Saturday afternoon, lunch for three, the principal guest is 74. Sunday, spending time with Ricci, she is 81. These are my friends.

When I was a young man, in 1991, I made friends with my first elder. His name was George, and he was 72 years old. I met George at our church and would spend hours chatting with him after the services. He tended to ramble, telling me loosely connected stories, interrupted by non sequitur and oddball details. I loved it.

George had been a soldier in the Korean war, an illustrator for Disney, and had loved and battled with women his whole life. He was a curiosity to me - free from the expectations of others, experienced in all things practical, an entirely singular individual. Most everyone else avoided him because he tended to go on for so long. George also had a potent body odor which turned people off right away. For some reason, I just didn't care. I liked him and felt like being around him was good for me, like pushups for the character.

He creeped out my sister and pretty much all the girls. He could be outrageously flirtatious and wouldn't hold back his opinions if he found a young girl attractive. By young, I mean under 18. Different times, for sure. I can't imagine George expressing opinions like that today when sensitivities to the inappropriate are understandably dialed up to the maximum. In this respect, I hope he was one of the last of a dying breed.

Creepiness aside, I respected George. I appreciated more than just his freedom of expression or his lack of concern for what people thought. He wasn't just a curiosity to me or something so strange and different that I couldn't look away – he was interesting, entirely dissimilar from everyone, cultured, well-traveled, and a throwback to a type of southern gentleman that now only exists in books.

He was also something of a weird mirror to me. I couldn't have explained it then, but I saw something in him I recognized. In most situations, I felt then and often still feel like an outsider. George was quite obviously out of place but could function like a neutron, twirling around the nucleolus of an atom, crucial to the whole but free to spin in orbit. I wanted, and still want, that freedom.

Once I hit high school, I started working and traveling on weekends. I went to church way less often than before. George and I saw each other about once per year, and I'm ashamed to say I thought of him less and less frequently. My senior year of high school, my mom told me he died; I don't recall even knowing he was ill. His wife asked me to be one of the pallbearers, along with his son and a few other men from the church. When I first met him, I wasn't big enough to carry much of anything, let alone the body and casket of a friend. So much had changed in so little time.

His death hit me in a strange place. A place, at that age, I didn't realize existed. I felt a new type of sadness, one which was lodged under the part of my body where I usually felt regret. I recognized what George was, and it hurt me to have only realized it after he was gone, so many years after we'd spent much time together. George wasn't a curious or strange *old* man; he was a man, a person like me or any one of my friends, just older, more experienced, and much more curious.

The men who carried his casket weren't the types to have listened to his stories; they were more likely to walk past him than stop and chat. They knew him, for sure, but avoided long-form conversation. I searched the faces at the funeral - almost none were as old as George's. His friends had been dying off for years, and the ones still living were in no shape to go to funerals. George may or may not have minded that we fell out of regular contact, but looking at the number of strangers in that church, I felt terrible about it.

Since then, I've made a point of cultivating relationships with my elders. I do my best to keep in touch and have a phrase I share with them occasionally.

If, for some reason,
goodbye extends into eternity,
know that I loved you
the whole time.

# Don't Blame the Welcome Mat

A strange popping sound made her stop cold as she walked out the door. She turned to look him in the eyes, eyes she was still getting to know, and asked flatly, "did you just fart?" He was not the brightest of young men, but when the chips were down, and it really mattered, he was bright enough. His laugh was relaxed and easy, "Ha, no, my foot caught on the edge of the doormat, see." He turned back and flapped the mat with his foot, which made a reassuringly similar sound to a pop of flatulence, and said, "but we should keep moving - before it stinks."

We'll call this woman Melissa, and we'll call this not-so-bright young man, me. Melissa and I met in a small, charming town in Illinois. I was thirteen, and she was much more than the first girl to catch me farting.

I'd been staying at my grandmother's house since the school year ended. Grandma was dying of cancer. My mom looked after her with all the empathy, skill, and patience she'd learned as a hospice nurse. I wondered if mom had anticipated some-day using those skills to escort her mother from the land of the living. In any case, she was prepared, and her mother was fortunate to have her there. She was slightly less fortunate to have the likes of me around - a thirteen-year-old pubescent maniac wandering the streets of her small town looking for a good time.

That small town, a place called Peru, Illinois, was a bit different from where I lived – another little town with an improbably exotic name – Hernando, Mississippi. In Portuguese, the word "peru" means turkey. While I don't think the city's founders intended to invoke the image of the noble bird by obliquely naming their town after it in a foreign tongue, I would like to believe they shared a commitment to the absurd. In fact, I'd prefer not to spoil the mystery by ever solving the puzzle of its namesake. I would rather assume that somewhere deep in the consciousness of midwestern Peruvians lies an inner drive to bestow things with confusing names. For instance, the bewilderingly christened baseball team, The Illinois Valley Pistol Shrimp, celebrate their home victories in Peru.

I almost feel compelled to apologize for the detour I just put you through, but considering you just learned that peru means turkey in Portuguese and that an organization called "The Pistol Shrimp" exists, I think there's a chance it was worth the trip. Anyhow, I was telling you about my grandmother dying of cancer via a story about a girl who caught me farting and a brief comparison of the small towns where we lived, so I'll continue.

The town where I lived, so named after the brutal conquistador, Hernando Desoto, does feature a charming downtown square. It does not, however, feature much of a walkable or tightly woven community. Or I should say, it didn't in the late 80s and 90s. It may now, but I don't care to find out. Back then, if I wanted to go downtown, I had to ride my bike past a pack of dogs who loved to chase me or along a highway of speeding rednecks who might love to hit me. Walking casually there was not a great option.

In contrast, the town of Peru was quite walkable and tightly woven. Grandma's place was half a block away from an idyllic city park that featured a large and spacious public swimming pool, a couple of baseball diamonds, a couple of basketball courts, and a playground starring a retro spaceship with a slide pouring from it. It was only a few short blocks from her house to downtown, and I could ride my bike almost anywhere in town a thirteen-year-old would care to visit. I played basketball and swam at the pool nearly every day. I'd also go to my great aunt Jenny's place to drink soda, learn the ropes of solitaire, or watch the baseball games from her upstairs apartment window.

I had another great aunt in town, Aunt Jeanie, or Death on a Cracker, as the kids called her when she wasn't around. I did not pay her any visits as I was convinced she thoroughly disliked me. One of my uncles lived in town, and I occasionally saw him. I also had a few cousins there, but they were older and had interests far afield from mine, so I was mostly left to my own devices.

It didn't take long for the young people of Peru to notice the new face in town. I stood out a bit. I was taller than the average kid my age, had longish hair, and dressed like a worn-out old hippie in tie-dyed shirts, dirty jeans, and ratty sneakers. Let me be clear, I was not, nor did I consider myself, some unique shining star basking in the glow of his radiant singularity. I was more of a low-rent sub-variant on the widely available teenage boy. A disheveled b-roll, printed for safety. If, for some reason, one of the good kids didn't make it, a guy like me could hold his spot in line. I saw the kids in Peru as "northerners," a bit more buttoned up, with cleaner accents, haircuts, and clothes. I'm not sure how they viewed me, but the girls I would meet sure noticed a difference in how I spoke and failed to comb my hair.

And meet girls, I did. Back home, I was new to the flirting game. I'd only had one girlfriend, one whose hand I'd only briefly held while no one was looking. She quickly drew it back to her side the moment her friends noticed us.

I looked at my grandmother's hands as my mother gave her pieces of chipped ice to soothe her dry mouth. Lying flat against the sheets, they were impossibly wrinkled and seemed physically spent, too worn down to even curl a little. I tried to imagine that happening to the hands of any of the girls I knew from school – it haunted me. That line of thinking, as it must, led my mind across the burning sands of painful musing. Watching my mother's hands as they did their work, strong, confident, purposeful, yet delicate, and capable of playing the organ in church, I had to drop the thread before I was over-whelmed by the pain of loss to come. I brought my attention back to the present sadness we were all facing and did my best to deal with it.

My method of dealing with the sadness was to stay out of the way. I was useless at the bedside.

Outside the home of my dying grandmother, I started making friends of a sort. There was a big, chubby kid called Henry. We were both thirteen. Like me, Henry was a smartass. He liked to sit around, drink sugary drinks, and talk shit. When I wasn't playing basketball or swimming, he'd be there with a can of red cream soda, ready to chat. We spent loads of time riding our bikes around town, just exploring and talking. He showed me all the cool places to get more soda, candy, or hamburgers.

Then there was the originally printed kid for whom I was the dirty variant. He was tall, clean, well dressed, and had all the same interests I did, but much better at them. With hand-somely chiseled features and Norwegian blue eyes, the girls all loved him. I'll call him Throckmorton, mostly because I don't remember his name, and he looked too perfect to have a name like Albert or Horace. Throckmorton disliked me tremendous-ly and openly. We played basketball together. After a few days, he started playing rougher than usual, knocking into me and throwing his elbows around. When I confronted him, asking, "What's the deal, man? You alright?" he told me, in a rare, uncharacteristically vulnerable way, "Since you came around, I can't get the girls' attention like I used to." This was news, as none of the girls hanging out in the park had said a word to me.

So, I decided to try my hand at flirting. First, there was a redhead named Sandy. She was the least shy of a group of girls I saw one afternoon at a baseball game and had made a long bit of eye contact with me on her way to the snack bar. What would be my big opening line as I walked up to the group, sin-gled her out, and spoke up? I'd silently agonized over it while Henry and I watched the game. Finally, I gave up on the clever one-liners and went with the super suave, "Hi, what's your name?"

It didn't matter. When her pale skin flushed with a red that nearly matched her hair, I knew I was safe to ask her, and most importantly, she wanted to tell me. She put out her hand to shake it, like I was meeting a bank manager, and said, "Sandy, what's yours?" Fortunately, I remembered.

Sandy was super Catholic and obsessed with volleyball. She was my age and had never had a boyfriend. She told me she once had a massive crush on Throckmorton but said he was a jerk and too cocky for her taste. We got along great, and I occasionally went to her house to talk on her front steps. I never saw the inside of her home, and that first handshake was our only physical contact.

Back at grandma's house, things were going downhill fast. My grandmother had been a nurse in her career and knew more about death and dying than most. She'd given birth to five children, only three of whom were alive that summer. She'd lost two of them, one as a child and one as an adult. My favorite uncle and my mother's twin brother, Jerry, had been killed in a horrible helicopter accident a few years earlier. She'd also lost two husbands, one young and sad and one old and wild – my grandpa. So, grandma was no stranger to pain, and looking back now, it seemed like she was ready for death and knew how to die – a skill I hope is embedded in the same genetic code currently instructing the hair on my head to abandon ship. Grandma was dying a little more every day, and even though I was busy playing, flirting, and making myself scarce, even I noticed.

The time I spent with Sandy was wholesome, sweet, and unrushed. We talked a lot about school and how different her experience was from mine. Not just the difference between a young woman from a young man, but the systems we were working with. My southern school, run by nuns and made up of one brick building and a flotilla of bone-white trailers adrift in a sea of Mississippi Delta cotton, was an archaic and quaint vision that made her laugh. Her school, on the other hand, constructed in the late 1800s by immigrants from Ireland, Germany, Poland, and Italy, was as hale and hardy as the people who built it. The stonework was perfect, the halls were spacious, and the floors were made to withstand brutal winters and endless snow-boot trampling. Her curriculum was also more solid and more demanding, leaving her with a firm understanding of history, especially that of the pernicious, slave-holding South, which the textbooks my classmates and I read from had all but glossed over.

One night, hanging around the edges of the baseball field after a game, Henry introduced me to Melissa – or Missy as I would come to know her. Missy was a year older than us, and a friend of Henry's older sister. She was not shy in the least. I did forget my name for a moment when it came time to tell her what it was. She was confident, not blushing even a little, and carried herself with a fighter's posture. It turned out she was a fighter, having taken taekwondo since she was a child. Her short brown hair, pulled back into a tight ponytail with a single wisp of hair dangling in front of her face, drove me mad. Within moments of meeting, she split from her friends and asked me if I'd walk her home. It was so bold I could hardly believe my luck! On the way, she took a detour through the park. I followed her to the rocket ship-shaped play structure in the middle of the playground. She walked right up to it, started to climb, then turned around and gave me a wink, nearly stopping my heart. I followed her clumsily, trying desperately not to start singing or weeping with anticipation.

The small metal rocket ship was painted in 1950s red, silver, and blue with all too modern rust filling in where the paint had been chipped by weather and rough and tumble children. The moon was taking a break, giving the stars above a chance to show us what they were up to. It was pure magic to me. Missy, however, was not interested in the magic of starlight, the romantic hue of the rusty ship, or the feel of the night air on her skin; she wanted to make out.

I had no idea what I was doing but had seen enough movies to know that whatever I did next, I needed to do it slowly. She put one hand on the back of my head, the other behind my back, and pulled me close to her. Our bodies connected in a way I could hardly believe was possible. When her lips touched mine, another piece of genetic code overwrote my programming and showed me the way. I won't go into detail for the simple fact that, even though I'm describing events that happened to me, we're dealing ultimately with the exploits of a thirteen-and-fourteen-year-old boy and girl, making out in a fake rocket. Let it suffice to say I was forever changed by that first kiss.

I couldn't tell a soul back home. My mom was exhausted from an effort and mental anguish I could scarcely imagine. Besides, sharing the thrill of my first kiss with her would have been weird, in any case. Grandma obviously had other, more pressing issues than her carousing grandson's adventures about town. My older sister Colleen, my usual confidant, wasn't there and had her own love life to consider. My other siblings, both older and younger, were not close in any sense, physically or mentally, so I had to wait until I saw Henry again. I wouldn't be seeing Henry for a while. That next morning, I had a date.

I woke up way too early, but not for basketball. I didn't take a swim, nor did I ride my bike to Henry's. Instead, I walked straight to Missy's house, where I had eventually escorted her the previous evening. She told me to come back in the morning and not to ride my bike, as she didn't want the neighbors to see it outside. After 10 AM, both of her parents would be at work, so I could come over after that. The way she'd invited me made my feet feel like the ground was missing. I brushed my teeth like never before, showered like I was trying to remove paint from my body, and put on the cleanest clothes I could find. Although the morning air was chilly, I was sweating with anticipation. At 10:01 AM, I was in her backyard.

I knocked sheepishly on the back door, afraid Chuck Norris might open it and roundhouse kick my lanky ass back to Mississippi. Instead, Missy opened the door, wearing a long T-shirt, which I would later learn belonged to her ex-boyfriend, and little else. She told me to come in.

I stood in her house like a dolt. It was a great deal different from any I'd ever seen. I could hardly land my eyes on a surface without wanting to look at something else right away. There were trophies from martial arts tournaments won by various family members and dark-themed sculptures on ancient but sturdy furniture. There were woodblock prints featuring ships at sea or angry samurai hung in rough wooden frames at odd heights. A super cool figurine of a Japanese villager in traditional garb with a wriggling fish at the end of a bamboo pole had a prominent spot on a high table behind the couch. It took all my willpower to take in the scene while trying not to stare at Missy's strong, tan-brown legs. I didn't understand that staring at her legs was precisely what she wanted me to do. One must live to learn, I'm told.

We'd hardly spoken the night before, so all I knew about her was that she was a taekwondo champ who would soon be a freshman in high school and liked making out. I quickly learned she wasn't in the mood for chatting that morning either. She poured me a glass of orange juice and sat on the couch near the fisherman. I followed her, leaving my immediately drained glass in the kitchen sink for fear of spilling the juice on the sofa and leaving a trail of evidence for some ninja in her family to track down and murder me. We picked up where we had left off the night before. Again, I'll skip over the details save for one - I said sayonara to my virginity that day on a trampoline in her backyard and would do so frequently for the remainder of the summer.

There may be some poetry in one creature discovering the ecstasy of sex while another approaches the threshold that separates the living from the dead. But searching for it is like trying to extract significance from one customer finishing his last soda as another buys his first. Yes, those things happen all the time - what of it? I was learning the joy of the female body from a bold and fearless young woman as my bold and fearless grandmother took a few more steps toward an indefinitely prolonged non-existence. These things must happen - essential elements of a story that writes itself, no matter what we do. So why take note? Why feel guilt, regret, sadness, or humor in any of it? If I knew the answer to those questions, I might have peace rather than the turmoil rumbling through my southern-fried brain.

One afternoon, exhausted from my efforts on the trampoline, I returned to grandma's to see several familiar vehicles lined up out front. My great aunt Jeanie, not to be confused with the sweet one, Jenny, walked right up to me, saying with naked scorn and disgust, "Where were you? You should have been here!"

My grandma died while I was busy having the time of my young life. I knew this pain was headed my way, but like most pain, you can't know ahead of time how it will feel. For me, the sadness of her loss was elastic, like stretching an old rubber band - resistant at first, with a long period of easy movement before hitting painful tension at the end of its travel. But there wasn't much time right away to think of my feelings, confused and guilt-ridden as I was at that moment, recently laid and more recently accosted by my great aunt.

I found my mom, who had just held the hand of her mother as she breathed her last breath. I was astonished by her poise and calm. Of course, she was emotional, filled with what I now recognize as a complex mix of sadness and relief, but all I saw at that moment was a woman of sublime strength, capable of giving care far greater than the pain begging for help, able to show a love bigger than the tiny world of personal want, and possessing a vulnerability beyond any impotent peacock-display of pride. She had gone through something primal and painful only to emerge bruised but stronger. I was sad for her, proud of her, and ashamed of myself. I felt like I was a mistake she must have made before she knew better. It would take a long time for that feeling to wear off. I felt awful for acknowledging my guilt before the sadness of losing my beloved grandmother. The gladness I felt for the end of her suffering also made me feel guilty. Should one experience relief from another's death? I didn't know. The strongest emotion on deck was pathetic and selfish anger towards my great aunt for making her pain my problem – what did I expect from an old woman who had just lost her sister? All I wanted in the world was to get back to Missy's house as soon as possible - a want which left me feeling even more guilty, but not so guilty that I didn't do it the very next morning.

The wild newness of the summer toned down from there. Henry and I got into an argument. When he accused me of not being a real friend and only caring about making out with "slutty Missy," I left his house and never spoke to him again. The neighborhood guys quit playing basketball with me altogether. Shooting baskets alone wasn't much fun, so, like Henry's house, I took the courts off my list of places to go. Although we weren't dating, Sandy stopped talking to me once she heard about Missy and me. Thankfully, Missy stayed interested enough to keep inviting me over, although I'd imagine she was relieved to know I'd be going home before too long. We liked each other's company and spent many afternoons on the trampoline and many nights wandering around the park, kissing in the big rocket and talking about death. It was the night before my grandma died that she heard me fart in the doorway. My uncle heard my excuse from the kitchen table and teased me about it later.

When my siblings arrived for my grandma's funeral, everything changed. I had little alone time and rarely saw Missy. I was ashamed to tell anyone about Missy and the trampoline. Our extended family filled grandma's small house after the funeral, surreptitiously examining the bric-a-brac she'd collected over the years. Under each figurine, decorative plate, or framed picture, she thoughtfully placed a small sticker with the name of whichever child or grandchild might enjoy having it after she passed. I had my eye on a small figurine of a burro standing around in a tiny desert scene. He was hanging around near a cactus with a blanket draped across his back, looking as oafish as I must have looked in Missy's living room on that first visit. To my great joy, the green felt base of the statuette held a sticker with my name on it. A few inches from that was another sticker bearing my cousin's name. His sticker was much older, likely placed when he was a child and showed an interest in the little burro. My sticker was added many years later, when her eyesight was good enough to notice me looking at it but not good enough to see the sticker she'd already put there. My cousin didn't want it, so I got to keep it.

Very few items from my childhood have followed me to the present day. I have no baby shoes, toys, clothes, or high school yearbooks. I find myself occasionally embarrassed for people who save these things - commonplace articles turned precious talismans, preserved and forever cherished for having once been used by the likes of the one and only "me." Objects tend to drift into and out of my life, sometimes in ways indifferent to whether or not I'd like to keep them. I knew I'd lose that burro eventually, so I gave it to Missy right away. She put it next to the Japanese fisherman in her living room. A strangely out-of-place anachronism, my Poncho Villa-era Mexican burro sticking out like a cactus-pricked thumb beside her ancient Japanese villager, yet, somehow, it felt right. An indelicate totem, with both stickers clinging to the bottom, gifted from one beautiful creature of delicate and free-form grace to another by way of a kindly, out-of-place buffoon. We said goodbye before the end of the summer, with her address handwritten on a piece of paper.

My mom drove home with her son, but without a mother. In the front seat, I silently pined for things not meant to last — grandmothers and first lovers.

Of course, I lost that handwritten address after sending a single letter in which I likely misspelled the word trampoline.

# Graceland

When I worked there, I never thought to ask why Elvis named his home "Graceland." I didn't ask for several reasons, I guess, but mostly I failed to because I was sixteen and, as I may have mentioned, very much a moron. Had I asked, I would have been as delighted by the answer then as I am now. As it happens, Elvis inherited the name from the family who sold him the property - a family whose aunt Grace must have been sorely missed by her surviving kin. Grace and her relatives were blessed and cursed by a last name with which I can truly sympathize - Toof.

Like the Couch family from which I come, the Toof family has the type of last name that easily lends itself to the cruel, yet funny, teasing of children. Even now, in the high-minded 2020s, the word cannot be typed into a word processor without being underlined in red, wavy lines, flagged as a misspelling of a more familiar term. Also, I can't be alone in feeling that consensus reality was seriously shortchanged, having been denied Elvis Presley's Toofland.

By the time I was hired at Graceland, the Toofs were long gone, and Elvis had been dead for nearly twenty years. His surviving relations left the property in the hands of an uncommonly competent cabal of corporate caretakers, successfully tasked with turning the grounds into a Mecca for Elvis fans, thus milking his legacy of film, music, and memorabilia for every possible penny.

These adept managers of legacy hired a team of talented people to run the joint. Those people then hired slightly less gifted people who could execute mid-level tasks without threatening the jobs of their superiors. Those people did the same, as did their subordinates. Follow that mutated employment regime far enough, and you'll find, at the bottom of this corrupted gene pool of hired goons, young weirdos like me.

Those young weirdos typically work in the no man's land between the parking lot and the grounds where Elvis slept, rode horses, parked his cars, and ate meatloaf. There you will find a whole world of Elvis-based delights. Tickets can be purchased for a tour of the home across the street. Devotees can visit Elvis's car museum, dine at a 50s style burger joint, walk through Elvis's private jets (the Priscilla and the Lisa Marie), or peruse several small exhibits in which these sturdy pilgrims could, for a fee, gaze upon the many treasures of the kingdom. These holy travelers could also leave behind offerings of even more cash in exchange for a variety of items lovingly machine-crafted in Southeast Asia and adorned with images of their fallen monarch.

To be fair, I don't blame the family for cashing in on what Elvis did. His fans find great joy in Graceland's existence. I was and still am an Elvis fan. Rather, I'm a fan of his music. Actually, I'd like to amend all of that. The word "fan" bothers me. I like Elvis, and I like his music. If he were alive today, I probably would not go see him in concert. Perhaps I might have twenty years ago when I was more prone to visiting casinos. I probably wouldn't buy any of his new gospel records, just as I didn't buy any of his older ones. So, to say I'm a fan is probably not accurate. True "fans" buy all the shit. I'm not likely to buy much of anything, so that leaves me unsure how to classify what I am relative to Elvis, or any of the musicians I like, for that matter. "Enthusiast" sounds too much like a term for amateur birdwatchers, and "supporter" suggests I can be counted on to write annual checks, which I cannot. So let's just say, as I've said already, I like Elvis, and I like his music.

Anyhow, I was hired in the summer after my sophomore year of high school. I had a car and loads of spare time for a job. I also needed cash to pay for my car - a vicious cycle I hadn't the wisdom to avoid for longer than I did. Several older classmates also had jobs at Graceland, and I was eager to join them. I had a massive crush on one of them, a pretty girl from Arkansas called Elizabeth. She was funny, laid back, and smart. She was one of my supervisors. My hands would sweat when she came around. I wasn't on her radar at all.

Working in that environment was formative for me. My job morphed several times over the summer. I went from working as a stationary clerk in one of the shops to being the guy who wandered around with a cash drawer to cover for other clerks while they took their breaks. I became familiar with the mechanics of this gift shop empire; my favorite was the one in the car museum.

After doing that for a while, I became restless. I found the stockroom where we housed the merchandise to be an unacceptably disorganized mess. Discontinued products in unlabeled boxes were clogging up the aisles where we stored other products like t-shirts, CDs, VHS tapes, figurines, watches, and bric-a-brac. I pitched my manager to let me do something about the mess. To move some of the older merchandise, he gave me the made-up title of "stockroom manager" and bestowed upon me a modest bit of agency to move products around and create displays in the various shops.

My first act was to create an ambitious display of discontinued mugs in the store closest to the main concourse where visitors purchased tickets. I carefully moved, then restocked a couple of existing displays to accommodate the new shelving system I needed for my presentation of deeply discounted mugs. Assembling the new shelves was a difficult task to attempt alone. It was made more difficult by the growing audience of slack-jawed gawkers milling about the shop and mingling with the flood of visitors in the concourse; my display was directly between them.

After a sweaty half-hour of carefully stacking thick-glass shelves on the metal frame of the shelving unit, I was finally ready to lay out my Elvis-themed coffee mugs. I started on the bottom shelf. Carefully stacking cups in a pattern that would show the images on either side of the handle while making it easy for guests to pick one up without fear of knocking over any others. I thought it was brilliant! Each shelf in the display was set up for a stack of mugs, two-high. On the top shelf, I planned on building a stylish pyramid.

The mugs were great. It would likely be my regular coffee cup if I had one today. They were thick-walled and tall. To one side of the handle stood a great shot of young Elvis in a golden Nudie Suit, and on the other side, a black and white shot of him dancing in "Jailhouse Rock." The display looked super cool, with every other cup showing Golden Elvis or Black and White Elvis. My plan for the top was equally ambitious, with the pyramid shape also featuring this vacillating pattern of bold gold or jailhouse stripes.

My pyramid was coming together nicely, and I had already handed over more than half a dozen of them to buyers who couldn't wait for the display to be completed. Much like the pyramid of cups, my confidence in the project was reaching its peak.

It was nearly 10AM, and the main concourse was absolutely jumping with visitors. The shop was packed, and people were everywhere. I had about six more mugs to stack before I could step back and admire my work.

What I didn't realize then, and am painfully aware of today, is that glass shelves do not like to have weight concentrated in their centers. In fact, the worst thing you could do to a glass shelf would be to build a pyramid of tall, thick-walled coffee mugs in the middle of it.

As I placed one of the last six remaining mugs, I heard an unfortunate sound: the unmistakable "TINK" of cracking glass. I looked at the bottom of the mug in my hand, worried that I might have set it down too hard and chipped either the bottom or possibly the lip of one of the others below it. The moment I shifted my gaze from the mug in my hand to the mugs on the shelf, I watched in horror as the thick glass shelf cracked completely and gave way.

As you've probably guessed, that brought my nearly completed pyramid crashing down on the shelf of mugs below, which also shattered and dropped on the shelf below that one, and so on, all the way to the floor.

The moment the crashing began, every other sound in the building, minus the unstoppable wave of Elvis music, ceased instantly. Every functioning ear within a forty-yard radius was then bathed in the cacophonous clatter of shattering glass, followed by a heavy silence. About one hundred people had a direct line of sight on me. I stood there like an idiot, up to my ankles, in a pile of glass shelves and destroyed coffee mugs. After the jangling noise had stopped and the pregnant silence was ready to burst, when I looked at the unbroken mug in my hand, I held it aloft and said, 'Don't worry, this one's fine. Super limited edition, actually."

I considered dropping it into the pile at my feet for comedic effect, but I was happy enough with the laugh I was getting, even if it was less with me than at me.

Misadventures in stockroom aptitude aside, I did manage to make some friends in Graceland's "upper crust." A member of Elvis's extended family, Uncle Vester, was "working" there with us. After years as head of Graceland's security, he was doing his best by the family name and hanging around the shops to promote his books - *"A Presley Speaks"* and *"The Presley Family Cookbook."*

Chef-Uncle-Presley and I got along great. We spent many hours of my summer chatting about his life in Mississippi, his memories of Elvis, his buddies, and what it was like to see so many people wandering around the place so many years after his nephew had passed. I'd dare say we were pals. I certainly felt like we were.

He told me about Elvis and *his* pals, known as the Memphis Mafia, and how, at night, they would play football at a local high school not far from the gates of Graceland. The school had a football field but no lights or bleachers, so Elvis and his buddies would circle the area with their Cadillacs, gifts Elvis was known to give his close friends. The gang would leave their headlights on to play in the dark. People from the neighborhood would come by to watch. He told me it was mostly housewives and their kids in the audience. Elvis got tired of running the Cadillac lights and ended up making, at the time, the largest private donation to a public school in Tennessee state history, and paid for a proper field, complete with stadium lights and bleachers. The only stipulation was that Elvis and his pals could use the field whenever no games or football practices were already scheduled. The neighborhood ladies were able to watch from the bleachers from then on.

Like many tourist attractions around the globe, Graceland is subject to seasonal highs and lows. The summer is, by far, the busiest time of year, but the absolute busiest *day* of the year comes in mid-summer with the Candlelight Vigil at the end of Elvis Week. Visitors from every corner of our planet flock to Graceland to pay their respects to The King on the eve and day of his death. Guests are given candles to hold while they listen to songs, tell stories, cry, and generally act weird as shit around the grounds of his house, the gift shops, and back and forth across the busy road which divides them. It is a 24-hour affair.

My managers asked if I would handle break duty again and invited me to stay clocked in for as many hours of the day and night as I cared to work. I was all in! I spent the next 24 hours meeting some of the most delightfully weird people I had ever met.

There was "K-Elvis," a Bolivian Elvis impersonator who looked and sounded just like a Sun Studios-era Elvis. He popped into the shop where I was doing a stint and played a spot-on perfect version of "That's Alright Mama" while standing on the counter of my register. His manager asked first if it was ok with me. Having absolutely zero authority to make decisions, I gave him my blessing and watched with rapt attention as the young man blew everyone's socks off.

After he climbed down to wholehearted applause from the audience, I shook his hand and asked him how he got turned on to Elvis. Instead of answering me, he turned to his manager, who translated my question. The manager anticipated my puzzlement, "K-Elvis don't speak the English." I asked him if K-Elvis understood what he was singing. After a giggling translation, K-Elvis erupted in childlike laughter. Through a full-toothed smile, shaking his head as he talked, the manager explained, "He don't know what he's saying. He just like singing the songs!"

Later that evening, while working in another shop, a woman in her early thirties approached my register with a question. She wore a simple yellow sundress with tiny blue flowers dotted about. Thin straps dangled the dress from her shoulders like the gentle vines of a French vineyard. Her long blonde hair was pulled back and pinned down by the sunglasses she wore that day. She was quite beautiful, with deep green eyes and lovely, high cheekbones. To a kid my age, I'm sorry to admit, she seemed a little old for me, but she was openly flirting with me, so I flirted back, thinking it harmless and exciting to be the object of such an attractive and mature woman's attention.

Her question was about a watch locked away under a glass display. It was shaped like a guitar and, as you can imagine, featured Elvis rocking around the clock with his arms functioning as the hour and minute hands. It was ridiculous and kind of cool. I pulled it out so she could try it on. She loved it and asked me how much it was. When I told her, I watched her excitement for the thing deflate like an untied balloon. "Oh. Well, maybe when I come back next year it'll be marked down a bit. If it's still here, anyway."

Having my finger on the pulse of our inventory, I knew we had another of these watches in the stock room, which had been damaged cosmetically but was otherwise intact. It had been marked for return to the manufacturer, but I knew I could still sell it for a discount if I wanted to. She was so cute to me. Despite being twice my age and a little bit Elvis-crazed, I liked her and felt a strong urge to please her. I told her about the damaged watch in the storeroom and that I only had to watch the till in that store for another twenty minutes, after which I would head to the T-shirt shop. On the way to my next relief shift, I could swing by the stock room, pick up the damaged watch, and then sell it to her in the T-Shirt shop at a deep discount in about 45 minutes if she was interested.

She was a little too excited about that prospect, making brief mention of Jesus Christ, something about magic, and how strong my hands looked when I helped her undo the watchband. A tiny red flag was waved in the back of my boner-driven, sixteen-year-old mind.

Of course, I ignored that red flag, fantasizing instead about her inviting me into some crazy motel room wearing nothing but the watch and a grin in the somber, post-vigil morning light. I stopped by the stock room, scooped up the watch, noted the inventory list, and headed to the T-shirt shop.

The place was a madhouse of bodies. Shoppers, mourners, impersonators, casual visitors, and sanctified, died-in-the-wool fans all rubbed elbows and did commerce with the young people working the registers. The T-shirt shop was a hectic place. Honestly, all the shops carried T-shirts and other bits of memorabilia, but the T-shirt shop only carried T-shirts. This singular inventory demanded special attention. Namely, the re-folding of shirts after customers invariably unfolded them to see what they looked like while standing in front of the exact same shirt placed helpfully on the body of a mannequin. The task was endless.

My routine in that store was rhythmic. I would find the chattiest and bossiest person in the group, show them how Elvis's mother folded his shirts and how he insisted that his maids fold them as well. I explained that the tradition had been passed along to the inmates of the gift shops across the street from his final resting place, and that this specific fold had even influenced the construction of the racks where the T-shirts were displayed. That bit was usually the clincher. After becoming the expert on Elvis' laundry, this type-A personality would then pass the method along to her friends (yes, it was a woman … every-single-time), thusly folding the lion-share of the shirts for me so I could focus on doing as little actual work as possible. My story was sneaky and bogus, to be sure, but it was effective nonetheless.

I was in the middle of this hustle when she walked into the store. Her sunglasses had been stowed away in her purse, and her long, thick, wavy hair effortlessly brushed against her bare shoulders like silk prayer flags in a soft breeze. I could smell a mix of her perfume and warm hair as she approached. Her eyes locked onto mine with what I perceived as naked sexuality mixed with something I couldn't quite grasp. Her voice, which was higher pitched before, was now being delivered in a slightly huskier tone. I was totally turned on, but nervous about something I couldn't pin down. It reminded me of staring at one of those paintings containing a central image you can't see until you let your eyes relax into it. I was in no state to relax.

I pulled the watch from behind the counter and completed our transaction in the usual manner. She paid with brand-new bills, pulled directly from the type of envelope banks give out when you make a large withdrawal. I counted them slowly, separating the bills for what felt like the first time since being printed. Oddly, I've thought of those bills a few times since that day, wondering how weird their lifespan must have been from that moment forward, having started their lives in commerce under such strange circumstances. What sort of odd-ball transactions would they facilitate as they were slowly separated, handed out as change, and passed between countless dirty hands over the rest of their lives?

She asked me how soon I could take a break. I told her I was on an hour-long stretch, covering back-to-back breaks for my coworkers - one of whom was grinning at me as I openly flirted with my customer. She told me she would be heading across the street before then to begin the serious bit of her pilgrimage but wanted to connect with me again after it was over. Ignoring the growing line of customers behind her, she started to tell me some seriously heavy shit.

"I've been praying that we would meet. There's this cutout photograph from a magazine on my vision board at home. The man in the photo looks exactly like you! He's tall, handsome, and looks like Jesus must have looked when he was young. You know, it was Jesus who sent me downriver to keep a vigil for "The King." He told me we would meet and that I would know you by the kindness you would show me. And now, here we are. You've been so kind to me, and I can't WAIT to return that kindness!"

I was blushing, conflicted by the sheer madness of what she just said and the possibility of getting laid. My brain knew what to do, 'Pull up, dummy! Get out of this right now!!!' However, an equally insistent manager of my anatomy had notes on the situation, which were hard to ignore. 'This lady wants to have sex ... you like sex. Case closed!'

"Give me your phone number," she said, "I'll call you in the morning."

In an uncharacteristic moment of clarity and freedom from libido, I lied to that beautiful woman, telling her I could be fired for doing that, but my manager would happily give her my contact information if she asked politely.

I didn't expect such a lame excuse to work, and fully expected, on the off chance that it did, there was no way my managers would ever give out the contact information of an underage employee to a total stranger.

Of course, only the unexpected transpired from that point forward. She stretched her lovely body across the checkout counter and planted a kiss on my cheek, promising to call me. My heart pounded like boulders in a landslide as she walked out of the shop. Even the next customer, who was likely just as crazy as the previous one, seemed to understand my sigh of relief when she left.

I did not receive a call from her the following morning. The reason for that was weirder than I could have guessed at the time.

It was sweet Elizabeth, the girl I had such a crush on, who was approached by the amorous Christian-single in her effort to procure my contact information after the vigil. I was somewhat pleased that Elizabeth knew I had been flirting with the woman, as one of my coworkers mentioned it to her when she arrived for work. That my name would even come up in casual conversation with her was beyond what my ego would allow my imagination to hope for. What I did not anticipate was that Elizabeth, in the sober light of day, would send the woman's request up the chain, with her blessings, allowing my complete contact information to be shared with this total stranger. Amazingly, a typo on the piece of paper this sensitive information was scrawled onto was the only reason I didn't get a call.

It did not stop her from getting my home address, though. Less than a week later, I was shocked to receive a large, brown envelope, courtesy of the US mail.

One of many regrets in my life is having lost that letter, as it was objectively the strangest piece of correspondence I've ever received. The contents of that large, legal-size envelope were as follows:

An 8x10 glossy, black, and white headshot for promotional purposes.

Another 8x10 photo, full body, full color, wearing the same dress she wore the night we met, conspicuously displaying the watch I sold her.

A business card with her job title and relevant contact information.

A two-page, handwritten letter, which I will do my best to summarize below.

Part bible-fan-fiction-erotica, part history lesson, and part manifesto, she repeated her claim that it was Jesus, to whom I bared a sexy resemblance, who made the "unbreakable" connection between us possible. The suggestively shaped tether of this connection was somehow the Mississippi river, with its nutrient-rich flow, connecting our great cities and eventually our bodies, which, once similarly entwined and flowing, could never be separated. Thanks to the divine nature of our relationship, like Joseph and Mary, Abraham and Sarah, and Jesus and Mary Magdalene before us, ours would be a historically relevant love marked by a mystical and sexual bond worthy of the greatest storytellers of all ages to come. Also, she really liked the watch and wore it daily, and the scratch across the face gave it character without interfering with accurate time-keeping.

Although her eccentricity was a bit advanced for my sixteen-year-old taste, I liked her. Honestly, the weirdly confused theology of the arrangement was the only turnoff for me. Without mention of divine entanglements, I might have rolled the dice and moved to St. Louis without finishing high school. Such are the triple and irresistible powers of libido, impulse, and Elvis.

The summer ended shortly after this encounter, and I had to leave my post to return to school. In my last week of work, I had one final coffee break conversation with Uncle Vester. Neither of us knew it then, but Uncle Vester wouldn't live to see another Candlelight Vigil. When I told him it was my last week at Graceland, he was bummed out.

"Ahh, man. That's too bad. You gonna come back next summer, or maybe for the holidays?"

'I'm not sure," I told him. "I'd like to if they'll have me.'

"Well, I'll sure put in a good word for ya!" I thanked him. We sat quietly for a moment, sipping and thinking. With his easy grin, he looked at me and gave me what I still consider the greatest compliment of my life. "You know, Andrew, I hate like hell that you're leavin', but if The King were still alive, you'd be drivin' a Cadillac for sure."

# Dreams with Dark Colors

Have you ever tried to untangle a string of Christmas lights hastily stored after the season's end? Or strained your hearing to catch a familiar tune or a voice you recognize through a din of sounds? For whatever reason, you just can't seem to tease them apart. In both instances, you're facing something that certainly *can* be done, but you might abandon the project before you succeed.

It's often the same with dreams. Tangled threads of free-floating thoughts are impossibly confused with errant fears, joy, troubling associations, and ideas from an ever-growing yet increasingly opaque past. Are they meant to be liberated from the impossible web of themselves? Or should we pick at them slowly until we find something less frustrating to untie?

I have a dream, a dark one, which is haunting me again. She comes and goes like a fever on a wave in a cloud over the petals of a poisoned flower. Burning, tumbling, nebulous, terrible, numinous, and acted out by a body that refuses to follow the brain's commands. I watch myself as I move under an influence, not my own. I want to turn left, but I continue forward toward a black and frightening door, viscous and glistening with what looks like sweat. The paint is clearly ill, and the door is heaving, like weak lungs under heavy skin, stretched too tight over a sickly frame. I hear it wheezing.

I reach for the handle, struggling against the urge to touch it. It glows from within, deep-black and textured. Carved delicately into the filigree - a model of the universe. Or are those unbound carbon atoms arranged in no particular order? I've never seen anything so horrible and yet so beautiful. I want to continue looking into the carving, but it's warm and pulsates as my hand closes around it.

Rushing fear and a strange noise come from behind me as if claws or nails are clicking in a chaotic rhythm across a wooden floor. I turn the handle to the left, and the sound grows closer. My head refuses to turn and face it, and my focus stays fixed on the door, which exhales an aggravated wheeze as it opens.

The clicking sound and the labored wheezing have followed me beyond the threshold. Everything goes black, and I'm in total darkness. I test myself against what I realize now is my own dreaming. I'll simply open my eyes and put an end to this madness, but the lids won't even flutter, much less lift. I try to raise my head - not even a bodily flinch finds its way to the surface, despite the effort. Arms and legs, nothing. I reduce my ambitions, aiming for a finger, or nostril, nothing still. Yet, the clicking continues, drowning out the tortured breathing of the door. The sound is everywhere now.

I become the clicking - my eyelids, shoulders, heels, and the bed underneath them clicking like ancient wooden cicadas, screaming their rhythms in an empty concrete cathedral. Echoing and repeating endlessly, increasing in speed terribly, until the waveform of click and echo find a common phase, canceling the wave altogether, collapsing into one incessant and impossibly rapid click.

I continue to struggle against paralysis. The click becomes a single tone, an urgent, high-pitched, and foreign alarm.

What is the half-life of fear? I begin to hear voices nearby. Serious and muffled, I strain to decipher them from the click-turned-tone. Constant and cruel, I attempt to scream. My voice, not even a node of dust in the empty expanse of space between the protons and annoyingly dispassionate neutrons I could have sworn I saw on the handle of the door.

I give up the struggle with my hopeless body. I discover imagination in the darkness and picture the handle of the door once again. Beautiful and strange, shouldering the expanse of every-thing, every-where, and all of time in such a simple contraption, crafted specifically to fit in the palms of my hands. I submit to fear, and in return, she leaves me entirely. The panicked alarm becomes a deep and reassuring chime, an endless sound, pleasant and gently reverberating off my bones and the skin of my skull.

The voices, dulled and muted, grow more frantic yet seem to be drifting away. Through the din, I hear a word I recognize. Well defined, with crystal brilliance, it clicks up my spine after I hear it — it is a woman's voice, and she has but one thing to say, "Clear!"

# Peabody Ducks

With warm sweat rolling down my back and trying to catch my breath, I heard someone scream. I shot my gaze toward the yell and saw several people pointing skyward. Following their fingers, I watched, deeply amused, as a semi-flightless duck glided slowly down from the top of a twelve-story building and landed in a flat-out sprint like a paratrooper dodging enemy fire. I looked to my friend and coworker; his eyes were wide with excitement. Without a word, we took off at a pace in hot pursuit of an escapee.

My friend Mario was a handsome, funny, and athletic young black guy who, like me, was working as a valet parking attendant at the Peabody Hotel, the twelve-story building from which the duck had just taken flight. The duck in question was very much in pursuit of its own agenda.

The Peabody is an old-world hotel, a throwback to the genteel, post-Civil War South when the transition from slave-holding monster to rich asshole had hit its full stride. The Civil War had been over for nearly sixty years when the hotel was constructed, and no expense was spared to make the place look as if the South had, in fact, risen once again. An ornate fountain crafted from Italian marble was installed in the center of the opulent lobby, merely a few steps from the bar and right in the center of the lounge. Even today, you can picture wealthy cotton traders smoking cigars and saying casually racist things about the state of the country. Honestly, the only difference between now and then is that the rich guys have diversified from cotton, and smoking indoors is no longer allowed. Of course, I'd encourage you to make up your own mind after a visit.

As legend has it, at some point in the 1930s, a different rich guy, after a hunting trip in Arkansas, got a little drunk and brought his live ducks into the lobby to hang out in that flamboyant fountain. Back then, live ducks were raised with their wings clipped and used as decoys to attract other ducks to be blasted from the sky. Evidently the hotel manager found this an improvement over the turtles and baby alligators placed in the fountain at various times by other drunken guests and so the ducks became a permanent feature.

The first "Duck Master," Mr. Pembroke, was a guy I never got to meet, but one whom many of my coworkers remembered. He was known to have been a character of epic scope and had a knack for separating "peckerwoods" from their cash with his charming and beguiling brand of hustle. Evidently, he got his act from time spent as an animal handler in the circus. That racket must have been truly wild in his era. Who knows what drove him to pitch the folks at the Peabody to let him try his hand at duck-based stagecraft.

The Duck Master is also sort of a doorman or bellman. His duties, as they relate to the ducks, are relatively simple. But before I go on about his obligations, I'll tell you what the day-to-day is like for the birds themselves, and briefly describe the spectacle of the famous "March of the Peabody Ducks."

First, there are five of them, four hens and one drake (or four girls and one boy, if, like me, you think like a six-year-old). These creatures live in a kind of opulent imprisonment they obviously did not choose. They spend most of their time asleep in a gaudy reproduction of the hotel itself, situated on the roof of the building. Every day, a guy in a waistcoat and top hat opens their literally gilded cage, walks them to an elevator with the help of a cane and some gentle tapping, then marches them along a red carpet to a fountain where they will spend the day swimming around and eating duck feed. This all happens with an audience of dozens of people and is accompanied by stupefying, vainglorious, and blaring music. Later in the day the red carpet is rolled out once again and the same cacophonous composition assaults the ears as the ducks are gently encouraged to board the elevator and return to their cage to spend the rest of the evening locked up. This repeats every day, all year long, even on Sundays.

The Duck Master, the guy in the waistcoat and top hat, has a weird job. It is he who does the marching, he who rolls out the red carpet, he who checks it for duck shit before rolling it back up again, and it is the Duck Master who is ultimately responsible for the safety of the ducks. These duties and a few more, which include feeding them and occasionally checking in on them while they are in the fountain, take up only a small portion of his time. For the rest of his shift the Duck Master is free to hustle at his leisure. This hustle often includes escorting guests and their bags to their rooms or acting as a concierge of sorts.

Inevitably, it is while the Duck Master is engaged in these side hustles that the ducks decide to mix up their regularly scheduled program.

One busy shift, I was helping a guest with a few bags when I noticed something odd. It was about ten minutes before the ducks were meant to be parading up to their palace, so the red carpet was unfurled, and a crowd was gathering to watch the incredibly brief show. Ten minutes is plenty of time for an enterprising Duck Master to make a few extra dollars and still make it back in time to wag the cane. As I deposited bags on a bell cart, handing them off to the captain of the bellmen, I saw the male duck, the drake you will remember, march himself, alone, down the red carpet, and climb into the next available elevator. Fortunately for the duck, he was not alone. Unfortunately for the woman who happened to be in that elevator, he was a rather ill-tempered bird.

I watched the number display above the elevator door, noting where it stopped – third floor. I hoofed it to the stairs and made it up the three flights in no time. Bursting through the emergency exit door, I saw the woman, clearly bothered, with her hair mildly tousled, clutching a purse to her chest. I approached her and before I could say a word, she desperately offered, in a comically posh British accent, "It's the drake! He's belligerent!!"

I managed to corner the duck at the end of a hallway and scooped it up. The poor disheveled Brit was correct; the drake's protest to my advance was quite cantankerous.

I saw several other instances of the Duck Master's dereliction of duty play out over the year I worked as a valet. Ducks out of the fountain. Ducks shitting on the carpet. Ducks wandering up to guests at their tables. I even saw a duck walk behind the front desk. But, by far, the wildest behavior I ever saw from a duck, took place outside the walls of the hotel. I'm not sure if the Duck Master was to blame for it, I'd like to think he wasn't, but there is a non-zero chance that he may have swung his cane a little too aggressively. However, you must remember, these birds are not pets. They are wild creatures, captured, pampered, then exchanged every-so-often to prevent the sort of madness that I witnessed in the valet lot that summer evening with my friend, Mario.

As I mentioned, Mario and I sprang into action once we saw the duck land. The crazy thing was pumping its tiny legs the second its feet were on solid ground. It had a twenty-yard head start on us, but we quickly closed the distance. I went left, Mario went right.

We ran past cars, then blew past the ticket booth. The sweet lady working the booth was wide eyed with excitement as she pressed her face to the window, amazed to see a sprinting waterfowl as it streaked past.

We chased the thing around in circles, and every time one of us got close enough to grab it, it would hop over a car or slip under one with enough ground clearance. Mario was enthusiastic about the chase, but sheepish about the catch; pulling his punches, so to speak, when he was close enough to grab the thing. Eventually we had it cornered. The bars of the ornamental iron and brick fence of the parking lot were too close together and too high for the duck to escape directly. I approached slowly from the left while Mario came in from the right.

The duck turned to face us, tail feathers to the fence. It shifted its huge, webbed feet like a bull situating itself for a charge. It looked oddly calm, unafraid, and seemed to be making calculations or possibly even evaluating our characters for weakness.

"I'm going in. Get ready!" I shouted to Mario. I was just about close enough to lunge, feeling mostly confident I could get my hands around its body before it could leap over or dash under me. As soon as I spoke, the duck took one last darting look at both of us.

I didn't make it a single inch closer; the drake made his move. Unfurling his wings behind him and launching his neck forward in a straight line to its full length, he made the fiercest noise a duck can muster, and lunged, with its beak and tiny teeth snapping like a brown-green feathery dragon, directly for Mario's legs.

Mario leapt as high into the air as I'd ever seen him jump — and I'd watched him dunk a basketball. As he leapt, pulling his legs to his chest with his eyes bulging out of his skull, he twisted mid-air so he could land behind the little demon.

The duck wasted exactly zero time. As soon as Mario was in the air, it leapt onto the hood of a car, then jumped as high as it could, pumping his wings until he was over the fence and gliding onto the sidewalk.

I followed the duck's lead, minus the wing pumping and gliding, and scaled the fence. I called after Mario as I landed on the sidewalk, barely able to get out any words through uncontrollable laughter. "Come on man, help me out."

Mario didn't have to say it with words; the look on his face very clearly said, "Man, fuck that duck!"

I chased the drake down Third street and watched it take a left on Beale, darting around the legs of startled tourists as it ran, hopping airborne, and gliding when it could. I saw it turn into a park with a small body of water. Gleefully, the intrepid man-duck made his entry into the little pond, paddled out to the middle, turned around and looked as if it saw something slightly more interesting over my left shoulder.

Sweating even more profusely with the combination of Memphis humidity mixed with an exciting yet fruitless chase, I shouldered my failure and made my way back to the hotel. I was greeted by Mario and the Duck Master. They both looked defeated and a little embarrassed. I told them what I had witnessed. We all agreed there was nothing to be done. The duck had won the day.

I saw the drake differently then. Like Steve McQueen in the great escape, he had been looking for a way out, plotting and struggling, ultimately succeeding in his most daring attempt. I visited the rooftop after my shift was over and looked over Beale Street. I could see the pond and its single occupant as it motored about happily, a safe distance from the shore.

I walked over to where the ducks were housed for the evening. The four ladies inside seemed to be enjoying the sunset, but I'm likely projecting — it was one of those powdery pink, soft blue, and marbled-white cloud ones, lovely really. I placed my back and head on their enclosure, trying to take the perspective of a duck in the coop. Turns out, it was quite possible for a duck to see that pond from any number of angles inside that cage. I wondered if the ladies could see their drake and if they gave a shit that he was gone?

Then it dawned on me, he was stuck out there. What would he eat? He couldn't fly, and if he tried his running trick again, how long before his luck ran out? The little thing was an easy target for a stray dog, a car, or even a hungry local. I felt bad for him, but also respected him. He'd made his choice. What a crazy leap of faith! Ditching his cage for a possible death sentence. Had the hens driven him to it? Was he compelled by the call of the wild?

I added those pointless queries to my growing list of unanswerable questions that evening. But I take comfort in knowing one need not face them unless confronted with off-circus-cane-wielding-hustlers, fowl-phobic-friends, or that rare flock of one, consisting of a single, belligerent drake.

# Curiosity Killed
# the Cake

If you're not a fan of stories about drugs, this one is not for
you. If tales of drug use are OK with you, but your tolerance
for listening to someone describe sex acts is low, feel free to
skip this one. I've heard of people for whom talk of doomed
desserts can be particularly unsettling; if you're one of these
people, then this is *absolutely not* the one for you. However, if
you like stories about sex, drugs, *and* ill-fated baked goods, feel
free to carry on reading.

The year was 1999, and I was 19. Like many 19-year-olds, I
was a moron. Little has changed since then, but I have learned
to respect a few things along the way. Way high up on that list
of things I did not fully appreciate as a young man but now
recognize as worthy of deference are the potent, life-changing
molecules found in a strong dose of LSD.

Before the events I'm about to describe took place, I had
experienced a handful of mind-altering trips, but none quite as
powerful as this one. At the time, I had only other morons my
age for company, so I learned a great deal less than I could have
if there had been a guide of some sort along for the journey.

On my first trip, my pals and I were wise enough to surround ourselves with musical instruments, warm lighting, pillows, mellow pot, and easy access to fresh air. On subsequent
trips, I spent time outside or in other pleasant settings. Some
trips were very troubling; others were filled with laughter and

insights into the increasingly curious problem of being a human animal. My experiences were relatively safe, somewhat planned-out, and not entirely representative of the impulsive behavior that typically guides my little ship.

It was a hot summer evening, and I planned to buy drugs in a parking lot where a hippie jam band was playing. I'd never taken LSD at a concert or in a crowded space of any kind. I was curious to have the experience.

The concert was on a small island theater in the Mississippi River, and the parking lot was on a steep bank with a large flat area where vendors had set up booths. Looking back through the foggy lens of memory, I gather those vendors were selling grilled cheese and patchouli sandwiches wrapped in thin tapestries and served on dirty flip-flops. I could be wrong about this specific detail, but practically every other element I relate to you from this point forward is spot-on correct-o!

I didn't have a girlfriend then, but I did have a friend with whom I occasionally had sex. She and I got along well, having known each other since we were kids, but we never dated. For some reason, when it came to the two of us having sex, I was a consistently horrible lover ... seriously, consistently horrible.

I called this patient young woman and asked her to accompany me that night. I have no idea why she agreed to it, but she did. She wasn't into psychedelic drugs, not even a little. She wasn't a prude, and she'd experienced plenty of other drugs, but psychedelics were not her thing.

I told her I was planning on taking a few hits of LSD and then going to the vendor parking lot to buy some opium and whatever else sounded interesting. She was cool with it and said she would drive us home if I couldn't handle it.

Before we left the house, I popped three tiny pieces of paper into my mouth, which some crusty wizard had dosed with liquid LSD. I'd tried this batch of LSD previously and knew it to be mellow, visual, and exciting. We hopped into my small pickup truck and headed downtown to meet our friends by the river.

For no good reason, I was wearing overalls, an old t-shirt, and a pair of sneakers. My friend was wearing something cute and sensible. She, of course, was sober, and I, as you know, was about to take flight on what I knew to be a challenging yet manageable dose of a potent psychedelic substance. At no point on our drive to the parking lot did she happen to notice that I was shifting the gears manually.

We found ourselves a parking spot, met up with our friends, and made our way into the throng of twirling hippies, loud music, grilled-cheese sandals, and tie-died madness. As it tends to happen with LSD, the sudden burst of super-stimulation made my dose kick in with a warm rush of sensations.

Within minutes of entering the crazed mass of people, I was transfixed by a particularly deranged creature making its way toward me. This bizarre figure, silhouetted by the setting sun, was of a tall, thin man with long, greasy hair. He wore a leather vest with no shirt underneath. His bare feet pounded the earth in filthy cloudbursts under an equally mucky pair of Navajo-print pants. What set him apart from the others was how he moved through the crowd; he seemed to be gliding, stumbling, moving forward, stopping suddenly, lurching back a few strokes, and then sailing ahead again with a half-sideways twist in his torso. This odd gait contrasted strangely with his unwashed companions' hopping and free twirling, dancing like stringless kites. I couldn't take my eyes off him.

He noticed.

In an instant, he was in my atmosphere, almost as if he'd sprouted from one of the dumb pockets in the chest piece of my overalls. His flashing eyes met mine, and our blinking seemed to sync up perfectly for a few too many flutters. He flashed an amber vial with a glass dropper. Without a word, I knew what he wanted from me. Without a thought, I tilted my head back, opened my mouth, and watched from the bottoms of my increasingly crazed eyes as the freaky character filled the dropper full of pure liquid LSD and squirted the whole thing down my tongue and into my throat. He smiled somewhat maniacally. Then, pleading through clenched teeth and a musty cloud of halitosis and beer, he said, "Good Luck, Brother!"

Good luck, my ass - goodbye was more like it.

I have no idea how much longer we were in that parking lot. I didn't end up buying anything. At some point, I lost my t-shirt and my shoes. I wandered around completely deranged, like a recently harvested farmer who'd accidentally planted himself and was heartbroken that an errant ear of corn had scampered off with his wife. Eventually, the noise and commotion of the parking lot overwhelmed me.

The heat was brutal. The incessant twirling of hippies felt sinister. Their flailing dreadlocks cut the air with evil purpose. The frying butter and sandwiches smelled like heavy, poisonous shit. Shoe leather slapping asphalt, out of phase and far out of rhythm with the noodling-nowhere-notes flowing from too many competing speakers, made my skin want to climb off me and cover someone with better taste. These assaults piled upon my senses like a car full of drunken clowns spilling out on the sidewalk before it burst into flames. I couldn't handle another moment.

We struggled back to my truck. I was in no shape to drive, so my friend climbed into the driver's seat, inserted the key, and gave it a turn. When nothing happened, I looked down at her hands to see if I could learn something about time and space. I stared at her feet, looking for an answer to a question I hadn't thought of yet, then looked into her teeth for what felt like a lifetime. I snapped back to attention briefly to hear her telling me in a loud and troubled voice, "I said I can't drive a stick!"

At first, I couldn't make sense of what she was saying. 'Can't drive a stick?' I said. 'Well, I'm not sure anyone can. They don't have any wheels, or engines, or ... '

"No," she said, "I don't know how to drive a manual transmission. I don't know how to shift the gears. I don't even know how to start this thing!"

I was flummoxed. I knew exactly how to drive this thing. I was also beginning to wonder if I could ever maybe find someone to teach me to "drive a stick." I painstakingly talked her through starting the truck before giving up.

'Let's switch seats!'

I asked her to scoot over and made the long and arduous journey out of my seat, struggling to open the door, unbuckling my seatbelt at the last second, finding the asphalt of the parking lot with not one, but both of my feet, failing completely to close the door behind me, then struggling to open the driver's side door. The high point of the exercise was climbing into the driver's seat with a sense of accomplishment one can only achieve after conquering some needlessly difficult task while extremely high.

"Ha!" I said triumphantly.

When I landed in the driver's seat, the truck was running. I could feel the tiny explosions in the engine through the old cloth and foam underneath me. I reached for the steering wheel and let my fingers curl around it.

Picture your hands right now, trying to hold onto a wedding ring like a steering wheel. Now imagine placing your right hand on the pointy end of a #2 pencil and preparing to shift a truck into gear with it. With these images in mind, you may have some idea of how the steering wheel and gear-shifter felt in my hands - tiny, breakable, wrong.

My body and mind were trying to tell me, in no uncertain terms – DO NOT DO THIS, DUMMY!

But as you already know, I'm a moron, so I did it anyway. In defiance of all instinct and in the face of self-preservation, I melted my left foot into the tiny pedal and mechanism of the clutch, gently adjusted the pencil of the gear-shifter into first, then lurched into a perfect and awkward stall-out. Undeterred and no longer parked in a proper parking space, I started my toy truck again and tried once more to get the thing in gear, up the steep bank of the riverside parking lot and out into the sweltering nighttime streets of Memphis.

After a few failed attempts, I managed to get up the hill and approached the exit. I almost couldn't believe it - I was driving!

Piloting my strange, bantam machine was suddenly effortless ... for about 12 seconds. Then, I saw them; a line of police cars and the policemen who drove them there, all parked at horrible angles and flashing every light those goddamned things had at their disposal.

All confidence was violently blasted from my mind, like one of those grilled cheese flip-flops from a hippie's ass-cheeks. I turned awkwardly into the street, then immediately back into another parking lot. I took the keys out of the ignition. I was convinced the cops had seen me, shirtless, crazy-eyed, and clearly out of my fucking mind. They would be coming for me! Any moment I would feel it, the mean arms of an ex-high school linebacker cop tackling my skinny ass into the asphalt in a well-deserved delivery of justice. Retaliation for my terrible taste and equally dangerous driving was, at that very moment, heaving its way towards me, sweaty, meaty, and with American Dairy Association breath; I braced myself for impact.

Nothing.

When I allowed myself to peek, my friend was staring at me with what most people would have seen as a puzzled look. I saw horror in her eyes.

I told her not to worry. I knew where we could get a cab.

We walked to the Greyhound bus station avoiding the cab-stand at the nearby hotel where I had once worked as a valet. Now shirtless and shoeless, I was exceedingly aware of the strangeness of my appearance. Sweating like an escapee and looking like a freak, I couldn't shake the fear of encountering a familiar face.

In my experience, cab drivers at the bus station have meager expectations; disheveled and crazed appearances are considerably less likely to raise any alarms with that lot. Of course, we got in the one and only cab piloted by a fundamentalist Christian who spent the entirety of our ride railing against "Drug addicts and crazies in the city!"

I nearly tore a hole in the ass end of my overalls, clenching my cheeks in fear that he was taking me directly to the cops who had been parked at the gate to the first parking lot. "Here ya' go, fellas, give 'em hell!"

Thankfully, he took us instead to my apartment, dropped us off in the back lot, and drove off with a handful of cash previously destined for a drug dealer's wallet.

I asked my cute friend if she wanted to come upstairs with me. She looked at me and said, "I'll come up ... your eyes look wild."

I fumbled with the keys until she took over and got us inside.

I'll never forget kissing her that night. It was passionate, tender, and filled with a strange power. We stumbled into my bedroom and fell on top of each other, sweating gloriously in the heat of a southern summer night.

It was incredible. After so many disappointing entanglements, we were now as one. Kissing and tumbling, a palpably electric passion crackled under my fingertips as I felt her body writhing and undulating with ecstasy. After an eternity of delight and tender lovemaking, we both began to take on serious momentum.

Our bodies were tangled in a cosmic way. Pounding and pulsating in perfect sync, our breathing was a rhythm section. Planets and their moons were drumheads, while suns and comets crashed like symbols. Her sweet, southern voice was like an angel's, singing a song of perfect orgasmic bliss. The squeaking of bed springs played like a divine horn section.

As the heaving, twisting and moaning peaked, I felt something like an explosion of pleasure and squeezed my perfect lover into my arms. I was on the verge of tears when, as if a record table had been violently bumped by a twirling hippie, her real voice, with absolutely zero singsong or angelic qualities, pierced through my ecstatic bliss.

"Did you just cum?"

And just like that, reality turned on the lights, grinning at me like a fully armed maniac in an armchair. I looked down and realized we were both tousled but fully dressed - a dark spot forming on the pant leg of my overalls.

It didn't take long for her to collect her things and leave. I was too high to be embarrassed. I felt amazing … I even giggled a little. "See you later!" I called goofily after her as she left, yet again entirely unsatisfied and understandably turned off.

Standing foolishly in my kitchen, I thought a snack might be interesting.

I opened the refrigerator and saw something so beautiful and striking that I couldn't tell if it was the LSD or the natural splendor of the object itself. My roommate had celebrated a birthday with her family the night before, and her grandmother had made her a small coconut cake. One perfect slice had been cut from it. I then remembered her telling me I could have a piece if I wanted one.

I suddenly wanted one more than anything.

Carefully, as if delivering the baby Jesus himself from the spotless womb of his improbable virgin mother, I transferred a practically shimmering cake from the refrigerator to a nearby countertop.

I paused for a few hundred years to enjoy the brilliance of the thing. It glowed from within, practically pulsating with radiance and natural perfection. As I studied it, I noticed the small pieces of coconut flesh, interwoven and layered, were beginning to move about. Writhing like tiny, flat, and perfectly white eels, the shavings rolled over and around one another in a seamless dance, covering the whole cake in a moving mosaic, save for one symmetrical void where my roommate's sweet grandmother had sliced out and served a perfect piece of cake for her special girl. I could see visible traces of love in the knife marks. The side walls of the space from which the slice of cake had been removed shimmered like wave tips at sunset, golden and delicious waves of cake carved by the knife of a benevolent grandmother-god.

I found I could make the mini and many eels move at faster or slower speeds by simply thinking the thought. I could make them dance, jump, or float. Then I found I could make the coconut pieces dissolve. As they disbanded, they began to smoke, with bubbles of varying sizes floating off the surface of the cake. I directed my now-powerful gaze away from the confection and let it land on the cabinet before me.

Glass doors with painted wooden frames were now releasing smoky bubbles. The old, cracked white paint of the cabinet frames seemed to be dispersing, bubble by bubble, into the air around me. I followed the bubbles as they rose and noticed every object in the room was dissolving and bubbling off, like a world made of soda. I still had some control over it, adjusting the color and speed of the bubbles as the ceiling, countertops, door frames, and then the trees beyond my kitchen window began to enjoy their emancipation from solid to effervescence.

A swaying cacophony of smoke, bubbles, and television static began to fill my field of view. I could no longer control it. The totality of existence was a mass of bubbling and dissolving surfaces, everything unrestrained from its previously rigid molecular structure, liberated by the foaming and floating of dispersed atoms. I closed my eyes, desperate for it to stop.

When I finally opened them again, I was relieved to see chipped white paint revealing years of landlords attempting to recover from tenants getting their wish to "paint the kitchen and get rid of that awful color." The simple cups, bowls, and plates behind the glass, solid and still, brought me powerful relief.

I then noticed a strange sensation between my fingertips. I looked down at my hands and puzzled over what I was seeing. I then began to weep a little, realizing that, while I was busy dissolving the kitchen with my imagination, I had been squeezing the tasty shit out of the most beautiful coconut cake ever made by a grandma's wrinkly hands. Where once a small sample of God's talent had proudly beamed its magnificence, a terrible and mangled heap of cake flesh, sugar, and coconut shavings lay in a pile of lifeless mush on a pastel-floral-patterned plate.

With tears in my eyes, I gathered the cake in my hands, and just as God sculpted Adam from clay, I molded the mangled remains into something not quite resembling, but not entirely dissimilar from, the gorgeous little mound of perfection it had once been. I then cleaved the once precious cake in twain. Like Moses parting the red sea, I made way for the chosen-Israel-ite-Birthday Girl's slice to be represented once more in relief, closing the back of the cake behind it so the Egyptian charioteers of my clumsiness could follow no further.

Once again, with great deference to the precious gift in my hands, but now with a well-earned serving of shame to fill the void I failed to satisfy, I gathered the plate in my sticky fingers and returned the defiled confection to its proper place in the kitchen.

The moment washed over me. I saw the whole night with new eyes. An ancient fool had resurfaced for yet another night of madness. This time, he danced in the body of a young buffoon from the Southern US. The clown in the good seats, slack-jawed at the ballet, his big head and bony shoulders fucking with the view for a brief spell. Not to worry, I thought to myself. Even fools need rest. Maybe I'll get a break from him now that I'm filled with a bit of shame? Can this fool teach me a thing or two about patience, being observant, being careful? Probably not.

Without washing my hands or changing from my soiled overalls, I made my way back to my room. I listened to records until the sun came up. Completely failing to fall asleep, I stared at the wild patterns of my sheets, contemplating how it would feel to live as a bee in a hive. And how I could know if maybe I didn't have nice manners.

# Ain't Goin' Back to Dee-Moines!

You can double-check this if you'd like, but to my knowledge, the distance from Memphis, TN, to Des Moines, Iowa, is, as far as I'm concerned, not far enough. The drive takes almost ten hours, and there is pretty much no good reason to go there from Memphis, or any location for that matter. If you happen to be from Des Moines and are reading this, please forgive me when I say Des Moines, Iowa is my least favorite place on the planet ... and I'm from Mississippi. That's gotta mean something!

The simple act of writing "Des Moines" shades the corners of my mind in a turd brown streak of fear and anxiety. I'll tell you how I ended up there in a fucked up, roundabout way, which, while thematically appropriate, is also the only way I seem to be able to tell stories. But before I jump into it, let me just say, although I'm clearly comfortable dangling my naked disgust for Des Moines in front of anyone willing to look, I am self-aware enough to recognize my poor experience there was almost entirely my fault.

It is difficult enough to be plagued by thoughts of things that cause fear and anxiety; the death of a loved one, horrible injury, financial ruin, etc. However, it is an entirely different and immensely more productive use of time to consider the emotional response of fear rather than the individual things that cause it. I'm not sure if it was hubris, childish naiveté, or just a result of being a moron, but when I was a young man, fear had a much weaker grip on my day-to-day activities.

One of the more pronounced effects of being a somewhat fearless moron is the sudden and impulsive abandonment of employment. Right out of high school, I landed a good gig at the Peabody Hotel in downtown Memphis, TN. I started working as an attendant at the health club in the hotel's basement but was soon offered a position as a valet. It was all cash tips, high-dollar cars, celebrity guests, and lots of fun.

The gig was a cakewalk. My nights were spent with a cast of characters who could fill a library of books. There was the perpetually sleepy and cool Charles. His gold-tooth-flecked smile was one in a million. It broke everyone's heart when he got shot to death during a card game in his neighborhood; his was the biggest funeral I had ever attended. I'll never forget Terry, a quick-witted redneck with a heart of gold, or my friend Mario, a smooth-talking, hilarious guy I once watched leap clean over a duck in abject fear of its snapping beak. Then there was our boss, Mr. Silas, a man with an impresario's commitment to looking sharp. He kept the gang of misfits who worked the front of house in line. I asked him once, 'Don't you get hot wearing that three-piece suit?' Without hesitation, he said, "Young man, I ain't broke a sweat at work since my last day in the cotton field." He wasn't joking.

But if Mr. Silas was the boss, Clarence, or "Big-C" as we knew him, was the chief. Big-C's official title was Lead Doorman, but he was really the face of the whole operation - a comical, round-faced hustler of a man who had more pithy sayings than any sage or guru, and a smile big enough to hide an entire sandwich.

Being young and easily impressed, I was amazed by the types of vehicles I was parking. Like the young bull in an old parable about impetuous youth, I asked, "Hey, Big-C, what's your favorite car?"

He looked at me with something like sympathy, took a breath, and said, "You know, Drew, I tried 'em all--Aston Martin, Cadillac, Bentley, Rolls, Lotus, Mercedes, and even a used fuckin' KIA! They all got something cool, you know what I'm sayin'? But man, don't nothin' drive like a rental!"

It took me years to fully comprehend the wisdom in that statement.

After about a year or so of working at the Peabody, where, in addition to making great money, rubbing elbows with Robert Plant and Jimmy Page, and getting a sweet hug from Maya Angelou, I was awarded Employee of the Month. One night, not long after the award ceremony, I decided to quit for reasons I honestly can't even remember. Instead of handing in a two-week notice or even seeking the advice of a single person on a planet of seven billion, I just handed in my name tag like it was a badge in some dumb-ass buddy cop movie and walked out on that sweet gig.

Being suddenly unemployed led me, as it has many times in the years since, to try something new. I got a job right away with a bicycle taxi company and found myself giving rides to corpulent and sweaty drunks for fifty cents a block in the mid-summer heat of downtown Memphis.

One busy night, after dropping off a couple of customers at a bar on the quiet end of Main, I paused to catch my breath before heading back to the more populated bit near Beale Street. As I took a pull from a water bottle, a wild-eyed and disheveled guy approached my bike and started screaming at me. The volume of his voice was nearly outmatched by the one-two punch of halitosis and rotgut liquor.

He grabbed the handlebar to my left and yelled, "Gimme all yo' goddamn money and get off that fuckin' bike!"

I was startled and briefly considered doing precisely that. Fortunately, instinct won the day, and I paused for just long enough to peek at his hands, arms, legs, and eyes. I looked him over, weighed my chances, and said, "Man, you don't have a gun, a knife, a rock, a stick ... Fuck you. I'm not giving you shit!"

I'd like to be clear, lest I give the wrong impression: I am NOT a tough guy. I've never won a fistfight in my life, and I'm not the kind of person who is looking to change that by brawling more often. But having fewer than twelve incredibly hard-earned dollars in my pocket and an obligation to return that heavy, gearless bike at the threat of significant financial penalties, I figured I'd try my luck on that sonofabitch.

"Fuck *ME*!? "Fuck *YOU*, white boy! Gimme the fuckin' bike!"

Now truly pissed off, I yelled and lunged at him with my pitiful fists balled up near my face. Fortunately for me, he jumped back like water popping on a hot skillet, then ran at top speed in the opposite direction. He didn't even slow down to round the nearest corner, skidding like a cartoon character and clutching a streetlight to help make the turn!

I was fine but spooked, nonetheless. I turned in my bike that night, minus the fee for the privilege of making a pittance with it, and never returned to the shop.

Being unemployed again so soon made me nervous. A childhood friend whose dad owned and was building what would briefly be the largest music store on the planet, Strings and Things, offered me a gig. They needed laborers for the job site. I'd never done any construction, but I was broke, none too bright, and willing to learn.

When viewed from here and now, the decision to quit a series of jobs for which I was qualified, only to land in a trade for which I was not, looks like the right move. It didn't quite feel that way at the time.

Fortunately for me, a job site laborer is not expected to have many skills. I swept up messes, carried heavy lumber, and assisted with the wholesale demolition of interior walls, floors, and fixtures inside the sprawling, former commercial bakery of a building. The demolition effort created an absolute mountain of construction debris, sloppily thrown onto the loading docks because the foreman forgot to rent dumpsters first. Two homeless characters sleeping behind the warehouse were hired to haul the trash away.

After three days, the pile had only grown, as the rate at which we demolished the interior outpaced their efforts two-fold.

The following day, someone arrived who would not only sort out that pile but would change my life. His name was Mickey.

Mickey was probably in his early forties, tall, extremely thin and angular, with a few too many missing teeth. He wore big, round glasses, old worn-out sneakers, blue jeans, and a surprisingly clean shirt for a guy sleeping behind a building. You could tell he had been a handsome youngster, still wearing his hair like an 80s rocker. I rarely saw him without a ballcap or a pack of smokes at the ready. One of those smokes often dangled from his lips as he talked.

He had spent the night behind the warehouse, sleeping near the other two cracked-out drunk guys who had been lazily dragging one or two boards at a time from the pile to one of the dumpsters, filling it incorrectly from front to back. I got to the job site early and was the first to meet him. He asked me, the lowest guy on the totem pole, if he could be added to the payroll to help with the cleanup effort. I asked the foreman when he showed up and got the go-ahead. Mickey didn't waste a second and got straight to it.

Before lunchtime, the two drunks had walked off the job entirely, as Mickey had insisted that they deal with the poorly loaded dumpster first before moving on to the giant and growing pile behind them. In a matter of hours, by himself, Mickey had sorted out their mess and cleared a path to the back of the dumpster, where he could streamline the cleanup and make better use of the space. By the end of the day, the pile was nearly halfway gone, with one of the two dumpsters filled and ready to be taken away.

Early the following day, I chatted with him for a bit, then walked across the street to the Piggly Wiggly to pick up something for him to eat for breakfast. He asked for a soda, refused water, and said he preferred doughnuts over an egg biscuit. I talked to him about working with us inside. He said he was interested, and I told him I'd ask the boss. By the end of that day, the other dumpster was filled, and for the first time, there was no garbage mountain. He had even swept up the area and set up a spot for lunch breaks, using empty milk crates and hammering together some two-by-fours with straightened nails to make a little table!

I asked the foreman to look at the loading dock. Clearly impressed, he asked Mickey if he was looking for regular work.

"Does the Pope shit in the woods? Hell yes!"

"Are you a carpenter?"

"Nope, I'm a wood butcher."

His answer, while self-effacing, was confident, honest, and what the foreman needed to hear. He was hired on the spot.

I liked Mickey, but he terrified me. He'd been a truck driver most of his career and had been recently released from prison after serving time for a drug charge that essentially wrecked his life. Clearly, he was smoking crystal meth again, drinking heavily, and eating like a child without an adult to enforce better choices. I didn't care about his criminal past, but I was afraid of what I saw in him. He was living proof that time could do horrible shit to a person. Despite my nebulous fears, we became fast friends. We talked about music, drugs, women, carpentry, travel, truck driving, military service, his past, hopes, disappointments, inmate sociology, and redneck thinking in general.

As it happened, he was much more skilled than he let on in the beginning. He knew a great deal about carpentry and could do almost every job in the building. Also, he worked harder than anyone else. They paired us up; I was his helper.

We were assigned to help build the acoustic guitar room. The store owners had purchased several truckloads of wood, stripped from an old house that had been part of the Underground Railroad. My job was to pull thousands of nails from boards that held a home together for over a hundred years. Mickey, after watching me flail about with the mechanics of the task, asked, "How's it going with them nails?"

Struggling and sweating, I lied, "I'm making out all right. Just getting the hang of it."

"Well, it looks like I'm watchin' a monkey tryin' to fuck a football. Lemme show you somethin'."

I handed him my hammer, and he picked up another board, teaching me a method for pulling nails that I still use. In fact, for a variety of reasons, I can't pull a nail without thinking of him.

After a week of working together, I asked him if he would like to stay at my apartment. Like a proper idiot, I did not ask my other roommates. He was thrilled and moved to the porch outside my room. My roommates were less thrilled.

Eventually, everyone got along with Mickey as all our interests intersected at getting fucked up. But things got crazy and weird real quick. Before Mickey joined us, we were all drinking too much and doing lots of drugs - smoking pot, dropping acid, eating psychedelic mushrooms, taking Ecstasy, and the occasional line of cocaine. My friends and I also shared a rented space on the outskirts of downtown where we played terrible music, got high, and lived like giant children. In a spectacular failure of creativity and inspiration, we called it "The Space."

Mickey loved it and took the drinking and drugs to a new level. I had never smoked any meth and wasn't particularly interested in it, so I passed it along anytime it came around. It came around increasingly often.

That changed one Friday after work. We had collected enough usable lumber from the demolition of the job site to build a loft in "The Space" and decided to make a night of it. I bought pizza - Mickey bought meth. Guided by curiosity and impulse, I decided not to pass the pipe when it came to me. I took a strong pull from the dirty brown foil for the first time. The hollow, metallic, chemical taste of the smoke rang alarm bells in my mind as I drew the methamphetamine cloud into my patient and long-suffering lungs – MISTAKE, MISTAKE, MISTAKE!

Mickey and our friends were wild with energy, pounding boards into place with furious and sweating brows. Every sentence seemed to be happening simultaneously, each syllable pushed out through gnashed teeth at top volume. Crazy eyes were the only eyes in the room. Music blared, and the pizza languished, untouched in the corner like a nervous and deject-ed teenager at a dance.

My reaction to methamphetamine was uncommon, to say the least. I was hungry and glad of everyone's disinterest in the pizza. I also felt tired, exhausted, in fact. The noise hurt my head, and the light in the room made me want to close my eyes. I slept peacefully on the dirty floor beside my guitars and amplifiers through some of the loudest and most frenetic construction ever performed at 3 AM. When I woke in the morning, everyone was still up from the night before, looking like dirty ghosts. I never smoked that shit again.

I didn't stop drinking or doing other craziness, though. Mickey and I would head home from work in my little truck, trek up the stairs to the apartment, and make something to eat. We ate terrible food, drank cheap beer, and smoked perfect joints while he talked. One night, while I was cooking, Mickey stretched the long telephone cable onto the front porch for a private conversation. When we sat to eat, he told me about his phone call – an unexpected chat with his ex-wife and daughter. Mickey had talked about them before but told me he didn't know where they were. That wasn't exactly true. He'd been waiting on a response to a handwritten letter sent through the U.S. Mail – a relic of the past and a lifeline for prisoners. He was overjoyed to have spoken with them. The conversation was a success.

I peppered him with questions about them and was moved to tears when he described the piercing pain he'd endured while in prison, unable to see his daughter, only to be stabbed again upon his release when he'd been denied visitation by his ex. We were both several beers and a whole joint into our eve-ning when impulse struck again.

"Where do they live?"

"Goddamn Dee-Moines, Iowa, man!"

"Do you want to go see them?"

"What the fuck do you think? Of course I do, but you know I can't!"

"You can't because she doesn't want you to?"

"No, because I can't afford it, motherfucker! You know I'm broke. She told me to get on a bus and come up there as soon as I can. I just gotta save some cash, and then I'll head up there."

"Man, forget that. Let's go right now!"

"Yeah, right."

"I mean it! Call her back. Tell her we're leaving now and will be there by morning!"

He looked at me like I'd just offered him a broken refrigerator filled with shit. "Are you serious?"

"Damn right, I'm serious. If she wants to see you, let's go!"

He got up from the table, dragged the phone over, dialed the number, and the three of us had a conversation: Mickey, his crazy ex-wife, and my nineteen-year-old idiot self. Not only did I agree to drive through the night, but I also agreed to take Mickey's wife, their daughter, and as much of their shit as I could fit into the bed of my truck back with us to Memphis. We were both still drinking.

I poured out the last quarter of my beer and switched to gas station coffee. Mickey took the first shift behind the wheel while I manned the map. We left Memphis with a full tank of gas and a pack of powdered sugar doughnuts at 9:30 PM.

The drive, in the light of day, is not particularly entertaining. You pass field upon field of monocultures, corn, cotton, and soybean mostly, broken up by shitty towns with dirty truck stops as the economic anchor. At night, all you've got is your imagination, AM radio, and, if you're lucky, a madman in the seat next to you telling you crazy stories. Mickey was an old hat behind the wheel, having been an over-the-road trucker through the 80s and 90s. "Well, before goddamn Reagan fucked it all up and de-regulated the shit out of it, anyway!"

We made great time, drafting incredibly close behind the big trucks to save on fuel.

He told me about a caravan of big rigs riding through the night in the desert.

"It was a fuckin' sight to behold, man. Thirty-five trucks rollin' one after the other. Only the rig in the front of the pack had any headlights on. The rest of the pack just had the trailer runnin' lights on. Each guy in the pack drove close as fuck to the guy in front of him. From the desert, it looked like a single truck with thirty-six trailers. Everybody took turns at the head. What a fuckin' feeling to be at the front of that pack, thousands of pounds of freight, and the next guy behind you so close he could smell the smoke from your cigarette. It was badass, man!"

I was too wound up with excitement at the idea of meeting his daughter and his crazy ex to get any rest while he drove. I took the wheel sometime after 2 AM - I felt drowsy immediately, and Mickey was snoring in the front seat within minutes.

I didn't turn on the radio so he could sleep, so I turned inward instead. My mind sprinted through memories--images from childhood, acid trips, books I'd read, sexual encounters, movies I'd seen, the color of my mom's eyes, how to frame a doorway, stories Mickey had told me, songs I was trying to write, songs I could never write, and so on. Thanks to the ceaseless chatter in my brain, I don't know if I've ever been bored. As a payment for that gift, I've never known stillness. That, too, was on my mind.

Stillness, silence, a chatter-free Hercules upon which Chatty Atlas could rest the globe of nonsense for a moment. I let my mind drift, trying in vain to clear it. I remembered a tape I had as a child about meditation. The speaker had a soothing voice and asked the listener to simply breathe in a counted rhythm, concentrating on nothing more than air in, pausing, then air out. Silence, stillness, the unsullied quiet time of never, now, and always. I let go of the pursuit of chasing a perpetually absent later for the briefest of moments. As we comfortably screamed down the freeway at seventy miles per hour behind an excited engine and a thick piece of automotive glass, my eyelids slowly covered my tired eyes, and the warmth of sleep let my busy mind off the hook and took the truck off the road.

I must say, the rumble strip installed on the sides of U.S. interstates is a system that just works. The violence and change in volume when encountering those terrible divots on the road's shoulder will rip a body from the splendor of sleep like a Band-Aid from burnt flesh. If, for some reason, these are not enough, a shrieking crackhead passenger will more than compensate for any force the rumble strips are unable to bring to bear.

My eyes couldn't wait for the lids to lift and practically jumped out of socket to get back on the job. Incredibly, I had the presence of mind to resist the urge to yank the wheel and instead managed to pull it as gently to the left as I could to keep from flipping the truck as the tires dealt with the change in surface. Mickey's impassioned swearing, as the Band-Aid was ripped from his much deeper sleep, didn't stop for another several hundred yards of safe driving.

That encounter was the closest to a horrible and violent death I had been in my life.

Mickey managed to calm down enough to sleep again after we stopped for some no-doze - a potent caffeine powder used by truckers who either don't want or can't find anything stronger. The high-octane caffeine jolt kicked my now sleep-deprived brain into imaginary overdrive.

I drove the remainder of the trip in relative silence, with only road noise and the rumble of a toothless snore to comprise my audio landscape. I pulled into Des Moines sometime after 7 AM. Hunger was the last thing on my mind. Calling our boss to explain why neither of us would be at work that day was front and center.

Impulse tends to shine a magic light on terrible choices. Sometimes, the more terrible the choice, the more influential the enchantment. What seemed like a totally reasonable decision under the mystical spell of early evening poor-choice-making looked appropriately ridiculous in the cold light of a respectable man's day. From a payphone on the edge of Des

Moines, I called a man I respected more in theory than I showed in practice: the foreman, my boss, and the father of my friend, who had given me the job in the first place.

I struggled to explain myself to him.

"You're in IOWA? What the hell are you doing in IOWA!?"

I had no hope of conveying confidence or a tone of certainty, so I tried pleading instead. "Um, yeah. I needed to take Mickey to see his daughter. He hasn't seen her in years, man!"

"I get that, but it's Thursday. It couldn't wait, like, one more day?"

His logic was sound, which pissed me off. I was getting dumber by the word. I gave up, apologized, and realized I'd be looking for another job soon.

Everything felt wrong. It wasn't just the weird stomach you get from being up all night drinking coffee and no-doze. I had a heavy feeling on my shoulders, like an invisible cloak stitched from consequence and emblazoned by every poor choice I'd ever made.

The feeling only got stronger as we rolled past several clean and well-managed Des Moines boroughs and made our way into a neighborhood the likes of which I had never visited, at least not on purpose anyhow.

I had grown up around impoverished people, but rural poverty wears an entirely different pair of boots than the rubber-soled sneakers of poor neighborhoods in a big city. Everywhere I looked, I saw signs of a major shift in priorities, to say the least. Trash blew around in whirling dervishes in front of the dilapidated homes, most coated in peeling paint, steel bars, and broken windows covered with aluminum foil and blue painter's tape. Worryingly skinny, dirty, and weirdly sexualized women were slinking around in front of gas stations and on the early morning street, while angry-looking men drove old cars at high speeds past my little truck.

We pulled up to his ex's house at about 7:30 AM. I could tell most of the people I saw had not had a good night of sleep in some time. I felt the same.

A powerful sadness gripped me as I pulled up in front of a house where several children were in the dusty yard kicking an old, brown stuffed animal back and forth like a soccer ball. Its flopping arms and legs flailed pathetically in the air as it sailed from shoeless foot to shoeless foot. One of the children, a girl of about four, stood out from the crowd. Her hair was the blondest and curliest in the bunch; it was Mickey's daughter. Blue-eyed, pale-skinned, and as cute as that stuffed animal must have been before it hit the dirt.

I looked into his eyes as I shifted the truck into neutral and pulled back the emergency break. They were filled with nervous tears, his jaw working back and forth while he worried his lips with his mostly toothless gums.

"What the fuck do I say to her, man?"

Being almost out of energy, and totally out of my depth, I had enough sense not to answer. We sat quietly and watched the kids joylessly kick the wretched toy. When the girl noticed us getting out of the truck, she shrieked and ran inside, excitedly yelling, "Mama, Mama, he's here!"

She reemerged from the house and was followed by a woman whose size made it immediately impossible for me to imagine her fitting into my small truck. Of course, it was Mickey's ex.

When she raised her arm to greet us, an ocean of flesh and fabric rippled with peculiar joy and was followed by a piercing midwestern accent through yet another toothless mouth. However, it was her crazy word choice that stunned me most. "Mickey, you sonofabitch! You look good enough to eat! Get in here and hug your daughter and your wife!"

"Did she just say wife?" I asked him quietly, silently wondering exactly how serious she was about eating him.

"Yeah, don't worry about it."

Mickey knelt to hug his beautiful little girl, and the two shared a brief and awkward embrace, filled with an exceptionally short-lived exchange of excited tears. Then the girl ran off distractedly to play with a ragged doll and her equally ragged friends. I heard her telling her pals, "That's my daddy. I've got a daddy now!"

Mickey and his possibly not-ex-wife wasted exactly zero seconds and popped into the nearest bedroom to do all the filthy things Mickey had been telling me he would do to her at his earliest convenience.

Nobody said a word to me, so I made my way to the nearest toilet.

It was in the bathroom of what I can objectively call a crack house where I encountered the fear I alluded to at the beginning of this meandering tale. A seriously troubling notion found its way into my brain, creeping out of that cloak of consequence and pouncing on me like a stealthy alley-cat on a newborn mouse. My naïveté suffered quiet violence in the teeth and claws of life's harsh reality.

I looked at my face in the cracked and dirty mirror. My eyes were dark, red, and weird, while the bags under them were heavy and dry. Looking into that horrible and familiar face, I was convinced of something unshakable and ghastly. It sounds ridiculous to talk about it now, writing comfortably, well rested in a chair I know and like, but when I tell you I was convinced, I mean my reality was, entirely and without exception, focused on the fact that I had died on that drive and was now suffering in hell for my shitty life.

*I'd been a shitty person, selfish and foolish, and now I'm dead, and this is hell,* I thought to myself, staring into the mirror. Tears streamed from my irritated eyes as the strange morning light poured in through the dirty bathroom window, making the redness even more pronounced and painting the typical brown/green of my irises a shiny, shark-eye black.

My fear grew in intensity. *I didn't swerve in time. The truck left the highway, killing me, Mickey, and who knows what else.* I was paying the price for it. A fragmented reality where even children were as wretched and broken as everything around them. I felt powerless, hopeless, like the filthy, hapless bear currently being ignored by the children, who had turned their attention to throwing rocks at the bathroom wall and singing a creepy rhyme about pooping which I'd never heard.

A fear I had only ever experienced while deep into a frightening acid trip was making my muscles twitch. I convulsed with tears and pain. The howling abyss, the skeptic's lament; not only was I wrong for doubting the existence of an all-powerful, all-knowing God, it turned out there was one, and only the darkest one. There was no benevolent master of time and reality, only a fey and horrible trickster hiding in our brains like the serpent in the ridiculous origin story, sneaking around convincingly, a juicy, poisoned worm in the fruit of the Tree of Knowledge. He had me now, and I was well and truly fucked, forever.

I focused on and felt the horror of forever in a new way in that bathroom, realizing no matter the punishment or reward, an infinitely prolonged afterlife could only be torture. Forever, a word made of hot nails plunged into tender organs, turning the screws on my fear like a madman, cranked up and high on the impotent pain of frightened weaklings like me.

The kids outside, bored by the fact that I hadn't screamed or cursed them for throwing rocks, gave up and moved along. The sudden silence was practically deafening. I was terrified as I opened the door and entered the hallway, scattered with candy wrappers, empty boxes, and pounds of dusty hairballs.

I stumbled to the kitchen and nearly vomited into a sink filled with dishes caked in dried and rotting bits of hamburger meat, grease, and ketchup stains. The refrigerator door was open. I pushed it closed, and it drifted open again. It was unplugged, unlevel, and empty.

I headed out to the sidewalk, truly afraid to approach my truck for fear of facing the reality that it could never deliver me from this punishment. I sat in the dirt on the edge of the sidewalk, tears still stinging my eyes, my throat aching from crying.

I watched a bird land on the telephone wire across the street, its black eyes shining like mine in the mirror. Was it crying, too? It stared at me for a moment, making an unusual and hauntingly long bit of eye contact before slowly shifting its feet and turning to face the opposite direction.

Mickey's daughter left the other kids and walked up to me.

"What's the matter with *you*? Why are *you* crying?" she said, indignant yet curious.

I looked into her little face and noticed how large her eyes were. They were as big as adult eyes. She'd seen a lot for someone so young. Maybe eyes are just big - maybe they grow at different rates depending on what they see in hell. I wondered if she was truly in hell or a mental construct meant to torture me for killing her dad. I didn't answer her.

She looked at me quizzically for a minute, but after a while, she sat beside me, put her sweaty hand on my arm, and looked right at me. "It's ok. I cry sometimes, too." I refocused my eyes and took her in. "I don't do it on the street, though. That's just weird."

The spell was lifted. I wasn't in hell. I was just being weird. An impulsive idiot set loose on a world I had no hope of ever understanding. These children were not in hell - they were in Des Moines, which was bad enough.

I wiped the tears of grief from my eyes so that tears of relief could have a place to land until I ran out of tears and could feel the shame I deserved. I chatted with the kids briefly, then joined them in tossing around the dirty bear. I heard a door open and a toilet flush, then joined the kids in some rock tossing. Mickey didn't disappoint and yelled, "Cut out that fuckin' racket!" The kids giggled to themselves, then burst out in full belly laughs when I threw the last rock, and Mickey howled, "GODDAMNIT!"

I gave him a minute to collect his thoughts and hopefully wash his hands before joining him in the living room where he and what turned out to be his actual wife were smoking meth and cigarettes.

I introduced myself, and then told him I was leaving. I gave him all the cash I could spare so he could buy a bus ticket, promising to send more money for the wife and kid when I got home. Without hesitation, I shook his disappointingly un-washed hand and left, pausing briefly at the nasty sink to rinse my hand on the way out.

I remember precious little about the drive home. I'm sure I was exhausted and found a place to sleep for a bit before facing the rest of the miles with only my recently traumatized psyche to keep me company. Mercifully, I find hours of silent driving to be a balm for various intrapersonal ills.

Looking back at that encounter with Mickey and his fam-ily--all of whom ended up joining me in Memphis, living to-gether on my porch, then in my room after I left--I genuinely mean it when I say meeting him changed me forever. Having such an excellent seat to witness his chaos, amidst the mo-mentum of his misfortune and poor choices as they propelled him faster forward than any drug, made me want to push my own life in different directions. It can come across as elitist or smug to suggest that watching another man flail about made me want to be a better person. However, the person I was ob-serving in free-flail wasn't Mickey exactly.

I have learned to look at people like mirrors, in a way. I am Mickey, and his wife and his daughter. I'm me, "Big C," all my bosses, and the unarmed crackhead who tried to rob me. I'm my customers, my friends, and ultimately anyone I'll ever know. There is no mistake I can observe that I am incapable of making. Everyone is everyone else. We separate ourselves and ultimately fight with others over what Freud called "The narcissism of small differences." I think this weird narcissism is one of the many mechanisms which make being afraid so easy. I fear pointlessness and the idea of "forever" because I want to be different, unique, beloved, and ultimately spared the cruel fate of the rest of my brothers and sisters. What could be more narcissistic than that, and what better fuel for fear?

I faced that fear at the ass-end of an ill-conceived effort to fix another man's problems. I was vainly attempting to be helpful without having a clue who *I* was or what *I* was doing. To be so fragile and incapable of asserting even a generous or kind impulse without crumbling under the weight of my own fear and apparent mental instability was powerful medicine for me. Realizing this, I decided I needed to do a little hard work and seek a method to get to know who I was. I left Memphis, my family, my whole life, and all the comforts and challenges I knew to find out who was living in my brain and what exactly he wanted with me. To be sure, I'm still working on that task twenty-two years later.

Mickey and his family spent several months living with me before I moved to New York. He and his wife split up again, and his poor daughter suffered through the turmoil of their toxic and abusive relationship. My heart breaks a little every time I think of her. The last time I saw Mickey was the day I moved. He used his years of experience securing heavy loads onto flatbed trailers and helped me wrap my mattress in a tarp and attach it to the bed of my truck with knots I was too dumb to untie. It was so perfectly and securely tied down that it acted as a waterproof lid for the rest of my belongings underneath it.

As I left, he had no profound words of wisdom, only a subtle but true piece of cautionary advice. He looked me up and down, chuckling, and said, "Try not to get too fucked up in New York. It ain't like the South up there; people might not be so gentle."

"Thanks, Mickey. I'll see you later."

"You better, motherfucker."

And that was it. I haven't seen him since. When I came back to Memphis for my twenty-first birthday, I met the woman I would marry, but Mickey was long gone, as were his wife, his daughter, and the girlfriend I once took him to see in Alabama. I can't picture him alive at this point, but I hope I'm wrong. His daughter would be in her late twenties now. If I think too hard about where she might be, my mind drifts toward sadness and fear, so I avoid it.

So, if you have a moment
And Fear ain't a problem
Spare a thought for a little one
Living alone
For one man's hell
Is another kid's reality

# Tiny Apartment, Big Landlord

I dislike the term "Van life." I spent two years living and traveling in a van and was never comfortable with the phrase. I've also spent forty years living in houses and apartments, and at no time have I been tempted to proclaim "House life" or "Apartment life." However, I would like to tell you about an apartment I lived in, in Brooklyn, NY, in 1999 and 2000.

I was one of about six white people living in a predominantly Hispanic neighborhood in Brooklyn, NY called Sunset Park, and I may have been the only person over six feet tall. Most of my neighbors were Dominican and Puerto Rican. All of them, it seemed, were persistently perplexed by my presence.

I rented my apartment from a large man called Mindi. When I say large, I mean rotund, corpulent, fleshy, stuffed like a sausage, practically bursting at the seams with adipose tissue stretching out his cheeks like a small balloon over a giant bowling ball. Mindi was a pillar of the Jewish community located about twenty or more blocks south of our neighborhood. He purchased the building in front of our apartments, pulled a demolition permit to remove a structure where my apartment was standing, then illegally constructed the ramshackle building where I would eventually live.

To be sure, Mindi commanded respect and insisted I pay my rent in cash, passed across his office desk at 10 am on the first of every month. His desk, when compared to his body, seemed tiny. Mindi, behind his desk, carried all the gravitas of a circus bear on a bicycle. It was outrageous, yet you had to respect the talent, difficulty, and potential bite of the creature dealing with the ill-sized object.

Mindi's face was a freckled, red butternut squash. His beard was always the same length. About two centimeters of scruffy hairs made their way through a layer of skin so taut it looked like it might pop if you poked it. His black yarmulke reminded me of a lace doily sitting on top of a beach ball. Every month, Mindi asked the same question through his permanently pursed lips, and yellowing, chiclet-shaped teeth - "How is the apartment, Andrew?" Every month I would lie, saying – 'it's great, Mindi, it's really great.'

That apartment, while fine for me, was anything but great.

The non-structural wall separating me from my closest neighbor was constructed of a single layer of drywall on either side of 2x2 studs. There was no insulation, so every sound made by my next-door neighbor was less muffled than a conversation conducted through face masks. I had two neighbors, in fact. One was directly next door. We could hear each other's refrigerators, which seemed to be timed especially so that at least one of them was loudly running at all times. My other neighbor was below me. He had a double-tiny apartment and somehow fit a pool table into the same space I had for my bedroom and kitchen. I heard every shot he took through the uninsulated, inexpensive flooring. We eventually became friends, and he tried to teach me to play pool. He gave up about two weeks in, saying, "When you first came over, I thought you were the worst pool player I'd ever met. I didn't think it was possible, but somehow, you've gotten even worse!"

The apartment layout was minimalist, to say the least; a single rectangle, about 10 feet wide by about 15 feet long. The entry door was on the far side of the 10-foot wall and was four inches from my neighbor's door. What I called the "kitchen" was occupied by a small, chipped porcelain sink, a two-burner stove, and a massive, old refrigerator. There was enough room in a small, blank-white-painted cabinet by the sink for a pot, a pan, a few dishes, a single cup, and a drawer for my fork, knife, and cooking utensils. Between the front door and the "kitchen" was the entrance to my bathroom, a remarkably small place where you could just fit in a toilet and standing shower. I had to brush my teeth and wash my face in the "kitchen," so I kept my toothbrush and toothpaste in the drawer with my fork.

The rest of the room was bare, but for my bed and a single window. The walls were drab, and I was told not to hang pictures, posters, or anything which might damage the walls. The only color on the walls was the window frame; it was fashioned from cold, black metal. I had a few guitars and an amplifier lying around the room and kept my clothes in neat piles by the wall opposite the window. I eventually bought a small plant and put it near the front door for a touch of color. I cut the outer layer of my cornea on that plant one morning, bending over to pick up my socks.

The one lone window afforded me a partial view of the city. I could see the rooftop of the next-door building, flat, white, and often slick with moisture, with an aluminum vent stack poking out of it like a periscope from a submarine. Four other buildings obscured most of the city. One was a high steepled church, triangular, colorless, and looming to the North and East. Three other rectangular and vinyl-sided structures obscured what would have been a breathtaking view. Almost supernaturally devoid of character and looking as if they had been constructed on the same lousy day about thirty years before my weird apartment had been glued together, the structures did little to inspire the viewer.

However, the view I was left with was interesting. I could see one of the twin towers. Of course, like nearly everyone else on Earth, I had no idea that the building would soon crumble to the ground in fire and concrete dust. I was simply enthralled by the fact that I had one of the twins all to myself. It looked as if only one existed, as there was almost no daylight between the South tower and the building obscuring my view of the enormous 110-story building next to it.

I often sat by the window, smoking a joint and staring at the building. I looked for the window washers, which I had watched previously from my brief residency at a desk job in the Empire State Building. I couldn't make them out from that distance, but I could see the sun as it glinted off the windows throughout the day. I pictured those windows, so precariously washed, to be the cleanest and clearest windows in the world.

At night, the sight was truly magical, even if I wasn't stoned. The glow of randomly illuminated windows and the way the crazy city lights reflected off the glass were mesmerizing. The few other buildings in my view, casually pitching out their own weird radiance, seemed to be speaking in code to one another as if through colorful beams of nighttime light.

I have a single photo taken from that window on a cloudy day. The drabness of my neighborhood is the star of the show, all gray-brown, soggy, and gloomy. The South tower is barely visible through the haze and fog, nearly indistinguishable without someone pointing it out. I wonder what that view might look like today. Is that slap-dash apartment still standing? Has Mindi been busted for bogus practices? Is he even alive? I wonder what bits of the city are now visible from that little slice of weirdness in what must be an increasingly gentrified neighborhood. The South tower I so admired has been stuffed into landfills and museums. And, like the tower, the man who once looked upon it no longer lives in a fixed address - continually repositioned and reinvented, depending on the view and the landlord.

# I swear,
# I love New York

When conditions are just right, it's possible to stitch together choice moments of the past to come away with a sense of having been exactly where you needed to be at precisely the right time. The rest of the time, you probably ended up exactly where you were going to be anyway, and either nothing particularly memorable happened, or you just haven't worked hard enough to punch up your saga. In either case, when we consider our personal myths, we have the luxury of picking at the allure of *possibility* or the ever-tantalizing *if only*, like flaky scabs on the bloody corpus of the past. Of course, 'possibility' and 'if only' are simply ideas, cut and pasted, after the fact - inaccessible, mechanically impossible, and representative of what is ultimately a masturbatory habit for the backward-facing hopeful multitudes, of which I am one. But whether we realize the importance of particular moments as they happen or tell the tale with flourish sometime down the road, we won't get the privilege of writing our own endings - so it pays to brush on a few extra coats of significance, whenever possible.

Just as it always is, New York City in the late 1990s was a wild place to be. It was a particularly crazy place for an impulsive young man from the Deep South. I was twenty years old when I arrived and very much in love with the idea that I was searching for something worth chasing. To say that I was aimless doesn't entirely cover it, but it's close enough.

I moved to the city in the summer of 1999 after abandoning an apartment in Memphis, TN occupied by a previously homeless friend, his methamphetamine-addicted girlfriend, and a few other friends to whom I've never adequately apologized. My oldest sister was living in Manhattan near 70th street and Broadway, and invited me to stay with her while I looked for a job and an apartment. Relations with my sister have always been fraught. Regardless of where she laid her head at night, her waking hours were spent on a roiling sea of emotion, ranging from seemingly unlimited, filial love for all beings, to a supreme distaste for those same beings. I was fortunate to catch her in a middle point between monstrous waves of affection and disgust. Another in a long list of sweet gifts from family and Lady Luck.

Her partner at the time, who I will refer to from this point forward as my brother-in-law, had a family apartment about twenty blocks south. I was eventually invited to stay there after having likely gotten on everyone's nerves for a few weeks. Every day, I scoured the classified ads of the Village Voice, looking for gigs and apartments. My generous brother-in-law loaned me a bicycle and encouraged me to buy a strong lock. I did and used that bicycle to great effect.

I quickly found work as a fundraising agent for the United Children's Fund. That job title is hilariously misleading, as I was essentially walking the streets of downtown Manhattan with a clipboard, a backpack filled with worthless trinkets, and a line of script to ply on the hard-nosed people invariably late for work in the big city. These busy people had the funds, and it was my job to sweetly ask them to part with a portion of them to help locate missing children. As you can imagine, a lanky, gregarious southern gentleman in his twenties was not the most welcome visitor upon the private thoughts and transit of people in a hurry. Despite the improbability involved, I was handed over the odd handful of cash and even received a few forms, filled out with accurate credit card information, during my brief tenure. It was strictly a numbers game where even morons could be successful, provided they had thick skin.

My most treasured interaction with a potential guarantor happened on my first day on the job. I approached a man sitting on a park bench, very much minding his own business. I had been in the area for a while and watched him eat his breakfast - a plain, cream-cheese bagel and black coffee in a blue and white cup delivering a simple message in Greek-style font. The message on these cups is unintentionally funny, but one I find hilarious, "WE ARE HAPPY TO SERVE YOU."

I marveled at how skillfully he rested that piping hot coffee on his briefcase, perfectly balanced on his lap, never spilling a drop as he munched. Waiting until I knew he was done with the bagel, I introduced myself and asked if he wouldn't mind my asking him a few questions.

With a heavy New Jersey accent, beautifully blending irritation with sarcasm, he got straight to it, placing special emphasis on repeating my name with naked disgust for my *southern* accent.

"Wha-da-ya- want, *Annn-dreew*?"

Young and foolish as I was, I could still read a room. I knew better than to keep going but was perversely curious to see how this man would react. Patting better judgment patronizingly on the head, I ignored it and continued. 'Great, thanks! So, I'm working for the United Children's Fund, and we're trying to support the efforts of those who locate and bring home missing children all over the world. We could really use *your* help.'

He removed his cup and briefcase from his lap and, with one hand, pulled out a crumpled pack of cigarettes. Plucking one deftly with his front teeth, like a horse taking a slice of apple without nibbling the fingers holding it, he lit the thing and inhaled a month's worth of smoke and half a second's worth of oxygen as he leaned back. Exhaling slowly, he squeezed out his response in a beautiful East Coast-sardonic cadence.

"You need *MY* help? OH, WOW, JEEZE ... please tell me, how can *I* be of service to the United-Children's-Fund?"

It was too late to run. I was fully invested in my willful knife-twisting, even though I knew the outcome would be negative. Honestly, I kept going specifically *because* I knew the result would be negative. In fact, I knew the more I pushed this man, the more violent his response would be. I just needed to hit the right notes. Instead of excusing myself with the apology the situation deserved, I obstinately leaned into my character. To match his crotchety and righteous revulsion, I turned up the dial on all available, earnest-nit-wit-charm and sang my tune.

"I'd be happy to, thanks for asking! So, we're working hard to raise money to aid in the search for missing children by appealing to the generous spirit and sweet nature of the good people of the financial district. Could I count on you to make a donation today? We accept cash, check, Mastercard, or Visa. Unfortunately, we're unable to accept American Express at this time."

That was the clincher. Playing the affable numb skull comes a little too easy for me. But it turned out that the absurd detail of not taking Amex was the key tone I needed. It was clear, if I stayed on it long enough, I could send this innocent man, who had equally effortless access to the short-fused, supremely sarcastic asshole, into a place where he could express his frustrations with clarity, eloquence, and sublime irascibility.

"Oh no, you don't take Amex? That's a shame, just a real shame," his schtick was falling apart. "Let me ask you a question. Are you fucking kidding me?"

I gave the note one last little tickling-trill, "No, sir, unfortunately, American Express charges a fee the United Children's Fund would rather not pay on top of our administrative costs. That's why we accept cash, checks, or ... "

He interrupted me by slamming his open palm down on his briefcase. "For fuck's sake, kid .... God damnit!" He paused to make another substantial withdrawal from his cigarette, letting his twitchy-eyed gaze settle on a cloud or bird somewhere over my shoulder, and finally breathed out an enormous plume of smoke, heated by coffee, bagel breath, and irritation. Without looking at me again, and through teeth and lips, lightly gripping a cigarette with an impossible length of ash still hanging on the unburned end, he let out a beauty of an insult.

"Andrew, I'd say you're a con artist, but you're no fucking artist. Just get the fuck outta here."

I was clearly the wrong guy for the job. It is an operation that requires the efforts of good-hearted, earnest people and not the curious meanderings of a goofball, intentionally testing people's patience. I lasted exactly two days and came home with less than thirty dollars for my efforts. This left me with sixty dollars to my name.

The following day I got a job with a bicycle courier company. Minus twenty dollars for a shiny new courier bag, I hustled packages all over lower Manhattan and quickly learned the ropes of that cutthroat business. I did my best to ride carefully but fast. The time you lose being vigilant in traffic is compensated for by efficiently getting into and out of office buildings. But being careful will only get you so far in New York City traffic. I was warned on day one to keep an eye out for people hailing cabs. The moment you see a person raise their hand, you should instinctively squeeze the breaks, as cab drivers and cyclists have a particularly adversarial relationship. Turns out, cabs have no problem pulling over in front of you without warning.

I encountered this phenomenon while hauling ass down the Avenue of the Americas, not far from the United Nations. Pedaling at top speed, I had the timing of the traffic lights on my side. I still had a long way to go and a satchel full of packages to deliver when I noticed a woman step out of a pack of moving bodies and shoot her hand in the air like she was trying to swat a fly. Before I could grab the handbrake, the big yellow cab ahead of me swerved hard right, slammed his brakes, and came to a full stop.

My front wheel hit the rear bumper and I went flying over the back of the cab. My bicycle stayed put. After skidding over the trunk, I landed painfully on my shoulder. Several packages scattered into the adjacent lane of traffic.

I'm no fighter, but I wanted blood. I leapt to my feet and moved out of the path of a city bus, slamming its brakes and screeching to a halt. I then turned my attention to the packages scattered about. My plan was to gather them, move my bicycle to the sidewalk, remove my helmet, then beat the cab driver with it until I felt a sense of relief. Some of that happened. With the first package in my hand, I saw the casually indifferent face of the woman who had hailed the cab, framed in the back seat window. A crowd was gathering around the wreckage of my bicycle, anxious to see a fight. My front wheel was bent at a horrible angle. Boiling with rage, I became increasingly aware of the sting of road rash on my arms and shoulder. Both package retrieval and bloodlust were interrupted by the sound of squealing tires. I watched, impotent and slack-jawed, as the yellow monster, with both driver and passenger inside, lurched back into traffic, racing to beat the red light so as not to combine a moving violation with reckless endangerment.

When the crowd realized they wouldn't see a brawl between a cabbie and a cyclist, they shambled off without a care. None of them offered to help with my bicycle or packages or even asked if I was alright. The honking and impatient gestures of the bus driver offered me one last reminder that I was in New York, not the genteel South, and that I should get the hell out of the road before things got even worse.

After handing off my packages to another rider who met me at a pay phone, I walked to a bike shop to replace the damaged wheel of my brother-in-law's bike. An hour later, I rode back to the courier shop to collect another round of assignments. My forty dollars in cash quickly turned into exactly zero. No kidding. The bike shop took $40 and told me not to worry about the $3.75 I still owed them for the used wheel. Even my Metro card was empty, and payday was several days away. So far, a week of work had cost me more than I had earned.

Back at the courier shop, the owner called me into his office to chat. He took one look at me and the road rash on my arms and said, "Hey kid, rough day? Grab a chair. You alright?"

'Yeah, man. I'm OK. Ready to get back on the horse. What's up?' I asked, more than happy to plop down for a rest.

He shuffled through papers on his desk as he spoke. "Look, I'll hire anyone. Literally, any asshole that walks into this office with enough brains to pile words together in anything other than a question gets the gig. But you, you're smart. You don't talk like a goon, and you look a lot less mangy when you're not all beat up - unlike the rest of the bums here." Gesturing with a distracted hand to a couple of guys hanging around and drinking coffee at a dirty lunchroom table outside his office, he continued. "You should go work for my pal in the Village. He's got a more high-end clientele and pays better than I do. I'll give him a call and tell him you're coming over now. Just don't embarrass me, OK? You're already replaced, so don't argue. Get moving and come back on Friday for your check."

I hustled to the East Village, trying not to get lost in the maze of streets and avenues. I felt like I was being timed. Everything in that business was accompanied by a ticking clock. When I arrived, I locked up my bike next door.

Several other couriers were hanging around the building's entrance. None of them said hello; one spat on the floor as I passed. I acknowledged the insult with as much indifference as I could muster, resisting the urge to take out the day's frustrations on a guy who would be a coworker if all went well. Nodding and looking into a pair of eyes I wanted to close with my fists, I climbed the stairs to the office.

A thin, bespectacled, and fast-talking man in his mid-thirties stopped me abruptly in the doorway. "You *gotta* be Couch."

"Yep, that's me."

"Jesus, he said you were tall. He didn't tell me you were so damn young and skinny."

I wasn't sure how to respond, so I grinned, tipped my head, and graciously swept my hands over my body in place of words.

"So, I'm told you can talk to people without saying, 'Motherfucker,' 'Ya-heard me,' or calling people a 'bitch.' That true?"

"True enough."

He was testing me, suspicious of anyone too clever or full of shit. Still standing in the middle of the room, he asked, "So, how would you get from here to the Port Authority on 42nd?"

There was a crowd of women at desks answering phones and busily scribbling. It felt like a trick question, and I figured he didn't really want to hear my dumbass route. I offered instead, "Careful as a motherfucker?"

"Ha! Alright, follow me."

I had to jog after him on the way to his office and marveled as we passed by even more women at cluttered desks, answering telephones and jotting things down on small carbon paper tickets. The place was clean for a messenger service.

"We deal with real time-sensitive shit here, and the customers don't want drug addicts or weirdos walking into their offices, frightening their clientele. Capiche? Keep your nose clean, drink some OJ, eat your Wheaties, watch out for cabs, and do what you gotta do to stay on my good side. Act like a pro, and I'll pay you like one. Act like a dick, and you go back uptown."

He had me sign a few documents and took a photocopy of my driver's license.

"Tennessee, huh? Wow, you're a long way from home. You ever fucked a cousin or a close relative?" Without missing a beat, he added, "I'm kidding. Jesus, *please* don't answer that! OK, here we go, you're knighted." He handed me the paper I had just signed and told me, "Go see Rachel for your first assignment. That's Rachel in the jean jacket, not Rachel in the blue sweater. She's in accounting. There's nothing for you in accounting. Give her this paper. Jean Jacket Rachel, not accounting Rachel. It's best if you just steer clear of Rachel in accounting. I can already tell she won't like you. Oh yeah, hit the sink and the first aid kit and clean up that arm. It looks like you got in a fight with the pavement and lost. Welcome to the team. Now move your ass."

I cleaned up my arm, applied a bandage to the deepest of the gashes, saw jean jacket Rachel for my assignments, then excitedly made my way to my bike to get a jump on my new gig.

I had chained my bike through the frame and the back wheel to a steel gate. When I approached the gate, all I saw was my ninety-dollar lock and a pile of metal and rubber shavings. The sulking couriers had all vanished. I went back upstairs and ran into the boss.

"What now? Did you forget to flirt with Rachel? Try that shit after hours. Ha! What's up?"

I told him my bike was missing.

"Ahh, shit. They cut your lock, huh? You gotta get a Kryptonite lock, man!"

I held up my intact and unmolested $90 Kryptonite lock for him to see.

"FUCK! They cut your bike!" He sat on the corner of Rachel's desk and shook his head. "Shit, man. I'm real sorry. There's about a 1,000 percent chance it was my guys. There's a guy with a truck and a generator driving around with an angle grinder and a Sawzall, chopping up locks and bikes to steal components and frames. My guys probably called him over to fuck with you. I can't prove it, and I can't do anything about it, but if you can get another bike, you've got a job. Welcome to New York."

I left without flirting with Rachel, put my heavy and expensive lock in my barely used satchel, and faced the four-mile walk ahead of me with considerable dread. I was too broke for the subway and beyond embarrassed, demoralized, and ashamed for losing my brother-in-law's bike.

As soon as I got back to the apartment, dropping my bag and heavy lock on the couch, I wanted to call my brother-in-law. I would have to find a way to replace his bicycle and another job, somehow. On my way to pick up the phone, it rang.

"Hello?"

"Andrew, hey, it's me," my brother-in-law must have known somehow and was calling to give me shit about his bike.

"Hey man, I was just about to call you. I've got some bad news."

"Oh yeah? I've got good news. You go first."

I took a deep breath, and before I could finish telling him about the bike, he interrupted me.

"Oh man, fuck that bike. It wasn't mine anyway. Some jerk left it in the apartment building, and the Super said I could have it. I never even rode the thing." Before relief could set in, he continued. "Listen, do you have a suit, or a sport coat and some nice shirts? Our secretary just quit in a hurry, and we need someone to man the phones. You interested?"

And just like that, I was off the hook for the bike and employed again. I would start the next morning.

My brother-in-law's office was on the 58th floor of the Empire State Building. His actual brother and a few of their friends had started a venture capital and money management firm, and I was to be their lackey.

If the cast of characters I had so far encountered in New York seemed to be fast-talking or foul-mouthed, the crew at T-Com, the fictitious name I'll be using for our office, made them look like monks on cough syrup and chamomile tea. These guys were consistently amped up; degenerate gamblers pounding caffeine and other powerful stimulants. Talking fast, telling jokes, and taking crazy risks with absurd amounts of other people's money.

Remember, this was 1999, and the first dot-com bubble was still being inflated. A select few of the more speculative ventures were not being propelled upwards at the same rate by that overblown marketplace. Those businesses were on their way to a crash only reasonable people who were not risk-addicted maniacs could see coming. A handful of our clients were beginning to realize this and had been calling so frequently and aggressively that the previous secretary lost her nerve and bailed on the job.

I remember getting into the elevator on my first day. I looked at the faces of the people in there with me; a guy from Pakistan, delivering bagels and coffee, a young woman from Cuba heading up to give a presentation, a Chinese tourist who had been separated from the rest of his group, and a South African lawyer repeatedly jamming the close door button each time someone got on or off the elevator. I wondered about the trajectory of a human life. How had the five of us, living such dissimilar lives which began so far away and having likely taken such drastically different routes, ended up in that elevator together? For the first time, I considered just how often that sort of thing is going on in our lives and what a wondrous thing it is to explore those intersections. It was a simple realization but felt profound for a young guy from the Deep South. My compatriots were less enthusiastic about my impromptu interview.

My desk faced the South Shore of the island, and I had an incredible view of the Twin Towers. I would marvel at the window cleaners, who I could see working on platforms dangled from the roofs of those massive structures. The office layout was stylish, decked out in muted black accents, tight woven gray carpet, and clean white interior walls separating us from the business next door. There was a large sitting area near the two private offices, and the partition walls were all glass, so the view remained unobstructed from every angle. Another partition wall between the private offices and waiting area led into the open floorplan where my desk, and the desks of the insane group of brokers, basked in the magnificent view.

When not staring out the window like a fool in the sun, I had a relatively simple series of tasks. I knew this job was meant to be temporary, as the guys preferred having a female secretary. But, thanks to my brother-in-law, they tolerated me while searching far and wide for the right candidate. I was free to search the internet for my future employment, so I substituted the classified section of an actual newspaper for the same classifieds on various websites. My only directives were to answer the phones enthusiastically, confidently, and purposefully while shielding the guys from angry clients. If my skill at reading a room was getting any practice on the streets of Manhattan, it would get a real tune-up in that office. I was meant to gauge the tone of voice for degrees of irritation, desperation, and sheer, violent rage. I had a vague idea of what it felt like to watch the value of one's portfolio take a sharp nosedive, having recently lost the entirety of my own net worth to a cab driver and a bike thief. The customers of our firm, which had invested their money so heavy-handedly into the now-defunct HipHopHut.com, were quickly becoming experts in that phenomenon on a much grander scale than I could imagine.

The main guy at the office, the boss of my bosses, my brother-in-law's brother, was handling a client who had entrusted the firm with several million dollars of seed funding for the aforementioned dot-com. That enterprise was practically guaranteed to tank. Even I, a guy with no clue what was happening, strongly sensed that the business was doomed. When the founders of the Hip-Hop-Hut, a company focused on selling hats, CDs, and t-shirts, arrived for a meeting in a caravan of large, black SUVs, wearing diamond earrings, gold chains, and flashing cash around, I got the impression that the investment money was being burned through on items which might not qualify as research and development.

This client, who I will not mention by name, was the heir to a large fortune earned by a family who had been in the adhesives business since just after the end of World War II. I can scarcely imagine the heir having to explain to his forebearers, whose company had been focused on the endless need for gluing things together, that it would be a good idea to invest millions of dollars in a marketplace for ill-fitting clothing whose appeal was limited to a small subset of the population.

When this gentleman would call, he was invariably furious. He was often the first voice I heard in the morning. I was told that under no circumstances was I to attempt to pass his call along to the boss. Absorb and deflect.

The guys showed me how to transfer a call on my first day. They also told me accurately that if I forgot how it worked, not to worry about it, as that function would rarely be of much use. Assuming the person was receiving calls, I could always just yell across the room, which everyone else did, pretty much constantly.

If you've ever worked in a busy office, perhaps you adapted your ability to concentrate on what you are doing or saying while several conversations are happening around you. I never did. In fact, to this day, I find it hard to concentrate when I'm near more than one conversation. That office was a challenging environment for me. I did my best, once again filling the role of the affable fool.

Day two, I arrived early. The boss was the only other guy in the office. He greeted me in the typical way.

"Hey, kid. How's it hangin'?"

'Morning, boss. I'm good. You?'

"Another day in the fucking promised land. Milk, honey, all that shit. So, the markets open in about an hour and a half, and it's gonna be a fucking bloodbath, everybody knows it. I'm expecting a call this morning, any moment, really. So, get your shit together."

'You got it.'

"Yeah, and if anyone really angry calls, I'm absolutely not here. I'm out all day in meetings. Tell 'em I'm busting heads at Hip-Hop-Hut, tell 'em I jumped from the roof, tell 'em any-fuckin'-thing, just make sure it contains my name and the phrase, *not here*! Clear?"

'Crystal.'

"Good man. You mind making coffee?"

The phone rang. I put my useless messenger bag on the back of my chair, took my seat, and caught the phone on the second ring.

'T-Com management, this is Andrew.'

Before I could finish, an aggravated voice interrupted me. "Andrew? Who the fuck are you? I know every asshole there. You're either new or faking a southern accent. Either way, I don't like it."

'No sir, just started yesterday.'

"Great story. Nobody gives a shit. Now put me on the horn with the boss."

The man's voice was loud enough for the boss, who was standing in front of me, to hear perfectly. His eyes were the size of hockey pucks, and he was practically jumping up and down, pointing his finger at the phone and shaking his head, and mouthing the words, "NOT-FUCKING-HERE!"

'Totally,' I said foolishly. 'Can I get your name and contact? I'll make sure he gets the message the moment he gets in.'

"Bullshit!" He spat into the phone. "I know that sonofa-bitch is there. He practically lives there. Just transfer me over."

'I'd love to, but he's just not here. I had to get the janitor to let me in. I'm the only guy here at the moment. Kinda strange, really.'

My story was weak, and he wasn't buying.

"Oh Jesus, another one. Shut the fuck up, put that asshole on the phone, and go learn from one of the other guys how to tell a lie."

I couldn't resist the urge to agree with him, so I leaned into another character. 'I agree. He is an asshole. Honestly, if he were here, I'd grab his stupid shirt collar and shove the phone so far up his ass you could talk directly to his colon. Sadly, how-ever, he's not available for over-the-phone proctology.'

My boss's face was priceless, both shocked and grateful. He stopped jumping around, stood up straight, gave me a nod of appreciation and a solid thumbs up, then headed back to his office.

The man on the other end of the phone laughed. "Ha, you're alright, kid. But I'm calling back every ten minutes until I hear from him. And if I don't hear back from that fucker before the markets open, I'm flying to New York, and you'll be getting your very own proctological exam from my foot. Understood?"

'Absolutely. Now, how about that name and number?'

"Don't overplay it, kid. You know who this is, and so does your fucking boss. Talk to you in nine minutes and thirty-eight seconds." He slammed down the phone and made good on his promise. I came to like him in a strange way, even though he never seemed to like me very much.

This job outlasted my previous gigs by over a month, and I spent my time searching for more suitable positions, listening to crazy stories from the guys in the office, and trying to find a place to live. Although I worked within arm's reach of intelligent and successful people who understood how to squeeze money from the market, I learned exactly zero about it. The vibe in the office was more casino than corporate. The stock market was a means to an end. In another era, these guys would have been shooting craps in an alleyway or playing three-card monte on top of a trash can. Fortunately for me, I was able to observe without getting too involved. I only got involved when it was actual gambling and not the Wall Street variety.

I should mention, my family has a fraught history with gambling. My Grandfather, on my mom's side, had a particularly trying relationship with games of chance. I think it was more of an issue with impulse control than a particular addiction. Grandad's scrapes with risk eventually landed him in trouble with both sides of the law. To pay off a gambling debt owed to the types of fellas in Chicago with whom aging debt is ill-advised, my grandfather robbed a bank with a starter pistol. After paying off the money he owed, he could have gotten away with the caper, Scott-free. However, the allure of relatively easy money was too hard to pass up. He robbed the same bank a second time and was, of course, recognized before he even walked in the door. The clerk, whose face he had pushed the starter pistol into on the previous occasion, told him that since his first visit, a silent alarm had been installed. The alarm had been triggered the moment they saw his car in the parking lot. The police were waiting for him outside.

I got a particularly nasty bite from the gambling bug when I was introduced to Off-Track Betting, or OTB, as I will call it from now on because OTB is way more fun to say and easier to write. About an hour or so before we closed the doors for the weekend, a guy I didn't know showed up in the office. He stood out by not wearing a suit or any gold chains. He was short in stature, lean, and full of nervous energy. Wearing one of those newsboy caps, a tight-fitting nylon jacket, blue jeans, and tennis shoes, he looked like the kind of guy who had spent the day at a racetrack. He even had a racing form in his back pocket and carried the ubiquitous blue and white coffee cup that my uncharitable bench-dwelling friend and all New Yorkers seemed to carry like a fashion accessory. When I hear about someone being "wound up tight," to this day, I picture this guy.

Everyone in the office knew him. They were old buddies from school and evidently had some sort of trade system in place. The guys would place bets for him on the stock exchange, and in return, he gave them rock-solid tips on upcoming races. I had no clue about horse racing, the OTB, or gambling. Even ignorant of the mechanics, I wasn't immune to the powerful pull of high risk, high reward. The degree to which all of this was illegal was something I didn't understand either. Turns out, it was all quite illegal.

It was payday, and I needed dough in a bad way. Almost all the money was already spent before the ink on the check was dry. I'd found a new place and would pay my first month's rent with my check. When I saw the guys writing down names on a big yellow legal pad and pointing at me, I knew something was up, but I didn't know exactly what it was. Another form of gambling was in the air, that much I knew.

"Andrew, get over here and say hi to Patrick."

Reaching out to shake his hand, I introduced myself.

He grabbed my hand like I might change my mind, then shook it like a dirty rug. "Hey, bud. Nice meetin' ya."

His New York Irish accent was unmistakable, and his accompanying frenetic vigor made me feel like something crazy might happen at any moment.

One of the guys chimed in, "You want in on this action, kid?"

'What kind of action?'

"What kind of action? Listen to this fuckin' guy." Patrick chuckled incredulously, looking at his pals. "Where the hell are you from? 'What kind of action' he asks. For Christ's sake, I come all the way up this fucking building to bring you the good shit, and this guy wants to know 'what kind of action!'"

My brother-in-law took over and laid out the scenario. It turned out we had about thirty minutes to place our bets on a race where Patrick had an inside line. I didn't quite know what that meant, but when he handed me an envelope full of cash and told me where to go, what to say, and how to place the bet, I got the picture. My Grandfather would have either been horrified or proud of me. Before I left, I told Patrick I definitely wanted a piece of the action. I signed over my paycheck to one of the guys in the office and pocketed the cash, fully prepared to place my own bet.

Patrick howled with manic laughter, "Look at the balls on the jolly white giant! Get moving, you big, lanky bastard! The clock's a tickin'."

With an obscene amount of dirty cash in my pocket, I hustled down the hallway to the elevator, remembering the rush of the courier's hustle. Once I was out of the lobby, I hoofed it, running at top speed to the nearest OTB, my sport coat flapping behind me like a gown on an escapee from a sanitarium.

The OTB is a slice of a bygone era, or at least it was. I haven't been to one since that day, and as I write this, that was well over twenty years ago. Old men pleading to television sets, dirty white floors, white and green striped walls, tickets crumpled in anger, and greasy racing forms discarded without hope litter the floor. The ever-present blue and white coffee cups filled the trash bin in the corner, with the slightest hint of whiskey wafting from one or twenty cups. The feel of great hope and terrible disappointment clung to the air like halitosis, and body odor clung to the sweaty man between me and the emotionless clerk behind the thick glass of the counter.

The clerk, a black woman with a face as beautiful as it was unemotional, was incredibly patient with me - a goofy white boy, sweating through his cheap shirt and jacket, with no clue how to place a bet. When she saw how much I was wagering in the first bet, she locked eyes with me, saying with naked surprise, "Well, look at you."

When I repeated the same bet with a significantly smaller, yet considerably more personal amount of cash, she followed up her previous commentary, accurately reading the situation. "Ah, there it is. Now, *you're* in the game, huh? Good luck, sweetie."

I took my little ticket and found a seat a few chairs from the big sweaty guy who had placed his bet just before mine.

"I hope you bet the farm on Red Letter Day."

I'd been instructed to lay down a bet on the Trifecta — wherein we picked the top three horses in order. Red Letter Day was not in our lineup. I don't remember the names of the horses we bet on, but that man's horse has stuck with me. To make this tale a little easier to tell, and because I've always wanted to name a racehorse, I'm making up the names of our Trifecta. Here they are, in order – Can o' War, Yer Majesty, and Scribbling Yeats.

Before I could even take out the race form to nervously read some of the other absurd and hilarious racehorse names, they were off, and the tenor of the room went from subdued elevator Muzak to frenetic rock and roll.

Straight out of the gate, Red Letter Day took a commanding lead, with two other horses between our three and the leader. My sweaty compatriot released a somewhat strangled cry of encouragement for his hopes and dreams in the form of a forceful yet down-toned whisper.

"Come on, goddamnit!"

A swift sideways glance towards the counter suggested the stern beauty in charge had laid down some ground rules concerning the shouting of obscenities.

My palms were sweating through my pants as I rubbed them nervously on my legs while we watched the horses round the first bend. From behind, Scribbling Yeats took the second-place position. But Red Letter Day looked strong, and

I felt like the smelly customer beside me knew something I didn't. To be fair, I always feel like anyone sitting beside me knows something I don't, but the sensation was more acute and came with slightly higher stakes this time.

Suddenly, Yer Majesty overtook Scribbling Yeats, and Red-Letter Day's lead was being whittled away, but not by much, with a little less than half of the race already behind them.

Ramen noodles were inexpensive. Maybe I could take out a loan from one of the guys or ask my sister for some grocery money?

Another dark horse came from the pack, overtaking Red Letter Day. He had the look of a determined champion. The jockey atop the beast seemed like more of a metaphor than an actual human pilot.

I was starting to wonder how to explain my craven bet and horrible loss to those who knew me.

The pack headed toward the last bend before the final straightaway. Out of the hopelessness of fifth place, Can o' War came screaming through the Frey, overtaking Scribbling Yeats, blasting past Yer Majesty and Red-Letter Day. In spectacular fashion, Can o' War took the lead over the Dark Horse. Red Letter Day slipped behind as the straightaway opened up for the final dead sprint. Yer Majesty and Scribbling Yeats were nipping at the heels of Can o' War, and The Dark Horse was right there with them. Red Letter Day looked spent, barely hanging on to fifth place.

I hear the sweaty man beside me crushing his ticket, wet and muted in his greasy paws. I'm not sure, but it sounded like he might be crying. But with my own fate hanging so precariously in the balance, I can't take my eyes off these impressive horses.

The fury of it, the back and forth of Yer Majesty, Scribbling Yeats, and the Dark Horse as they each struggle to get ahead. Can o' War leads by almost a length; he's gonna take the win! But I need the other two to fall into place for it to count.

The big guy lays his head in his hands and slumps over.

The heat and ferocity of the beasts, and the rhythm of the jockeys, urging them on, is something you can practically feel, even in the plastic chairs of the OTB. The Dark Horse falls behind the furious Yer Majesty, as Scribbling Yeats looks like he might just take the second-place spot. The final moments see Can o' War cross the finish line for the win! At the last possible moment, Scribbling Yeats loses second place by a nose hair to a steaming and frothing Yer Majesty!

The Dark Horse, and the struggling Red Letter Day, finish fourth and fifth.

An unpuckering and release, unlike any I'd ever known, rushed through the muscles of my body, chased by electric waves of euphoria and relief. For the sake of the unspoken rule, whose enforcer was watching from behind thick glass, I growl in muted-animal joy, "YESSS!"

Through my periphery, I see Red Letter Day's biggest fan curling up in the agony of defeat. Without taking my eyes from the screen, for fear that I've somehow gotten it all wrong, I get the sense he's physically morphing into the question mark, punctuating the question he's muttering, over and over, "What the fuck?" Even this desperate plea is delivered in a forceful whisper rather than the bitter bark it deserves; the lady behind the counter must have ruled that joint with an iron fist.

And why not ask the question, "What the Fuck?" It's as effective as yelling at a television, pleading for your horse to win. Yet, I won. The undeserving, exceedingly fortunate man prepared to collect an enormous sum of money from the OTB while the losers in the room faced the vicious and lingering feeling of having literally bet on the wrong horse.

I wish I could tell you now that I reached out to the poor fellow who had lost his ass on Red Letter Day's defeat and offered to buy him a sandwich, a beer, or even a cup of coffee. I had that impulse but resisted it, unlike the urge to gamble, to which I quickly gave in. Instead, I hit up a pay phone, called the guys at the office, and told them to get down to the OTB to give me a little cover. I didn't want to travel alone with so much cash.

My winnings, which were substantial for me, allowed me to refill my coffers, make the deposit for my new apartment and permitted me to purchase a used bicycle for my brother-in-law (who refused it, re-gifting it right back to me). I even had enough for a couple of journeys I had planned, including a trip for my 21st birthday – the same trip where I would meet the woman I would later marry.

Are the concepts of justice and luck simply fictitious coping mechanisms for our species to coalesce, cooperate, and collectively dream, or is there more to it than that? Fact or fiction, these concepts hold great sway over how we perceive our lives. I'm picturing the well-known statue of Lady Justice, blindfolded and holding a scale in one hand and a sword in the other. What would a statue of her ideological counterpart, Lady Luck, look like? We must, for the sake of this paragraph, ignore the fact that both beings sound like they were given racehorse names. However, we should consider that Luck is also blind. Perhaps she would not be blindfolded, suggesting she could peek like Lady Justice, but maybe born without eyes at all. I can see an eyeless figure with wild hair, wearing a flowing robe with strong, slender, and powerful arms. Her ears would also need to be omitted, and we might as well get rid of the nose so as not to provide prejudice for the malodorous or sweetly perfumed. One hand clutches a flaming torch with menace and terrible purpose, translated by a white-knuckled grip, the bulging veins of her marble hands, and the suggestion of a random swinging motion by way of her robe. The other arm, still formidable yet gentler, like the arm of a sock-hop waitress, is held aloft. A large, golden plate covered with sparkling treasures rests atop the pyramid of her fingers. Of course, her sandaled feet would need to be standing on different things as well. As you might expect, one foot could be covering a twenty-dollar bill while the other is indelicately squishing a pile of shit.

Are we where we need to be right now, at this very moment? Or are we always where we need to be? Some *times* do feel more special than others, as Lady Luck spills a touch of her infinite treasure into our laps. This treasure may or may not soothe the burns previously received by her literally senseless flailing. In either case, we play the game with the hand we're dealt, and the only justice we have the right to expect is that which we find within ourselves to share.

The man who insulted me led me to the cab driver who injured me and left me even more broke than before. Those insults and injuries guided me to the thieves who stole my bike, a theft that left me free to work in an office in the Empire State Building. That maniacal pursuit dropped the OTB and a rare and beautiful bet into my lap. That windfall would eventually lead me to the woman with whom I am so fortunate to share a life. So, of course, I ended up where I was going to end up anyway, *and* I was in precisely the right place at the right time. I have a sneaking suspicion; this might just always be the case.

# Organic Let Down

"**S**HISHKABOB! ICE COLD LEMONADE!!" shouts a sweaty Greek man in the booth next to me. The fragrance of sizzling lamb and onions confuses the air, already sweet with roasting peanuts and the chemical smell of hot pavement. Several city blocks are closed to vehicle traffic, and the roadway fills instead with colorful booths and people on foot. Such is the magic of a street fair in Manhattan.

I was in Chelsea, handing out free apples and pears for my employer – an organic produce home delivery service. My insightful boss was convinced he could sell more people on our service simply by exploiting my folksy, redneck-adjacent charm. At 20, my interest in sales was about the same as it is now, near zero. But I was unafraid to approach people, had no problem being ignored, and was getting better at being persuasive with every attempt.

I noticed a woman in a red sundress walking with what I assumed was her mother. They ambled, much like I would imagine mothers and daughters have done since the first market opened in the Fertile Crescent thousands of years ago, casually judging every last item on offer. I saw her from almost a block away. That was my method; when I wasn't engaged in conversation, I'd scan far afield to identify likely customers, interesting characters, or attractive women. It's the same method that once caused Joey Ramone to reluctantly pluck an apple from my outstretched hand like a crippled king delicately accepting his third favorite pair of house slippers from his least favorite attendant. The woman in red was in the attractive woman category by a Manhattan mile.

The gig was simple: all carrot, very little stick. I offered free organic fruit to passersby, engaged them in conversation if they accepted, and then told them about our special - a one-week trial for only $9.99. My boss got a kick out of hearing my southern accent saying nine so many times in a row. It was hokey, but a good deal I was happy to shill. For less than ten bucks, a box filled with a week's worth of organic fruits and vegetables would show up at your house, minus anything you said you didn't like. If you wanted to continue the service, you could. If not, no big deal. You just had to call the office to cancel. These were early days of the dot com boom, so the online form wasn't quite up to modern standards. I signed up hundreds of new customers that summer street fair season.

I singled out the attractive woman and her lilliputian mother through the crowd of moving bodies. "Would either of you like an organic apple or pear? They're free?" The mother was old enough to have been raised by depression-era parents - an obvious mark to whom free food is reliably irresistible. She stopped cold, looked me up and down with masterful skepticism, and said flatly, "No."

She pulled at her daughter's elbow and kept moving. The daughter, Bella, I would soon learn, in her soft cotton sundress with a subtle floral print, hesitated. Slender and fit, she moved with careful poise. Up close, I realized she was older than I was by at least a decade. As she looked up at me, a sliver of hair fell from her ponytail, delicately brushing against her neck where it met the teacup of her collarbone. Her perfume, subtle jasmine, rose, and something warm I couldn't identify, brought a little subtlety to the otherwise heavy aromas of the street. She resisted the pull at her elbow and said, "I'd love a pear. You say they're organic?"

Her increasingly cranky mother rolled her eyes and walked past us, shooting Bella a look that clearly said, "Fine, but don't buy anything from this creep!" The shouting Greek bellowed his crazy ingredient list into her ear as she shuffled down a few booths to linger and pretend she wasn't watching.

I did my best to keep it professional. Not openly flirtatious, but not wholly anodyne either. I asked Bella lots of questions while talking about food and the benefits of growing it without chemical intervention, speaking with nitwit conviction, sincerely, as if I'd grown them myself. She was observably healthy and, like most vegetarians, let me know about her diet almost immediately. She signed up for the service, took an apple for her mom, and moved along. Brief and delightful, I thought that would be the entirety of our entanglement. I was wrong.

Back at the office, my duties included follow-up phone calls with new customers. When Bella's name came across my desk a few weeks later, I relived the thrill of meeting her as I dialed. All native New Yorkers, my colleagues often listened in on my calls, amused by the friendly kid with the funny accent chatting up their cynical brethren.

By the end of our conversation, they were all standing behind me, literally clapping, as I put the phone back in its cradle. I had a dinner date with Bella the following night. My coworkers teased me for the remainder of my time there, amazingly never protesting what was clearly unprofessional behavior. "Nicely done, Casanova." I can't imagine what they would have done if she'd turned me down.

We "dated" for about a month when I suggested a trip. My brother-in-law had a timeshare in the West Indies on the island of Antigua. He offered me his free week, so all I had to do was cover airfare, and the place would be ours. Bella and I agreed on a Thanksgiving getaway.

I put "dated" in quotation marks for a reason. It would take a second month of "dating" to realize I had not met a single one of her friends, and our "dates" were basically takeout food and sex, followed by her hustling me out the door at sunrise. To be fair to her, I was 20, and she was 35. I don't blame her for being embarrassed to introduce her pals to a southern guy who had so recently been a child. She also never let me see her bedroom, which I found even more isolating and demeaning than her reluctance to introduce me to anyone. We spent our nights on her couch like hungry, horny house guests.

I didn't have the wisdom to realize how painfully aware she was that I didn't have any wisdom. We could make each other laugh and were both in our "sexual prime" (whatever that means) - this should have been enough. But as I mentioned, I was lacking in the wisdom department. Honestly, I'm lucky she let me sleep inside.

We bought tickets, inexpensive for her, not so cheap for me. But as the holiday drew close, I liked our arrangement less and less. She was becoming increasingly condescending and pointed to my very real lack of worldly experience as the source of almost every problem in my life. My college sophomore philosophy and unsophisticated worldview just made her irritable. Insecure already, it was too much for me. I'm sure I was insufferable, unable to grasp the concept that, on the spectrum of suitable partners, I landed somewhere between a vibrator and a gigolo. I was someone's lover; I should have been thrilled. My sexual history did not recommend me for this type of work. Yet, like a fool, it hurt my feelings, and I turned pouty when it finally dawned on me that she wasn't with me for my singular personality. Having her attention was a strange way to learn a much-needed lesson; being young and weird doesn't make you interesting, and being needy is just annoying.

I suppose it would have all been a bit easier if we'd discussed our arrangement on the front end, but how unsexy is that? Completely oblivious, I honestly thought we'd connected on a deeper level. It would have been simpler if I had relaxed and spared her from my desperate energy. Eventually, I found that I didn't like being around her at all. I had choices to make and had already waited too long. My problems have often been born of poor timing and ego - the Bella situation was no exception.

We met for lunch about three weeks before Thanksgiving. My eyes have no respect for timing, and told the truth right away. I stalled for as long as I could, making it to the delivery of our drinks. Before her sandwich order reached the kitchen, she drew it out of me.

"I don't want to go with you to Antigua."

At first, she thought I was joking. When she realized I wasn't, a sudden, heavy tear pierced the foam of her untouched cappuccino. "How can you do this?" I had no answer, maintaining eye contact with her flushed red left cheek. "Have you even considered the fact that you are *ruining* my holiday? I mean, who's gonna go with me now? At the last fucking minute, I mean Jesus, I can't go by myself!"

*Well, shit* - communication breakdown - "Um, so that's the thing, you're *not* going. I don't want to go *with* you. I *am* going by myself."

"WHAT!?!"

Her eyes were a loaded double barrel shotgun, dead-set on a fat, panicked little duck. "I know, I know. Look, I'm sorry, but it's my brother-in-law's place, so either I go, or it sits empty." I had to get control of my voice, at least, never mind the situation at hand. She was freaking me out with that stare. "I'll pay you back for the ticket if you don't want to find somewhere else to stay, but there's no other way to say it. I don't want to spend the holiday with you, and I don't think we should see each other anymore."

I am not a cruel man. At least, I don't think I am. I didn't want to hurt this woman, I liked her much more than I could have admitted, but I couldn't lie to her. I wanted her out of my life; more accurately, I wanted out of hers. Her embarrassment and hurt hardened into anger. With a bitter hiss, she said, "I'm glad my friends and family think I'm going out of town for work and not a romantic getaway with an immature and under-legal-drinking-aged jerk." She yelled at me a little more before leaving; I understood.

After she left, I felt a sense of relief typically reserved for hearing something like, "Great news, it's *not* cancer!" Canceling her trip was a shitty thing to do, for sure, but what else could I have done? I couldn't lie to her for the length of time it takes a busy Manhattan restaurant to make lunch; no way could I have pulled off lying to her all day for a week. I wonder if a dishonest compliment is indeed worse than an honest insult? If I were more honest, I would have admitted I was too self-centered and insecure to handle not being particularly special to her. But that sort of honesty takes wisdom. You get what you pay for with twenty-year-old weirdos, I guess. And yes, I ate both of our sandwiches, even though hers was vegetarian.

When we met one last time in the lobby of her apartment building, I felt like the biggest piece of shit in New York, if not the world. I handed her a check to cover the cost of her airfare. She took it angrily and asked me if I was still planning on going alone. I was so mentally unprepared that my dumb face settled into an absurd tear of a smile that understandably pissed her off even more. She rolled her eyes at me and walked to the elevator. I haven't seen her since.

I spent a week alone on that island, nearly broke from the unexpected expense of two plane tickets. I made due, riding the bus, swimming in the sea, nearly drowning in it, wrestling with multiple existential crises, drinking rum, and eating mostly fruit or spaghetti noodles with no sauce – at least I know how to make myself feel special. I took a little comfort by telling myself Bella would have hated it.

# There are Landfills
# in Paradise

Antigua, like many islands, is a crazy-making place. The roads are narrow and winding and feature more farm animals than stop signs. I was puzzled by the goats and skinny cows wandering freely with frayed bits of rope dangling from their necks. A local, equally perplexed by the young white boy on the bus, explained it to me through a giggle. "Law says 'dem gotta be tied up. Law don't say what to. So 'dem rope don't tie to noting', HA!" Naturally, the animals hang out in the road, as they seem confoundingly compelled to do, wearing tattered old necklaces.

I got the sense that maybe the island was like a racetrack, where one-way traffic made better sense, but the locals got tired of having to lap around the island every time they forgot something and decided to risk going against the flow. And risk it they did. Each new blind corner had me sending apocryphal prayers to St. Christopher, the Devil, Ganesh, and the lesser-known teenage Jesus who learned to tend bar in Kathmandu. We dodged animals, cars, and other buses and scraped the edges of cliffs as elephant-ear banana plants splattered against the neglected side view mirror. The driver's eyes closed when he laughed, and he laughed a lot.

I arrived at my brother-in-law's timeshare in a nervous sweat. Twenty years old and dumber by the minute. Carrying my single bag and stupid twelve-string guitar, I found my way to the check-in hut. The European expats who ran the place were amused by their unlikely guest - an American man-child, arriving on foot, dressed in thrift store clothes that almost fit, carrying an insufficiency of provisions and an overabundance of musical instruments.

I asked them about the beach with curious enthusiasm. The way they admitted to me and each other how seldom they visited the water was awkward for everyone. Almost like they accidentally slid headlong into the truth that the island had completely lost its charm. I also didn't like the way they asked me what I planned on doing for food.

Most of the guests at this small hotel were old and wealthy enough to have rental cars. I, of course, was neither and counted on riding the bus. The husband told me, "This is not something white people do on the island." I'd already gathered as much on my way from the airport. They also told me that I'd missed the only opportunity to get any food, as the grocery store was back in town, and there were no restaurants nearby. "Oh, and the bus doesn't run again until morning. Welcome to Antigua," they said, with the joylessness of bummed-out Germans missing the hearty sausage, strong beer, and reliable public transportation of the motherland.

I was up before the sun the next morning, hungry but excited. I followed the beach to a large outcropping, crossing over a low-tide gap, carrying my camera and shoes in a waterproof courier bag as I waded through the ankle-deep and salty water. I took photos of the locals (a family of goats) and watched the sunrise over the island, marveling at the colors of the sea and clouds as they changed by the second. I explored, climbed around, and tried not to think about food. I made it to the bus stop just in time to see that I'd missed it. I decided to walk to town.

Crippling fear had caused me not to pay enough attention the previous day. The route was the last thing on my mind as the bus driver chattily careened through corners and took stabs at breaking land-speed records on the narrow straightaways. So, of course, I made a wrong turn. Passing a ramshackle brothel, where the women outside seemed as tired and worn out as the sun-faded railing of the porch, I waved as they drank coffee and ignored me. Strolling with numbskull-glee through the shack-filled village next to it, where every face I saw looked as confused by my presence as I was by the necklace-wearing cow following me, I was too amused to realize I was headed the wrong way. The road ended at something I had not considered and to which I had not yet had the horror of contributing – a landfill overlooking the sea.

I'd seen landfills before. Coming from the rural south, they were a part of my life from an early age. The big machines pushing trash around reminded me of cats rolling their turds in a sandbox. In Brooklyn, I'd watch the trash barges haul their loads from Manhattan to Staten Island, giggling childishly to myself as I said the phrase - *shit ships*. This tropical island dump had all the same trademark features as the ones I'd seen in the US. A cyclone fence with windblown candy wrappers and Styrofoam cups forever stuck in the diamonds - The terrible, pungent smell of rotting food and mud - and the lonesome crushing sound of huge diesel-powered contraptions rolling over discarded lawn furniture and exploded trash bags. Several bizarre facts set this one apart from its continental counterparts.

First, there was the fence. Like the rules concerning cows and rope, the fence looked like it had been constructed strictly to the letter of the law. Standing alone, without a gate or a single corner, it was just a twenty-foot length of chain-linked metal and posts, like a windbreak, constructed to tick the box next to the rule - *landfill must have fence* - maddening and hilarious at the same time.

Then, of course, there was the view.

If you put your hand just below your eyes, the view from the dump was the best I'd see on the island. The extra elevation set the viewer well above the sea, opening up an expanse of deep blue water and smaller islets so charming and serene it broke your heart to know it was inseparable from the stink of the place. Palm trees and dense jungle-like foliage grew as close to the massive trash hill as possible - an overwhelming force slowly descending upon the dump. I forgot all about being hungry.

As for the local population, I'd never seen anyone living anywhere near a dump state-side. American landfills are so bleak and heavily regulated it doesn't seem possible. Not to mention the fences around them are connected on all sides, topped with razor wire and feature gates that lock at night. This beautiful island landfill, however, was not uninhabited. Several people picked through the rubble, carrying ratty satchels and heavy sticks to overturn larger debris. I saw lean-to structures in the forest and people moving through the trash heaps like homeowners moving through their gardens – surveying the territory with the curious air of proprietorship.

The contrast between shit and shine was captivating. I moved deeper in. I thought the locals in the village were perplexed by me. These guys avoided eye contact altogether, like a fart in an elevator or a racist uncle; it's best not to engage. My bovine companion abandoned me at the entrance, grazing instead on the opposite side of the road. I rounded a hill, separating myself from the roar of the tractors, and could hear the sea again. I also heard something I did not expect, a human man singing a bizarre tune.

The voice was more growling bear than trilling bird, but the tune was up-tempo just the same. His singing synched rhythmically with his movements. The man wasn't simply digging through the trash – I could hear him dancing with it. A phrase of the melody would hit a beat just as something heavy smashed the ground, or a word would sweep along as he dragged objects from place to place. Nearly hypnotized by the weirdness of it, I climbed on top of a mangled refrigerator to look for this strange crooner. My head crested a nearby mound, and I looked straight into the most tortured pair of eyes I hope I'll ever see.

The bits you would expect to be white were a sickly yellow streaked by deep red veins, converging on filmy, pitch-black irises. As tortured as they were, his eyes were the first I'd seen on the island that didn't seem surprised to be looking into mine. The rest of the guy took some time to absorb. For one, he never stood still but held my gaze as if it belonged to him now. He continued to sing, growling every line with maudlin creole menace. The only English words I recognized seemed to be the hook of his tune, " ... now it mine!"

Instead of having 100,000 individual hairs, he only had to deal with a single giant dread. It looked and moved like a massive worm, emerging from the back of his head and keeping an eye on his six. He had the wildest beard: dust-covered, but still as black as refrigerator feet, with a single bleached white chicken bone twisted impossibly into the bushy hairs sprouting from his cheek. His bare chest rippled with sinewy muscle fibers and more scars than I could count. He wore a pair of filthy black dungarees with cracking mud caked around the knees. His feet were bare and looked more like large wooden reproductions than the real thing, complete with comically large soles and toes.

He continued to weave about, growling his tune, looking into my eyes with unknowable emotion; I stayed put. He eventually turned his gaze to the ground, his song catching on the upswing as he dipped down, snatched a small piece of pink fabric from an open bag, lifted it into the air, and danced a kicking jig. At the end of an ecstatic spin, he seized my gaze once again. With both hands, he showed me what he'd found, a pair of pink panties, small enough to have belonged to a little girl. His grin was as troubled as his eyes. His few remaining teeth were either yellow, black, or a shade of green, more unripe banana than spring grass. In time with his strange rhythm, he danced into the panties, one leg at a time. This new accessory seemed to please him wildly, yelping, " ... now it mine!" as he snapped the band around his waist. He twirled and shimmied away, pointing at random objects, kicking up tiny dust plumes, and sending cans and empty cigarette cartons flying in all directions. He vanished behind another trash pile, taking his peculiar tune with him.

My mind was one more shredded piece of debris, unceremoniously hauled out to sea by the outgoing tide.

I took out my camera. One of the machine operators noticed me and sped over to the refrigerator carcass. At top speed, honking the tractor's hilariously puny horn, his body half in the cab and half out, he waved his free arm wildly, screaming at me, "No Photo, No Photo!" He stopped about three feet from me, "*Da fuck you are doing, hah? G'won, white boy, g'won!*"

On the road back to the main highway, where I'd made the now glaringly obvious wrong turn, I saw the bus pass again. Too unsettled by what I'd just seen in the dump to feel upset by my poor timing, I kept walking, ignoring the waveless stares of locals.

What the fuck had I just witnessed? A landfill in paradise? A dancing wizard? A nutcase? Myself? Was that man my father, my brother, everyone I'd ever known or would know? Was *he* special? If he isn't, then for sure, no one is! How did he end up there? Wasn't he once a pliable baby, soft and vulnerable in a pair of loving arms? Where was his family? Am I his family now? Is he alright in there? Is anyone alright anywhere? It was all puzzlement and zero answers. I'm afraid little has changed.

Notions of life's pointless pageantry, hopeless equality, endless sameness, and the lie of individuality collapsed into one another like rotting debris in a plastic bag – impossibly tangled, inseparable, ruined. My body filled with a lonesome sadness so complete I had to crouch down in a ditch for a spell. Painful tears gave me perverse pleasure, like stretching a bruised muscle or puking out the last drop of poison.

When I finally made it to town, I spent almost all my money on rum, fruit, and spaghetti. The chicken was affordable, but I couldn't stand the idea of facing the bones.

# Ain't No Heroes Here

Cocaine, when hoovered from the end of a house key into an oversized nostril, tastes like spoiled mint, unripe apples, and gasoline. To verify this rare flavor combination was as I remembered it, I sniffed a small powdery pile for the fifteenth time that day. My friend and navigator put the bag back in his pocket as we checked each other for unsightly white boogers. Only then were we mentally, physically, and spiritually prepared to emerge from the back of a beat-up Dodge van to handle the finest organic produce in all five NYC boroughs, New Jersey and Connecticut.

If any or all of this sounds like a terrible idea and/or a gross combination of inputs and outputs, well, that's because it was both terrible and gross. That's not to say it wasn't fun, though - it was. I'll tell you how we got there.

It was 1999 in Brooklyn, NY. The navigator and I spent our days working in the offices of a company called Urban Organic, a rag-tag home delivery service. I was a recent hire and a transplant from the Deep South, but my friend was a Brooklyn native. When I got there, he'd been an office manager at the company for a few years already. Neither of us showed up that day expecting to be driving around in Manhattan.

Urban Organic's service was novel then, with most of our business done over the phone. It's worth remembering organic food was not widely available at grocery stores just yet, even in New York. After signing up with us, our customers received a week's worth of fruits and vegetables delivered straight to their door (or as close as we could get). This was pre-Amazon and at the tail-end of the first dot-com boom and bust. The idea of having items other than pizza or Chinese food delivered was taking hold in a big way. For example, a nearby company was advertising the promise of a big-screen TV, a DVD player, a copy of Raging Bull, and a large Pizza – all delivered in less than two hours! I never met anyone who tested it, but I wouldn't have been surprised to learn it actually worked.

Our warehouse was in Park Slope, Brooklyn, a part of the city on its way to becoming increasingly homogenized and almost insufferably hip. In 1999, the waters of gentrification were rising, and even though I was poor and lived in a cheaper neighborhood, my white, lanky, young presence helped further erode the seawall of cultural diversity.

The crew at Urban Organic was a mixed bag of misfits, alcoholics, people with anger management issues, and a few regular, well-adjusted, tax-paying citizens who just wanted to make a living without violating too many laws or social norms. There were the packers - a disparate group of zealots responsible for receiving shipments, stocking the refrigerator, and preparing boxes of produce for delivery. These guys haunted their territory like wolves in a forest. The drivers represented their own outrageous subset of delinquency, angrily menacing the streets of the greater New York Metropolitan Area, simultaneously hauling packages and navigating terrible weather while in the grip of some of our planet's most aggressive driving.

The office team was somewhat segregated from the others and populated by young, ambitious folks like I was before I knew any better. In fact, one of Woody Allen and Mia Farrow's charming and beautiful daughters worked at the computer next to mine - a gracious and funny young woman who never made mention of her family. I quickly made friends with two brothers working in the office, one of whom was my navigator on the day I'll be describing throughout this text. For the sake of his privacy and to spare him from embarrassment, let's call him Duke. We remain friends to this day.

Duke and I shared a few common interests: drinking, playing music, flirting with women, and an affinity for drugs - especially cocaine.

Cocaine was easy to find, and Duke had connections to the purest, uncut Colombian powder. The Fishscale-perfectly white and free from baby laxatives or other pharmaceutical fillers. After trying what Duke had to share, I quickly realized I'd only ever taken sub-par cocaine. One of the guys working the packing line also sold coke, but nothing pure. Like most things worth enjoying - bagels, pornography, broccoli – it's worth it to hold out for the good shit, but for young, broke, and impulsive idiots like me, *some* is better than *none*.

The difference between sniffing bad cocaine and the real thing is similar to the difference between drinking green tea and slurping truck-stop coffee. A nice cup of green tea gives the drinker an energized but not jittery buzz. Gulping down truck-stop coffee, on the other hand, often ends with a jumpy weirdo squatting on a toilet. Real, uncut cocaine is powerful but imbues the sniffer with a slightly crazed-yet-measured sense of what the Spanish call "Fuerza" or force, as gringos would say. Alternately, cocaine cut with fillers has similar effects but tends to amplify the craven and maddening aspects of the real thing. It is also, like truck-stop coffee, often a shortcut to the sudden and aggressive shits.

On the day in question, both Duke and I were at our desks, busy trying to look busy. Neither of us was high, and neither of us planned to get high at work. Part of our jobs included maintaining regular communication with the delivery drivers throughout the day. Customers often called in to find out where their order was or why it had shown up with so many bruised apples. To manage customer expectations, it fell upon the office goons to radio the drivers for answers as the day developed.

As the morning progressed, we noticed one of the drivers was late - an issue that required the boss's attention. His introduction to this narrative deserves a paragraph, at minimum, so here we go.

Charlie, Charles, or Charlie Urban as we knew him, was a New Yorker through and through. Born in the same part of town where we operated, he cut a distinct figure - tall, slender, red-haired, with the slightest hint of slouch in his shoulders. His uniform rarely varied - white tennis shoes, faded blue jeans, a t-shirt, and a leather jacket. When they rounded on you, his big Irish eyes suggested he knew something funny about you that nobody else had thought to mention. His Irish roots were deep, and he knew poverty and hardship in a personal way. That hardship, along with what growing up in New York can do to just about anyone, made him an intelligent, mercurial, and iconoclastic figure. For example, he was sober but employed more alcoholics and drug addicts than most bars. He ran an organic food company but almost exclusively ate powdered doughnuts and White Castle hamburgers while drinking diet Pepsi and smoking Parliament cigarettes. I never once saw him eat a fruit or vegetable.

I asked him to join us at a nearby bar one night after work. He declined, saying, "I don't drink."

"No problem, I'll bet they've got diet Pepsi." You see, I thought I was clever.

"Tennessee," he looked at me with an implied wink and grin, "you don't walk into a whorehouse for a kiss." Wise and funny, Charlie Urban. Oh yeah, he sometimes called me Tennessee – fucking awesome.

Through the long row of windows in the office, we could see the delivery vans and the big worn wooden table where the packers worked. I watched Charlie slink around the table, smoking and chatting with the guys, scratching his head and looking around like he was searching for something. His eyes locked onto mine.

"Yo, Tennessee!" flicking his cigarette into the street and motioning me to join him on the warehouse floor, Charlie looked serious. "Hey, you've got a driver's license, right?"

"Yeah, I do. What's up?"

"I'm short two drivers today. I'm taking one of the routes, but I need somebody to head into Midtown. You know your way around?"

"Sure," I said unconvincingly.

"Hmm … well, no problem, it's easy. We got maps, and it's all streets and avenues, so no biggie. You wanna deliver today?

"Absolutely, sounds like fun!"

"You know what … it might be a little tricky closer to the village. This is a busy route. Let me find somebody to navigate and help run boxes." He walked into the office and asked around. Lucky for me, Duke didn't have his driver's license, but he did know his way around the city, so we got paired up.

Duke and I looked over the manifest and agreed we had a long busy day ahead of us - 120 stops. A brief, clandestine, and very stupid conference ended with Duke heading to the packer's table to score an 8-ball of coke to help get us through the day. Unfortunately, the only coke on offer was far from "the good shit."

"Tennessee! Grab a map and a radio, and call in if you got questions."

Crisp, clean, and poised, Duke and I climbed into the van, sending a jaunty salute to our Captain as we drove off. He gave us a wink and looked pleased with his last-minute choice to wrangle the two young office guys into the harsh fray of home delivery.

Before we hit the city, we pulled over to look over the map and took a couple of bumps each from the bag. Within minutes, I felt crazy, like I could just throw each box from Brooklyn straight to the address on the label.

What followed was eight and a half hours of madness, violence, and questionable degrees of customer satisfaction. Starting with what Duke still refers to as "The Turn!"

To fully understand "The Turn," you need to know a thing or two about driving in midtown Manhattan. For one, it's madness. The painted lines on the roadway, elsewhere known as "traffic lanes," are simply there to remind you that staying between them is for suckers. Cab drivers and delivery drivers are locked in a largely unspoken forever war. And the odds that a cyclist will do something to endanger himself, piss you off, or both are high. Combine these factors with heavy foot traffic, an overarching aggressiveness in the population, and a city-wide sense that everyone is running late for something important, and you get a traffic scenario that is, if not deadly, at least uniquely nerve-wracking.

Duke and I were making good time. For sure, we suffered no lack of energy and the relative ease of occasionally being able to double park while Duke ran boxes into apartment buildings made things easier. But cocaine is not the sort of drug that lends itself to wise, measured use. We were both taking bumps at an increasing rate. Sweating profusely, running back and forth from buildings to the van, feeling the obsessive-compulsive thrill of watching the pile of neatly stacked boxes shrinking with each stop, we didn't notice the spinning of our machine begin to wobble.

We found ourselves traveling north on Park Avenue, near 57th street, needing to cross over to the West side of the park. I'd missed the turn where it would have been easiest to do so. The streets of New York City have this annoying feature of alternating one-way directions, and occasionally you encounter two streets in a row that are one-way in the same direction, but head in the opposite direction you need to go. If you are in a stable frame of mind, this is no big deal. You just keep going until you can make a safe turn, then double back. But when your state of mind is less than stable, it's a different story. Especially if you're sweating through your skin like sausage on a hot grill, grinding your teeth to dust, desperate to find a place to piss, and anxious to empty the old van you are driving of its perfectly stacked boxes. However irrational it may seem, there is a chance you might begin to take these unpredictable one-way streets personally.

On a whim, I chose the right-hand turn option, but missed my first shot, encountered a few more confusing one-way streets, then ended up on Park Avenue again, in almost the same place as before. This probably only took a couple of minutes, but time was no longer moving the same for us, and the need to turn left was growing desperate. Sitting in the far right lane at Park and 60th street, anxious to make a left, I started to squirm. There were six lanes of traffic on Park Ave at this point. Three northbound and three southbound - all divided by a tree-and-shrubbery-lined median. All we needed in the world was a left-hand turn, but I had positioned us in the worst possible place for one.

Thanks to low-grade and pharmacologically questionable cocaine mixed with a naturally reckless and impulsive personality, I was forced to face my inner ugliness head-on. I wanted to explain to Duke what I was about to do. Instead, I blurted out – "HOLD ON TO YOUR SHIT!"

From that far right lane, as the cross-traffic signal turned yellow, I made a last-second visual sweep of the intersection to confirm no vehicles were traveling in either direction. Then, like trying to kill a snake with my boot, I smashed the gas pedal with full force, turned the wheel hard left, and went for it. Tires squealing, the top-heavy van tilted on its wheels like a fat dog running around a corner. I careened through the intersection like a getaway driver trying to shake the cops. G-force momentum made Duke and I scream like teenagers on a carnival ride. The neatly stacked boxes rearranged themselves to match the scrambled neurons in my drug-rotten brain. We crossed all six lanes before the light turned green, seriously traumatizing a pedestrian who would forever have good reason to fear crossing the street. Even in the throes of that wild moment, I couldn't help but notice the face of a cab driver waiting for the light to turn green, shaking his head in disgust while I confirmed his suspicions that all delivery drivers are totally fucked.

Two stops later, we were still jangled from "The Turn." While leaving a five-story walkup, carrying two empty boxes a customer had asked me to return, I was running out of the building like the kid least likely to qualify for the track team. I misjudged the stairs leading to the sidewalk, made an awkward leap with about six stairs to go, then landed horribly on my ankle, spraining it with a pop that sounded like snapping every stalk of celery in our van at once. Watching from the van, Duke wretched.

I hobbled along, brushing dirt and bits of gravel from my body where it had gracelessly hit the ground, laughing like a madman as I climbed into my seat.

Duke, a much calmer person than me, even when high as a kite, looked freaked out. "Jesus Christ, man! Your ankle just buckled like it was on a hinge! Are you all right?"

"Probably. Maybe. It's gonna hurt if I stop moving for too long. Fuck!" Thanks to years of being a klutz, I had lots of experience with sprained ankles. This would be, by far, the worst one yet.

Of course, the radio chose that moment to chime in. "Duke, Tennesse, come back." It was Charlie. "Where are you guys?"

He'd done some creative shuffling with the other drivers and was waiting for us uptown. He said we could make better time if he drove the van while Duke and I ran boxes.

I suddenly remembered that I couldn't afford to lose my job. "Goddamnit, I'm high as shit! What do we do?"

"Me, too. Don't worry, we'll be fine." Duke was much more experienced but not wholly free from the shackles of totally stupid decision-making. We agreed that we shouldn't have any cocaine "on" us, so we put it all inside us instead and sniffed up the remainder of the 8-ball.

"Wow! What the fuck happened to you two? You guys look like shit!" Charlie was facing two guys who scarcely resembled the crisp, clean young men he'd watched drive away only a few hours earlier. Both of us were unusually sweaty, and I was dirty from my fall, with dried blood on my shirt, hands, and elbow.

"Just working hard, boss." Duke chimed in. "Oh, and Andrew probably broke his ankle, but he's still moving, so we're good to go!" His voice sounded much higher now that Charlie's sober ears had joined us.

"All right … " Charlie said, suspicious and knowing. "Tennessee, stretch out in the back, Duke, you're on the map. Let's move."

The sun had set. Darkness and street lights battled it out as I hobbled from door to door in the crisp Manhattan evening. Working with Charlie, as tweaked out as we were, Duke and I managed to keep it together. My ankle was so swollen it looked like I'd taken a grapefruit from one of the boxes and stuffed it in my sock. I knew I had to keep moving or it would seize up on me. As cheap and dirty as the cocaine was, it did a fine job of keeping me from focusing on the pain … for a while.

We were nearly finished, and traffic had died down considerably when, traveling north on Central Park West, I saw something I couldn't ignore. Central Park was to our right, and a seemingly endless mountain of buildings was to our left. By the park, on the sidewalk, I saw a large man struggling to overtake a much smaller woman. Duke and Charlie were chatting in the front and hadn't noticed. I yelled out as we sped past them, "STOP THE VAN! PULL OVER, PULL OVER!"

"What the fuck, Tennessee?" Charlie asked as he hit the brakes and maneuvered to the curb. But before the van stopped rolling, I was already on the sidewalk, struggling through a hobbled and now incredibly painful run toward the ruckus on the corner. I started yelling at the top of my lungs, "LET HER GO, MOTHERFUCKER!"

The woman thrashed about as the much larger man struggled to maintain his grip on her wrists. Her hair was long, brown, and greasy in the orange hue of the lamplight. I couldn't see her face, but she was making strange noises, somewhere between strained grunting and a scream. I thought she may have been injured already. I was closing the gap as quickly as possible and bummed out that the man hadn't reacted to my first plea. I stupidly yelled again, trying to add a little gravel to my voice, "GET YOUR FUCKING HANDS OFF HER NOW!"

I was within three feet when the man spun around, reaching into his coat with one hand. I instinctively made a pointless show of ducking and making my body a smaller target for the gun I was sure he was drawing on me. But instead of a gun, he pulled out a cell phone and yelled at me, "Take this and call the police! This is my daughter, and I need help!"

"What!?" I wasn't prepared for anything, really, but I felt more prepared to face a pistol than whatever *this* was. I directed my focus now to the woman, "Hey, is this your dad?" Hair continued to obscure her face, and her guttural sounds were less like words and more like what I imagined Mongolian weightlifting would sound like. She *was* small for a full-grown woman; maybe he was telling me the truth? Still, I wanted to tackle the man and smash his face into the sidewalk, just in case, but I hesitated. "I need to know, IS THIS YOUR DAD?!?"

The man kept insisting his phone on me, "TAKE THE PHONE! PLEASE, CALL THE POLICE!"

With one hand now free, the small woman brushed the hair from her face just enough for me to realize two crucial things — she *was* a teenager, and her pupils were even more dilated than mine, suggesting she was extremely high. The whole thing was suddenly a little clearer. The man had probably come home from work to find his daughter tripping on LSD, they both lost it, and now the two of them were locked in a struggle at the end of which there would be no winner. I looked up at the buildings to my right and noticed that half of the balconies had people on them, and half of those people were holding telephones to their ears.

I was once again reminded of just how high and stupid *I* was. I suddenly had to face facts; talking to a bunch of cops would be a terrible idea. So, to the man I would not be tackling and the teenager I would not be rescuing, I offered, "Oh no, man, she's fine. Just give her some bananas and a little space. Maybe tell her you love her and that it's OK to be scared. Hey, sweetie, it's alright if you're scared; you can handle it. OK? Look, yeah, um, I'm guessing the police are probably on their way already, so you won't be needing me, right? Good deal. You guys are gonna be fine. Good luck, bye-bye."

I saw Charlie and Duke standing by the van, shaking their heads like the disgusted cab driver had done as I streaked past him making "The Turn."

"Nice work, hero," Charlie said sarcastically.

"I know, I know," I said, exhausted. "But we should get the fuck outta here ... and fast."

"Yeah, no shit." We climbed back into the van, and Charlie gave me a well-deserved earful of solid wisdom and common sense. Duke and I gave our beleaguered teeth and jaws a break from grinding as we laughed at Charlie's keen and hilarious insight into what an idiot I was. Blaring sirens and flashing lights passed us as we left the scene.

I like to picture the mostly satisfied customer who called me the following morning - carefully opening her wholesome box of organic produce shortly after I left her house and frowning slightly when encountering the apples. If only she could have heard the true story of how they earned their bruises rather than the off-white lie I delivered through a stuffy nose. With my foot propped up and wrapped in ice, I shamefully offered, 'Oh, I'm sorry to hear that. We can toss a few extras into your next delivery to make up for the damaged ones. But remember, organic apples often look more like the real thing than chemically treated ones – bruises, blemishes, and all.'

# A Bridge Too Far

October 7th, 2001: a beautiful fall day in Memphis, Tennessee, and a horrible one in Kandahar, Afghanistan. The US was still reeling from the attacks on September 11th, and the new reality of heightened security was on almost everyone's radar. I say almost everyone because there will always be a cross-section of the population who, even though they live in the modern world and hold down jobs, do not bother to read the news, listen to the radio, or own a television. Two prime examples of that subset were my sweet girlfriend and me.

Three bridges spanning the Mississippi River connect Memphis, Tennessee and West Memphis, Arkansas. Two are interstates, I-55 and I-40, and one is for railroad traffic. The I-55 bridge has a lovely catwalk underneath the roadway that spans the length of the bridge, with access points to climb down onto the massive concrete pylons below. It was technically off-limits to the public, but people walked across it all the time. On that lovely fall day, my girlfriend and I decided to go to the river and walk under the I-55 bridge.

To reach the catwalk, you had to climb over a fence, scale a ladder, then shimmy along a narrow metal walkway overlooking the river below for about a hundred yards or more before reaching the pylon. It was worth it, even on a cold and cloudy day. On a crisp and sunny fall morning, the payoff is huge. Standing in the open, above the mighty river as it rushes below you on its way to the gulf, is a powerful feeling. We made the most of it, lounging around in the sun, smoking a joint, and pissing off the side. At one point, my girlfriend even took off her top to give the city skyline a peek at her boobs. In short, we had a great time up there - the very picture of youthful exuberance and joy. After about an hour or so, we decided to head back and get some lunch.

The catwalk jogs around a few corners before the long straightaway that leads to the entrance/exit. I was in front, with my girlfriend behind me. Once we rounded the last corner, I noticed the shape of a man crouched down in a defensive position at the end of the platform. The moment I saw him, I knew we were in trouble. I said as much to my girlfriend, "Babe, I think we made a terrible mistake. I'm not certain, but I'm pretty sure a cop is looking at us through some binoculars."

*Of course, this was a bad idea,* I thought to myself. Paranoia dry-humped my raw nerves as I slowly crawled my way toward the man in black. My worries began to take shape, remembering - *The whole country is on high alert, and I'm crawling around on my hands and knees under a major interstate bridge over the Mississippi river ... precisely the sort of thing every redneck within 100 miles is expecting from a terrorist! I'll be on the "No-Fly" list if I'm lucky. If not, I'll be in Guantanamo Bay.*

When we reached the end of the platform, we were about fifteen feet above the parking area. My vehicle was surrounded by a grab bag of law enforcement vehicles, the likes of which I'd never seen. The local FBI had a couple of guys there, as did the County cops, the City cops, the Coast Guard, and the Railroad cops. I didn't know the railroad had its own police force!

Fortunately, none of them were aiming their weapons at us. It looked, from our perspective, like they knew exactly what they were dealing with. But due to the climate, they had to make a show of force out of the exercise. I'd reached peak stupidity, and the assembled lawmen knew it.

A local cop was the first to say anything. He handcuffed me, then separated us for on-the-spot questioning. *Well, this is it. This is where I go to prison,* I thought. When, instead of being shoved into it, I was pushed against a police cruiser, something in me relaxed a little. If I were going to be arrested, I'd be in the back of the car, not leaning against the side of it.

For good or ill, I knew I had one thing going for me. I'm a white guy - not brown, not particularly tan. I didn't have a big beard then, and the last name on my driver's license, while weird, is not "foreign." While many of the officers around were black and had good reason to be eager to turn the screws on a privileged white boy, they would at least not associate me with the insanely and unfairly profiled "Arab-looking guy" so derided in the culture at the time. I recognized even then, many years before the woke masses demanded it of people without much melanin in their skin, the absurd and unearned advantage of simply being a white man.

The questioning began right away. An angry, serious, beefy, African American officer, showing off for the FBI goons, laid into my girlfriend. She was crying. Remember, we were both high. Fortunately, I had only brought one joint and had flicked the butt end of it after we smoked it. I was extra glad of that while I was being patted down by the officer *not* asking me idiotic questions. The one making the ding-dong inquiry was either not worried about showing off for the FBI or thought that asking me, "So, who told you it was OK to come up here?" was some kind of brilliant line to lead with.

In any case, I decided to be a sweetheart to the guy. I called him sir, never let a frown cross my brow, and made sure my answers conveyed two simple facts. One, I was embarrassed not to know that the USA had started dropping bombs on people in Afghanistan that very morning. Two, I realized just how dumb it was to be under the bridge at all, especially with the new information I had about the escalation of violence around the globe. In other words, I slipped into a very well-worn personal groove and showed my hand as an affable halfwit prone to doing dumb, yet harmless, things.

I navigated his easily spotted "trick" questions but never took the upper hand, never acted like a smart guy, and basically rolled over, showed my belly, and did everything I could to highlight the fact that we were two dumb young people enjoying their day off in an admittedly reckless but ultimately innocent way. The officer understood this and admitted they had been watching us from the moment we climbed onto the pylon. The Coast Guard and Railroad police had already left. Now it was just the local goons and the FBI guys they all wanted to impress.

My poor girlfriend, on the other hand, was having a much more difficult go of it. The large, angry guy questioning her had asked her something, and her answer didn't cut the mustard.

He approached the car where my interrogation had fizzled out. The two cops who'd been questioning me were relaxed and looked like they were ready to move on. My handcuffs had even been removed. "I need to talk to you!" he said, pushing his thick finger into my skinny chest. He barked, "Come over here!"

I followed him to the side of the FBI cruiser where he'd been questioning my girlfriend.

"Now, she doesn't seem to want to tell me, so maybe YOU will; what did you put down out there?"

I had no idea what he was talking about. Hanging on to the character I'd developed with the other two knucklehead officers, I politely told him exactly that.

"Now look here!" he said, turning again to my girlfriend, "We *ALL* saw you put something down up there! What was it?

She was red-faced, frustrated, and completely shaken by the exchange. I could see she was about to snap. Before I could say anything to her, she angrily blurted out, "We didn't do ANYTHING!"

*Shit, well, prison jumpers look comfortable. And I've always wanted to have big muscles. Looks like I'll be getting my chance.*

"Don't you yell at me, little lady!" The officer was pissed. "You're the one trespassing on federal property while the whole damn country is on alert, not ME! You need to check that sassy attitude and answer my damn questions!"

I realized what it was all about; the big cop was loving this. They all were. They were supposed to be on high alert, and their system had failed. We could have blown up the bridge twice in the time it took them to respond. Two stoned young people had managed to infiltrate the "secure perimeter," and now every agency with a stake in preventing "acts of terror" was getting the chance to mobilize a response. The angry cop just needed to flex his muscles. I also noticed he hadn't mentioned seeing her bare breasts. I felt safe when I helpfully interjected.

'I did take my jacket off while we were out there. I put it down for a while but picked it back up before we left. Is that what you're talking about, sir?'

"Yeah, that's exactly what I'm talking about. I told you we had eyes on you from the start. I just wanted to see what you'd say."

I didn't really follow the logic, but I knew better than to question it. I just wanted them to stop asking my girlfriend any more questions. I leaned into my character and offered an apology. 'We're both terribly sorry for choosing today of all days to make such a stupid mistake. I understand you've got a job to do, and you've got our full cooperation.'

"Hmm, full cooperation, my ass! You're lucky we don't arrest you both right now!"

'Yes sir, thank you for that.'

The big angry cop told his lackeys to hurry up and get us out of there. He told us to leave and never come back. I thanked him again.

Just before the officers who had our licenses were about to hand them back, another squad car pulled up. When the other officers saw who it was, a sense of deflation rippled through the ranks. The FBI guys chose that moment to drive away. The older model squad car parked at an annoying angle, lights still blazing unnecessarily in the noon-day sun. Out of it creeped one of the most obnoxious individuals I've ever encountered. Thankfully I don't remember his real name, but for the purposes of our story, I'll call him Officer Dickcheese.

Dickcheese oozed from his car like he'd been poured into it as a prank. Once standing, he hiked up his service belt, gripping the revolver in one hand and the leather expanse of his handcuff case in the other. Tall, angular, thin, sucking on a gnarled and sickly-looking toothpick, wearing dark, mirrored sunglasses, and desperate to compensate for lack of control in his early life by being overbearing in the middle of it, Dickcheese was quite obviously disliked by everyone there. The officers who took our information quickly handed us our licenses and walked away to avoid him.

He walked right up to both of us and said in a saccharin and nasally voice, "Do you two have any idea how STUUUPID this is?"

I knew we were in the clear. The cuffs were off, our driver's licenses were back in our pockets, and we were free to go. I was personally out of obsequious nicety and just wanted to get the fuck out of there like they told us to. When I realized how much everyone there despised this guy, I was inclined to follow suit.

'Yup, real dumb.' I meant it in more ways than one. I could tell he missed the subtlety of what I was saying.

The guy had hauled ass at top speed from miles away the moment he heard there was action at the bridge. I could tell he hadn't driven all that way for nothing - he wanted to give us a piece of his mind. "You know, if you'd been on the railroad bridge, they got orders to shoot on-site! You two would be DEAD!"

In the vacuum of his eyes, I could practically see the reflection of the bullies who tormented him in school, teasing him about his big ears, his nasal voice, or any of the things shitty little bully imaginations can get a hold of. I felt terrible for the kid who had endured this but was currently disgusted with the adult he'd become. I looked into those sad eyes and found myself saying, "Well, it's better to be lucky than good, I guess. So, your boss told us to get out of here and never come back ... we'd like to do that now if it's OK with you?"

He recoiled at my annoying answer and said he needed to check with his superior and that he'd be right back. He walked a few steps away and made a call over the radio. I suspect he thought we wouldn't hear it. We probably wouldn't have, but being surrounded by multiple cops with their radios on, we heard him say, "Come on, isn't there some way we can bust these guys?"

I saw the big angry officer place his thick slab of a hand on his forehead, shaking slowly like it hurt a little. He called out, without using the radio, saying perfectly loud for all to hear, "Dickcheese, just let 'em go."

Amazingly, I never did make the "No-Fly" list. I did manage, eventually, to marry the girlfriend, though. As instructed, we never returned to crawl under the bridge. Instead, we crossed the length of it using the pedestrian walkway that was eventually built on top - where it should have been all along, really. Oh yeah, and the war fell apart and ended almost twenty years later; it turns out that was real dumb, too.

# They Say Bad Things Come in Threes

There is a belief called triaphilia, a fear that bad things will happen in threes. The origin of this is, of course, religious in nature and should be viewed with the suspicion it deserves. But when three bad things happen to you in a relatively short period of time, it's hard not to give the theory at least a passing glance. In my case, the three terrible events that marched through my young life - a breakup, a death, and a burglary — did me no end of good.

I don't mean to suggest I enjoyed any of those tragedies individually. That's weird and dark, even for me. I mean to say I benefited from each troubling event in ways that weren't obvious in the moment but have insisted I take notice as time shoved me down the road.

Let's start with the breakup.

My now wife and I had only been dating for a few months when we moved into our first apartment. It was for sale when we rented it, but the landlord assured us our signed lease would insulate us from crazy rent-hikes or flat-out eviction. One morning - almost noon, really - I was up and smoking a joint, plucking my guitar, and staring out a window when an unfamiliar car pulled into the parking lot. Two of the three people who got out of it I did not recognize. One of them I did — my high school guidance counselor.

When the trio eventually crowded my tiny kitchen, like the stoned and jabbering idiot I was, I started to ramble, attempting to justify my life's decisions and resulting outcomes to my former guidance counselor. She smiled, listening patiently, then introduced me to her husband and their real estate agent. "Um, it's OK, Andrew. We're looking to invest in a rental property. We're thinking about buying this place." They eventually became our landlords.

Tiffany and I lived there together for about a year before I fell apart. I started to write that I'd been unfaithful, but looking at it spelled out on the page, UN-FAITHFUL, it felt wrong. First, the "UN" bit of it represents only twenty percent of the word, while One hundred percent of what I did was shitty. I think a more robust word is in order; betrayed will do. Besides, unfaithful sounds like a word made up by people who want to soften the blow of their own treachery, lying, or selfish behavior. What I really did was sleep with a friend from New York while there on a visit. I'd never done anything like it. I tried to convince myself I could do something dishonest and it wouldn't matter so long as I kept it to myself. I could not have been more wrong.

Living under the weight of the lie was just gross, like morning breath in the evening or putting dirty socks on clean feet. I truly loved Tiffany and cursed myself for lying to her. I also cared for my friend a great deal more than I had shown and had lied to her as well. She would never have slept with me if she knew I had a girlfriend. I was the bad apple, the lying, selfish asshole I had always tried not to be. Tormented by my terrible decision for about a month, I confessed. A confession I later realized was given more to relieve my own guilt than it was to protect or honor my partner. Self-centeredness piled up at the foot of our broken relationship, like the dishes in the sink after she moved out. It was more than a mistake or a lack of judgment, though. To call it a bad decision doesn't really cut it. I had been a *bad* person, embracing lies and selfishness over the hearts of others.

I felt like garbage, and I went a little wild with distraction. Desperate to make sense of having such a spacious place all to myself, I moved my bed into the kitchen, making a tiny bed-room out of the nook where a table would usually go, then turned the bedroom into a music room.

Living without her, something I had practiced for twenty-one years, was suddenly much more difficult. There was no relief, no jubilant celebration of living single. I shoveled selfish experiences into a new hole in my life. Where my partner no longer laid her head, I stacked a piano and some instruments. Where we had shared our meals, I put my bed.

If life didn't feel shitty enough, shortly after the breakup, my older sister, Colleen, and I paid a visit to our dad. He'd been ill and wanted to see us. Dad had always been barrel-chested with thick forearms and full, round cheeks. But we were confronted with a sickly and gaunt-looking man who had lost too much weight too fast, and whose muscles were in total atrophy. Something was terribly wrong. We both cried on the ride home.

My dad's health history was spotty, to say the least. He had rheumatic fever as a child, and his family physician limited his physical activities for most of his young life. When the Vietnam War came around, he was treated like cannon fodder, and the same physician who had previously insisted playing baseball was too risky for his health, signed a release paper paving the way for the draft board to send him to a Marine boot camp. Against all odds, he made it through basic training, took the oath, and became a Marine Corps private. His commanding officer took one look at him and knew he was too ill to serve but knew making him a Marine would give the poor kid from Flint, Michigan the health benefits he desperately needed. The extreme physical effort of boot camp enlarged his heart and damaged its already weakened valves. He would undergo several surgeries and receive one of the earliest versions of the mechanical heart valve.

His physician, the same man who had kept my father alive for much longer than anticipated, was now concerned that one of his heart valves was leaking, causing him to waste away. A plan was devised to replace that leaky valve. A battery of tests was performed before the surgery. One of them, a check of thyroid function, was so crazily off the charts the physician wrote off the result as "machine error." Unfortunately, the simple test was not repeated.

On the day of his surgery, my older sister, brother, stepmom, and I joined him while he was waiting to be wheeled down to the operating room. We chatted uncomfortably before the nurse came to take him to surgery. Each of us hugged him and wished him luck. Like all the hugs I'd shared with him before, our hug was awkward. He hugged my brother last, and when he did, he started to cry. We heard the young nurse laugh at something he said as she wheeled him down the corridor – funny guy.

Touching my dad had always been weird but took a decidedly self-conscious turn after one of our weekend visits. As he dropped us off at our mom's house, I leaned over the front seat to kiss his cheek. He tensed up immediately, "Don't you think you're too old for that?" At eleven years old, I wasn't exactly sure how to take it. He might have been right, but it hurt me somewhere deep, more like a loss than a rejection. I certainly never kissed him again, unsure which show of physical affection might be age appropriate. We were strangers with friends in common, shaking hands at parties but not close enough to hang out independently. I didn't have the wisdom to purge that awkwardness from our final embrace. Would it have been much different had I known it was our last?

I later learned he was convinced he wouldn't make it. He'd shared the same opinion before each of the many surgeries and procedures endured prior to that one, so no one took it too seriously. He was reassured by my siblings, my stepmom, and his physician. I had nothing to add, so I kept quiet as usual.

We would all spend the next several days in and out of an ICU waiting room, standing for a few minutes each at his bedside during visiting hours. His surgery was relatively successful, although they forgot to deactivate his defibrillator during the procedure and were surprised by it as it shocked his grossly enlarged heart. I took that as a bad sign. Unfortunately, it was his recovery from the surgery that was unsuccessful. He was intubated and semi-unconscious for the brief and tortured remainder of his life.

I was working at my sister's restaurant as a bartender and managed to keep my shifts, distracting myself from worry by working in the evenings and drinking. I worried my father might die. I worried about the terrible suffering he was enduring. I worried I would have to keep living with the weight of our failed relationship hanging on my shoulders, unsure if he knew I loved him and unsure what my love for him meant to me. You know this kind of worry; it's got no real name or purpose. It just lingers shapelessly in the heart, like a pulse, or more accurately, a missing beat.

At home, my sleep was fraught and uncomfortable. Instead, I stayed up through the night, making music and writing a song that would play on a loop in my head for about a month. In the hospital waiting room, I installed myself in an oversized reclining chair, which could stretch out flat like a bed, and managed to doze off throughout the day. I used the same chair every visit, claiming it like one might at home, slowly leaving an imprint of my tired and uneasy body. The memory of that weird vigil comes in hazy vignettes featuring my dad's friends arriving to talk to my stepmom and brother. I could barely keep my eyes open and only got up when it was my turn to stare wordlessly at him during visiting hours.

I looked into my dad's eyes two more times before he was carted off to the morgue for an autopsy. Once, on a visit to his room with my brother, we stood by his bedside and talked to him. He was sedated and usually wouldn't even stir. My brother spoke to him. I stood there like an idiot, not knowing what to say. Years later, when we scattered his ashes in the Mississippi River, I experienced a similar phenomenon, silently staring at remains with nothing to say as they floated off somewhere else. During that visiting hour, as soon as my brother spoke, my dad woke up. Terror and confusion shot through the red, bloodshot veins and the narcotic-yellowed bits of his eyes, which would have otherwise been white. His gaze darted around the room, pleading for help. Craning his neck and reaching for my brother, he gagged on the tube which had been down his throat for days. He was too doped out and disoriented to make much progress. My brother touched his forehead and spoke reassuringly until he closed his eyes again, relaxed his neck, and laid back. Beads of sweat had formed on his skin, and my brother's fingers came up damp from touching him. He casually wiped them on the sheets of the hospital bed as he slowly pulled his hand back.

The last time I looked into his eyes, I was with my older sister. Dad was blind in one eye and had a funny way of dealing with it. As kids, when my sister and I had a surprise for him and asked him to close his eyes, he would cover one eye with his hand and leave the other open. Dad said it was the same as closing it. I could have sworn he changed up which eye he covered from time to time. When my sister asked him once, "What's it like being blind?" He took a moment to consider, then replied with pure dad-genius saying, "Imagine trying to see out of your ear."

On the day he died, my sister and I walked into the room and took our places next to him. Colleen, who I have always considered bold and oddly daring at times, bent down and pushed one of his eyelids open. The eye had the same yellow and bloodshot aspect as before, but this time his pupil was much different. It had an unoccupied quality, like a house after a family has packed up, dusted, mopped the floors, and driven away, leaving it empty. "He's not here," she said. I'm still not sure if she was looking into the good one or the blind one.

The last moment I saw him technically alive, my brother and I were in the room for a visit when several nurses barged in, telling us they needed to move my dad immediately for testing. For whatever reason, they let us walk with them as they wheeled him out of the ICU and down a corridor to a service elevator.

Three nurses, one short and muscular, one angular and attractive, the third a vague, nurse-shaped blur in hospital scrubs, chatted awkwardly with us while we waited - the same sort of strained conversation everyone who talks while waiting for elevators ends up making, but somehow with even less eye contact. As they shoved him into the elevator, one of the bed's wheels wedged itself in the gap between the floor and the car. Scrambling without addressing the central issue, they floundered clownishly - impatiently snapping at each other like an act in the saddest circus ever. The door was trying to close on the gurney, beeping impatiently to hurry the hell up. A machine, plugged into my dad in some uncomfortable way, chose that moment to shriek its own urgent song above the fray. We shouldn't have even been there at all, but we were both taught, by the man quickly vanishing in the unmoved bed, not to stand around watching people struggle without helping. We lifted on the edge of the gurney to de-weight the stuck wheel, telling them, *Push now!* Nurse Muscles snapped at us, "DON'T TOUCH IT! LET US DO OUR JOB!" I stepped back, staring into his eyes, briefly considering leaping across my father's nearly dead body to strangle him a bit. The pointlessness of that conflict, and all of them really, took on a sharper focus after the door closed and the three stooges were out of sight. There is chaos in death, even for those with lots of practice.

Less than an hour later, he was dead ... my dad, not the sassy, muscular nurse.

Back in my quiet house, I drifted from room to room, searching in vain for something, anything, as comfortable as that hospital chair. Instead, I tossed and turned throughout the night in my bed in the kitchen.

The morning after he died, I stared out my window at an enormous oak tree - a tree so tall and decked-out with massive branches a whole family of fat raccoons lived in it without revealing the exact location of their home. I tried to picture the acorn it once was, likely buried and forgotten by a squirrel, well over a hundred years before my father took his first breath. Did you know they lose almost 80% of the acorns they bury?

Unsatisfied with the images in my mind, I imagined my father as a fetus, growing in the womb of my poor grandmother - a woman who, like the most forgetful of squirrels, planted her own forest of sixteen children, thirteen of whom would branch out beyond the sapling stage. Coincidentally, her rate of success was almost perfectly inverse to that of squirrels – roughly 80%.

I found myself troubled by the improbability involved in every moment of human life - growing from a goo of cells - materially almost nothing, really - into a big, dumb body. A miracle so incredible we *must* take it for granted to get on with the business of living. And what of my dad's journey? Once powerful in motion, despite severe poverty and rheumatic fever, tripping up his stride, propelled by the power of wit, luck, and charm, drawing the short stick of the Vietnam War draft, nearly finished by Marine boot camp, shadowed so close-ly by death it counted down his moments from a spacious perch in his enlarged heart, a heart which ticked weirder by the day. Catching love on a train, succumbing to the evolutionary impulses which produced too many children, meeting some success, fighting some failure, crawling the Earth's surface for a taste of travel, he hardly had time to stop and check the rose bed for weeds. And then, just like that, his clock stopped, and death revealed the truth to yet another person who won't be spoiling the surprise for the rest of us. Powerful images of the tiny growing big, struggling against a lifetime of gravity's pull, and weighing competing interests, while trying to take notice of a few prized, yet fleeting, moments before dying on a ran-dom Saturday in February. Life in a nutshell.

Beyond the sadness, disbelief, and denial of loss lies a hol-low place where, for me at least, imagination whispers all the lies a man needs to hear to keep moving toward his own final moment.

This void was soon filled with music. I was pretty sure my dad never even knew I played. I didn't have any of the hard-ware for cymbals or a stand for my snare drum, so I suspend-ed my kit from the ceiling with twine; the ungrounded and resonant tones matched my mood. A friend gave me a piano. I didn't know how to play the drums or the piano and was a marginal guitar player, but I managed to chase down sounds I liked on those instruments, recording songs about loss, doubt, godlessness, and wandering through life without a clue how to live it. The song that played in my head as my father died on that hospital bed, I chose to perform at his funeral service instead of talking. Even dead, I didn't know what to say to or about him.

In addition to the drum set and the piano, I had six guitars, a cello, two amplifiers, a recording console with microphones, a record player, a banjo, a stereo, and a monitor system with speakers in every corner of the room. Fortunately for her, my poor neighbor, an alcoholic in her late fifties, was usually passed out drunk when I made the bulk of the noise. Loud, late-night music, fueled by beer, liquor, pot, and bad singing, assaulted the thin wall between us. My friends would come over and we would terrorize the air with meandering and noodling in search of a good song. Our finest work was a slow song - the best part of the track played by a cricket with a microphone placed near its body as it clacked soulfully and with desperate purpose above the pointless human noise.

Two weeks after we recorded that beautiful insect's expressive beats, I came home from work sometime after midnight on a Friday to find my back door unlocked. I walked into my kitchen and saw an amplifier in front of the refrigerator. Something was wrong. In the music room, my heart broke open like a glass jar hitting concrete. The window unit air-conditioner had been shoved in and was lying in a heap, a chunk from the stained wood floor gouged out by a sharp corner as it landed. I briefly worried for my landlords, wincing at the damage to their newly purchased floor.

The drum kit had been clipped from the ceiling, leaving slack and lonely pieces of twine, twitching in the breeze sneaking in from the same window the thieves had climbed through. Newly exposed dust, which had accumulated under the guitar stands and the now missing pieces of equipment, looked as empty and hollow as a dying man's eye. Nearly every possession I had ever cared about was gone, and every note I had ever recorded had vanished. I called the police, wondering what to do with my expectations. I know now that I should have tossed them out that open window.

When they finally shuffled into my apartment, I was reminded of when a bunch of unruly teenagers picked my pockets at a county fair while I played a game. We were there with my dad, who insisted my sister and I wear the "nice" clothes he bought, not the jeans and T-shirts we preferred. When I approached a police officer to tell him I had just been robbed, he looked me up and down and said, "Well, they probably thought you could afford it," essentially blaming me for looking like a rich guy's kid. I was too angry to know he couldn't care that the money was earned by cutting grass and washing cars, the clothes were not my choice, and that none of that was the point.

The cops who came into my burglarized house might as well have been the same guys from the fair. When I told them what had been stolen, they asked if I played music at night. "Well, thieves hear that, and it's like an advertisement for free shit!"

I gave them my statement, providing a timeline of events and a list of everything that was missing. I asked if they were going to dust for prints.

They laughed.

"Nahhh, man. That's television and murder stuff. It's not what we do."

So, what DO you do?

"Pass your statement to a detective. He'll probably call you Monday."

*What do I do until then?*

"At least they didn't steal your air-conditioner! I'd put it back together or at least close that window. It's hot outside."

The emotional fallout after a breakup or a death is profound, the kind you feel in your bones, more like a chill or a phantom ache than a bruise or blunt trauma. Post-robbery emotion is similar but edgier. Raw, like freshly peeled and gravely skin after a fall. Vulnerable, like being nude in a church. Unsettled, as if I'd been suddenly relocated but not told where. Uncomfortable, metaphorically sitting on my balls. Ruminating and regretful, considering the missed opportunities and warning signs which might have prevented this most recent disaster. But above all, I was angry. I couldn't sleep and contemplated spending my nights prowling the streets like a wolf, seeking out any no-good thief I could find to tip the scales of justice, just a bit more in the right direction, by way of my pathetic yet rageful fists. *THIS*, I thought, *I could do something about!*

I decided not to wait for a phone call. On Monday, I went to the police precinct to find a detective. The guy they assigned to me had a desk on a busy floor in the upper reaches of the building. I was surprised when I was told he was late for work. No one else was. Obviously, he was the butt of nearly every joke in the office. Smart-looking, gun-toting detectives with files under their arms and steaming cups of coffee in their hands shook their heads and chuckled as we walked by. I'm sure we were a picture to behold; a lanky, long-haired white-boy-weirdo and the short, black, bespectacled, well-dressed detective who couldn't solve the case of the ringing alarm clock.

It became clear, quickly into our interaction, his dress, his patterns of speech, and his exceedingly self-important demeanor were meant to compensate for being generally bad at his job and roundly disrespected by his peers. I felt for him. But if some are at the top of their games, there must be those of us who are at the bottom. This was my guy, the absolute worst of the best.

I gave him the same statement I'd given to the uniformed officers at my house and his sergeant only moments before. He took notes which, when I saw them, made my heart sink. I'm no detective, but I would think when handling an investigation into a burglary, the first note wouldn't be the occupation of the victim or the detailing of his or her physical statistics. The word burglary, misspelled, didn't appear until halfway down the page. It would have been just as effective if he'd used a crayon rather than a pencil, drawing pictures of cops and robbers instead of notes.

I suggested we start looking in local pawn shops and music stores. He put down his pencil, amazed by the sudden arrival of a great idea, and told me we could go right then. We stopped by the coffee machine on our way out just as one of his coworkers took the last of the coffee cups. The now in-accessible, half-full coffee pot seemed to jeer at my cup-less detective. Our momentum continued to struggle as he spent the next several minutes searching for a cup. Eventually, he abandoned the mission, pretending he had been there simply to verify that no more cups were available. Standing there like a fool while my detective searched in vain, I realized he wasn't the only joke flying around the office. I felt the eyes and could hear the giggling of the other assholes in the precinct. Another minor discouragement, but my spirit lifted as we headed for the parking garage to get in his police cruiser.

His personal vehicle was parked in a nearby lot, while the car the city provided for him was stored in an enormous build-ing filled with similar cars - most of them black sedans. We walked confidently down one of the aisles, chatting about the likelihood of finding the stolen instruments in a music shop versus a pawn shop. When we reached the end of the aisle, my detective, who could barely see over the tops of the parked vehicles, stopped and put his hands on his hips. I watched as puzzlement crept across his features like nervous lizards over hot rocks. We tried another aisle. No luck. I asked him what we were looking for. "My car" was his first retort. When I asked him to be more specific, he didn't really have a great answer, saying distractedly as he stood on his tiptoes, "A black sedan."

After having given my complete, detailed, and thorough statement three times already, I was irritated that my detective couldn't be bothered to share further details about the missing vehicle, but I was still clinging to a quickly dulling optimism. I hoped the two of us would be working together in a relation-ship of mutual assistance, like a buddy cop comedy where a lanky hippy and a black Mr. Magoo-type character would solve the crime, culture-clashing all the way. Instead, at the end of the next aisle, he gave up.

"I can't find the car. Let's go get my personal vehicle."

That was two abandoned searches in less than ten minutes. There were still many more aisles of cars to search and dozens more black ones. When he turned on his heels and started to walk back towards the elevators, my enthusiasm finally gave up the ghost. I told him I would go looking on my own and would get back to him if I found anything and asked that he do the same. He gave up on me as well and went back to his desk, a quitter, through and through.

I managed to channel my anger in a more productive direction and solved the case alone. I found several of my instruments at a lousy music store dealing in stolen goods not far from my house. I set up a sting operation with the store manager and a friend, gathered security camera footage, and ended up watching the thief remove a couple of my instruments from the trunk of his car in the store's parking lot. I followed the thief back to his house – it was only two blocks away from mine and on the same street! I wrangled every friend I had at the time to surround the place. After calling my detective for the fifth time that day without an answer or a callback, I gave up on him and called 911. When the uniformed police showed up, angry that I was calling, I was nearly arrested for disturbing the peace as I demanded the burglar open the trunk of his car. The police made us leave the area and let the burglar go, even though the tags on his car did not match the vehicle's registration. I was beyond disappointed. On a whim, I sent the thief and his family a pizza. I'm unsure what psychological effect this had on him or the people he lived with, but it felt right. He was arrested many weeks later - the car and the instruments were long gone.

I still have one of the instruments I recovered from that bogus music store - an electric guitar. I sold it to a friend in New Orleans a few years ago but recently bought it back from him. I first purchased it when my dad was still living and before my wife and I shared our first kiss. It's curious how an object, particularly a musical instrument, can carry such personal weight. When it is resting in a corner, I can picture the younger version of myself who searched for it over two decades ago. It never made a single sound for my father and was making too many sounds when I broke two hearts at once. And now, all these years later, the sounds it makes come from a heart, growing like a forgotten acorn, repeatedly damaged and mended by the madness of existence, swaying in the wind.

I looked up the word triaphilia in a library on Vancouver Island, Canada - a place I would not have visited at all had I not become single, fatherless, and involuntarily liberated of my possessions in such a short period. I saw those three things, even from the close time-space distance of less than a year later, as something else. In Spanish slang, there is a word for it "Malegria" - a little bitter, a little sweet, a little loss, a little hope. More than twenty years later, I see those three losses as the skeptic's equivalent of a blessing. You may already know this, but sometimes it takes a little muddy water to truly appreciate the clearer stream.

# Stupid Cookie

"**Y**ou know why you arc here?" No one answered. Collectively, I believe the group thought the question rhetorical. "OK, I tell you." The voice, thick with a Barcelona accent, continued. "You are in Spanish cookie commercial … "

At twenty-two years old, I could have passed for a basketball player – if not a shooting guard in the NBA, then possibly in a European league. I was working at my sister's restaurant as a bartender and not exactly at the peak of my physical prowess. Still, I had what many professional basketball players have going for them, height and youth. These two attributes, coupled with insatiable curiosity, made me a perfect candidate to play an extra in a television commercial.

One of my regular customers, a guy called Martin, waited for a lull in the action on a busy Friday night to pitch me on the idea. He worked in television and movie production and was hired to shoot a commercial for a company in Spain that sponsored the NBA star, Pau Gasol.

The company paying Gasol to endorse their product made some sort of energy bar. If the production budget was any indicator, the company was either nearly broke or spent the lion's share on securing Pau's name and likeness - unless, being Spanish as well, Pau was doing the gig for the honor of supporting the confections of his countrymen. I don't remember the name of the energy bar, but for the sake of this tale, let's call it Galleta Tonto, which roughly translates to Stupid Cookie.

Galleta Tonto could not afford any NBA players to share screen time with Pau, so the pros were out. College athletes would have been great, but they're not allowed to get paid to play basketball, even for a Spanish energy bar commercial. So that left the crew of Galleta Tonto searching around Memphis for guys who looked like basketball players. My pal, Martin, was kind enough to ask me if I'd like to be one of them. "It only pays 100 bucks, and it might take all night, but it'll be weird, and I get the sense that you like weird shit." He knew his bartender. I agreed and planned to be on set the following weekend.

I played basketball in high school, so it wasn't out of character. My final game as a student ended on a terrible note. We were losing by several points to a team we should have been beating easily. Our coach was frustrated. I had a job at the time as a photographer for college fraternity and sorority parties and was scheduled to work later that evening. I managed that job, three nights of practice per week, sometimes two games per week, and five days of school. I was a busy guy and worked hard. Many of my teammates were in the same boat, working odd jobs, playing on the team, and trying to keep up their grades. Our coach, by all metrics, was an asshole, even in the best of times. He was a pedantic, condescending, passive-aggressive, and generally unpleasant man. He was also my English teacher. I much preferred him in the classroom to the court, as he encouraged us to write freely, daily, and to a high standard of specificity. There is little doubt he would dislike many aspects of this telling. On the court, he was irritable, impatient, and not exceptionally competent. Still, as much of a prick as he was, I squirm when I think of my behavior relative to his.

My last game was near the end of the season. As I mentioned, we were losing, and the coach called a time-out. He'd been screaming discouraging and less than constructive critique for the whole game, more like an angry spectator than chief strategist. In the huddle, rather than manage us or give any useful feedback, the coach started telling us how lazy we were. An already low-level irritation in me was quickly stoked into a raging aggravation. Sweating and breathing heavily, thinking about the late night ahead of me, and looking into the faces of the demoralized guys getting yelled at in front of their friends and families, I'd reached my limit.

I loudly interrupted the coach, saying, 'Jesus Christ, man, that's enough! Not one of you is lazy, OK!' The coach, eyes bulging and his translucent skin turning beet red, looked like I'd just kicked his mother in the crotch.

"What did you say?" he asked pointlessly, infuriating me even more. "You're out!" he belched, "Sit down and shut up!" Pointing to another kid in the huddle, he yelled, "You're in!"

Impulse took over, and I let him have it. I looked him right in the eye and said, 'I'll do better than that.' Looking at my now former teammates, I told them again, 'You're not lazy.' Looking again at the man I would have to face on Monday in the classroom, I said, 'Good luck, I'm outta here.'

As calmly as possible, with the electricity of conflict making my heart flutter like sand in the wind, I walked to the locker room, changed, and emerged dressed for work. My now former teammates were on the court and not doing well. As I passed by the coach, I restated my case in broad terms, telling him, 'This is bullshit.' Two days later, I handed in my uniform and apologized for swearing but not for the sentiment behind it. My grades, to his credit, did not suffer.

Four years later, I walked into that same gymnasium, prepared for my role as a numbskull extra in a commercial for Galleta Tonto. It was weird, but it only got weirder from there.

The high school gym was exactly as I remembered it, minus the crowds in the bleachers, or the smells of popcorn, spilled cola, and steaming hotdogs. The bleachers were occupied instead by a smattering of cardboard cutouts in the general shapes and colors of human spectators. Even to a first-timer on set, it looked absurd.

A film crew was busy setting up the court, staging lights and cameras, while the primary actors and about a dozen extras milled about, shooting hoops at the other end of the court. I joined them.

Several were grown men in their thirties, but most were around my age. One of the guys was showing off, perhaps hoping Pau would notice his skill and ask him to join the NBA. He was sweating like he'd been playing for the championship, crisscrossing and shooting long-range jumpers from nearly half-court. At one point, while I was taking a shot, the guy leapt from several feet away and blocked it, slapping the ball into the bleachers and knocking over one of the cardboard audience members. It was ridiculous, yet somehow fitting to be there in that gym, getting my shot blocked, more pointlessly than ever, by a kid with such wildly misguided ambitions. He apologized, saying, "I just can't help myself, sometimes," a sentiment I understood completely.

After about an hour of talking and taking turns shooting the ball, one of the crew came over and asked us to take a seat in the bleachers. I sat between a super tall and muscular guy in his mid-thirties and a cardboard cutout of a lady with no face.

The crew member, a Spanish woman, serious, purposeful, and driven, was preparing us to meet the director. She had the personality type that naturally lends itself to toting a clipboard filled with action items and holding her subordinates to account. I pictured her at home stalking the ranks of her cats like a general while reading them entries from an ever-growing to-do list before leaving for work. Her lovely dark hair, pulled back into a ponytail so tight and clean, coupled with severe military posture, made me wish I'd been more disciplined in my life. I was confused, though, by her word choice, "Prepare yourself to meet the director." I looked around to see what preparations we were expected to make and noticed no one else knew what she meant, so I relaxed and considered myself prepared. It turns out I was not. "I introduce to you, Tobias." When none of us clapped as he made his stately way from behind the bleachers, she made a note on her clipboard.

Tobias was of another breed. A Picasso of a man, important, strange, and endowed with an artistic streak so desperate to be recognized, it grabbed you by the lapels and breathed a sangria-scented aria in your face until you complimented it sufficiently. His accent was outrageously Spanish, and his English seemed almost deliberately chopped up for comedic effect. He welcomed us like dinner guests in his home; his tone was more fitting of a congratulatory toast than a director's instructions to a rag-tag group of extras.

He began, solemnly flipping the tassels of his scarf from one shoulder to the other, "You know why you are here?" As I mentioned before, no one answered. He relented when the pause grew so pregnant with grave sincerity that even the wood pulp lady next to me seemed uncomfortable. "OK, I tell you." I'm no expert, but I don't think language and cultural barriers erect walls that high; I can't imagine a culture where a dozen men would show up to an empty high school gymnasium on a Saturday night with no clue why they were there. Either Tobias thought we were twelve of the dumbest people ever to tie up their laces, or he just liked the drama; I honestly couldn't tell. He continued in his earnest and lugubrious tone, "You are in Spanish Cookie Commercial with famous basketball player, Pau Gasol." He trailed off at the end, tipping his head and waving his hand in flourished genuflection to honor the sacred name his unworthy lips had just uttered.

He then laid out the scene we were to act out. There were two guys dressed like coaches, several players wearing either black or white jerseys, and a couple of other guys dressed like 1930s photographers. He marshaled us into those groups and stood there, eyeing us with both awe and a touch of disgust. The scene was already peculiar, with Tobias getting weirder by the sentence. "It is the *END* of the game," Boris Karloff in his prime would have thought the guy was overselling it, "and the stakes are *VERY* high!" He continued with his oddly timed emphasis, "*YOU* are very excited!"

And that was the totality of our direction. We were then marshaled to our marks at the other end of the court by a ponytail so perfect and capable we had no choice but to obey. A row of chairs had been strung together where the players who were not in the game would react to whatever Tobias had in mind for action. The tallest extras, all wearing black jerseys, were on the court, waiting for the star to arrive. I was also wearing a black jersey. We were once again addressed by the severe woman with the clipboard and introduced to the star of the show, Pau.

Pau Gasol walked onto the court and was easily the tallest person in the building. Demure and somewhat shy, he said hello to everyone. I noticed the young guy who had blocked my shot earlier was standing with his chest poked out like a soldier presenting himself to a general for inspection. Tobias approached Pau and whispered as he placed his small but meaty hand on a tiny portion of Pau's unusually long back. I pictured Rasputin poisoning the ear of the Czar.

Pau and the primary players ran through their bit. Wearing a white jersey, Pau would blow past three hapless defensemen and leap from a great distance to dunk the ball. They did this a few times, with Tobias whispering to Pau after every run and looking through his outstretched hands to frame the shot, ignoring the actual camera behind him.

Satisfied with the action, Tobias then addressed the extras once more. "OK now, you," pointing at one of the coaches, a few of the guys in black jerseys, and the young sweaty shot blocker, "you can all go home now. We change the angle, and you can go." Just like that, they were done for the day. The deflation and disillusionment in the overly-eager young man's face were painful to see. He approached Pau and shook his hand before shuffling off in abject disappointment. Pointing to me for some reason, Tobias said coldly, "OK, you four, follow me."

The coach, the two other guys wearing white jerseys, and I followed him to the row of chairs at the edge of the court. Remember, I was wearing a black jersey. "SO, you are here," guiding the coach into the first chair. "You are here," placing me to the right of the coach. "And you two sit there." The two guys in white jerseys were to my right.

Snapping his fingers, the woman with the clipboard handed each of us a small towel, including the coach. "Now, you

244

have the towel, Pau dunks the ball, and you are very excited."
He said this without the dramatic flair of his previous speech.
Feeling satisfied we were sufficiently inspired and directed, he
turned towards the cameras across the court. I was confused
and called out before he could get too far away.

'Excuse me, Tobias, I have a question.' He turned around,
approaching me like I was a child with a poopy diaper.

"Yes? What is the matter?" Tobias was a close talker and
crept so far into my personal space he felt more like a garment
than a separate human being.

'Uh, well, in American basketball ... ' I was stammering,
nervous at his proximity, and unsure of his vision.

"Yes?" He said, impatiently

' ... Um, well, typically, that is normally, opposing teams
don't sit together like this.' I gestured pathetically toward the
white jerseys on the bench while touching my black one.

"No!" He said, looking almost hurt and a little sorry for my
lack of imagination. "You have the towel, yes? It is the *END*
of the game. The *STAKES* are very high." He was breathing
into my ear from a few inches below, waving his hand as he
spoke. "Pau dunks the ball, and you are *VERY* excited. You
understand?" His tone was more conspiratorial than irritated.
I didn't, but I also realized I didn't have to understand. Not my
problem, I thought. I thanked him and told him I was ready.

Take after take, Pau leapt through the air and dunked the
ball on the hopelessly outmatched trio of players. Each time,
the 1930s cameramen fired the flashes on their cameras while
the coach and the two guys on Pau's team would jump, wave
their towels, and make whooping noises. Of course, even
though the stakes were high and my team was getting dunked
on, I joined them in their excitement. We were there for hours.
After the clipboard general told us our checks would be mailed
right away, Tobias left without saying goodbye. And just like
that, it was over.

I never did see that commercial, but my pal Martin told
me it ran for a bit on Spanish television. When I asked him

how they handled the fact that a guy from the opposing team was sitting and celebrating with the winners, he laughed. "They shot it in black and white and blurred out the background. You just see Pau dunking the ball. Probably could have done the whole thing in a couple hours with half the extras."

My bizarre reward for having been a part of some of the most pointless moments in basketball history, twice in the same gymnasium, seems reasonable - one painful memory of needlessly swearing at an authority figure and 100 dollars more than a cardboard cutout of a faceless spectator - a fair price for one stupid cookie.

# Sam Hotel

Tending bar came naturally to me. That's not to say I was any good at it. I likely wasn't. Remembering the names of drinks was as tricky as remembering the names of the people who ordered them. Oh, and forget about describing the type of leather wallet or ass-end of which fruit a wine is meant to taste like. No, what made it a natural fit for me was something less concrete and more guided by ephemeral sensations than any particular skill. It helps that I learned how to bartend while taking psilocybin mushrooms every day for about a month.

Keep in mind this was about two decades before the term "microdosing" became part of the lexicon. If somehow you're not familiar with microdosing, essentially it involves ingesting a sub-perceptual amount of a psychedelic drug on a regulated schedule. The promise and premise of this trend, similar to herbs or vitamin supplements, is that microdosing can potentially address nearly every possible ill which might befall the mind of man. What I was doing was not precisely "micro." I would eat either a cap or a couple of stems every morning. I did this for the first month of my training behind the bar. This was less for the betterment of an otherwise well person than the stumbling machinations of a craven nitwit who heard it from a friend that it was "nice to eat just a little bit every day."

My daily dose, unregulated, non-uniform, and always covered in a spoonful of peanut butter, was not sub-perceptual, but it was way less than the perceptual flood which would have washed my dirty mind clean if I'd eaten them all at once. Why, then, did I do this? Honestly, I don't know. I'm a creature of impulse and tend to follow my wandering mind like a lost kid behind a security guard in a department store. What resulted from being just a little high as I learned this new occupation? Well, it seared into my mind that tending bar was a fun and essentially low-stakes affair—a sensation that would last for over a decade.

On my first day, Harrold, an older, beloved, and affable man universally appreciated for his aloof and easygoing personality, was my only guide. Harrold was notorious for telling people he had to "take out the trash," a thinly veiled code for going outside to smoke a little pot. He showed me how to set up the bar - where things go, arranging glassware, cutting fruit, stocking beer, wine and liquor, ringing up drinks and food, etc. The bulk of his advice for making drinks was exceedingly straightforward. "So, bartending is pretty easy. Most drinks have the ingredients in the name - Gin and Tonic, Vodka Soda, Rum and Coke. Everything else is in here," he said, handing me a dog-eared and greasy-red covered *Mr. Boston's Official Bartender's Guide*. "Seems like you've got it under control. I'll be right back. Gotta take out the trash." And that was that - I was a bartender.

I picked up the rest by trial and error and by watching Harrold. My Martinis were fine, and my gin and tonics a bit strong, and my bullshit answers to what a wine might taste like were passable. Honestly, the big difference is that wine nerds fail to deliver their answers with the sense of embarrassment or shame which should accompany being unequivocally certain about something as subjective as taste.

In short, I could pour drinks, deliver meals, and keep the place clean. If I had any skill, it was for making people feel welcome.

About a year into my tenure behind the bar, a young person, only a year or so older than me, walked into the bar and confidently sat in the only open seat. It was uncommon for a guy my age to drink there. My sister and brother-in-law owned the place, a popular and unusual restaurant for a town like Memphis, TN. It had a ten-seat bar, tables without salt and pepper shakers, and white cloth covers on them instead. It was best known for serving seafood, but catfish was nowhere to be found on the menu. The only fried item was Calamari, and at no point were the patrons encouraged to throw peanut shells on the floor. The bar was mostly a placeholder for people to gather while waiting for their table to be ready. Some regulars would eat at the bar, but they were usually older and could afford the higher price, which was well outside the drinking budgets of most of the people I knew. The average age of our patrons was somewhere around fifty. I was twenty-two.

"Hey man, whatcha drinkin'?" I asked, likely polishing a glass or wiping something to keep my awkward hands occupied as I took my chances on prolonged eye contact with the wild-looking young man who had calmly walked in like it was his regular bar.

"You got any sherry?" He was casual and relaxed, wearing a loose-fitting, well-worn T-shirt, jeans, and Italian boots. I could smell his body, and his aroma suggested he'd either been exercising, working hard, or fucking. I would later come to know which of these activities was most likely. Hint: it wasn't work or exercise.

"Like cooking sherry?" I asked, unaware of the fact that there were many types of sherry and that we did not, in fact, have any of them.

His face said *Great, another idiot,* but from his mouth came, without hesitation, "No, Amontillado, or if you have it, an Oloroso Cream?"

He might as well have been speaking another language. He obviously lived in another world of awareness and confidence, carrying the same 'I truly don't give a shit' attitude I'd only ever known in elderly people. He gave up on me and ordered a draft beer instead. I poured it and introduced myself. He didn't even blink when I told him my name, then introduced himself. "Sam." He said it with the tiniest of grins. People in Memphis knew him as Andy or Andrew. From that moment, we were pals.

He was back in town after a long stretch of moving around and had lived in some of the same places I had, namely New York and Portland, OR. We bonded over the usual subjects, music, drinking, and flirting with just about every woman we met - although he was much better at each than I would ever be. Thanks to him, my taste in and awareness of the variety of ways alcohol could be enjoyed grew by leaps and bounds.

Sam was extremely handsome. His laugh was infectious and suggested he got more about the joke than most people. He was philosophical, preternaturally funny, well-read, adventurous, and confident in ways I could not imagine. Sam was also insecure, deeply troubled by something I didn't have the wisdom to identify, and in constant search of something I didn't have the imagination to contemplate. He could sing and play guitar without much effort. His ability to paint and draw was a talent he barely scratched, and his gift for poetry and prose made me hate reading my own clunky sentences.

My girlfriend had recently moved out, and I'd converted my bedroom into a music room with a piano, guitars, a banjo, a cello, and a drum set. The drums were suspended by lengths of twine from the ceiling, and the cymbals seemed to ring on forever with the slightest strike from a stick. Sam was with me the day after I discovered that all of it, except the piano, had been stolen. He joined me in a Quixotic, yet nearly successful, search for justice and helped me recover a couple of the guitars. Sam was there with me the night my father died. We were drinking together the night a bandmate asked me if I'd like to hike on the Pacific Crest Trail, and he lived in my house for several months while he avoided his inconveniently rent-seeking landlord.

He took me to his apartment to show me why he didn't feel inclined to write his landlord any checks. As we climbed the steps, he stopped at his mailbox. It was comically overstuffed with junk mail. Catalogs, coupon rags, bills, nothing of any value to any living being on the planet, all jammed into the box and spilling out like a lanced boil frozen in time. The bills and flyers clung to one another like a colorful barrel of monkeys suspended mid-fall. He laughed out loud and pointed to the absurdly overstuffed letterbox, "Are you fucking kidding me? What the hell is wrong with people?" Good question, I thought.

In his apartment, I noticed an alarming number of unfinished carpentry projects. The ceiling showed signs of old leaks, and some of the roof decking was replaced by hand-painted plywood advertising a BBQ joint downtown. Those pieces of plywood were the remnants of a sign he had painted for them. "What's the deal here?" I asked.

"I haven't paid rent since the roof started leaking," he told me.

"Really? How does that work?"

Laughing easily, he said. "The rain pays my rent."

"Are you supposed to be doing the repairs?"

He had a way of answering questions that closed off inquiry without admitting anything. "Sometimes. Here, take these." He handed me a bag of clothes and an old guitar.

We loaded these and a few more items into his van. Neither raindrops nor Sam paid me any rent.

My time with Sam vacillated between hilarity, madness, and bouts of manic anger. Like the time I abducted him from a bar with the help of two drunk young women. I grabbed him from a barstool, hoisted him onto my shoulder, ran through the bar, kicked the front door like an outlaw, and tossed him into the back of his van. The girls fished the keys from his pocket, playfully grabbing more than just his keys, and forcefully yet teasingly taped his hands behind his back. I drove off while the three kissed and tumbled, howling and laughing like wild animals.

There was the time he slid at top speed down the side rails of an escalator on the soles of his worn-out boots. It looked crazy and sounded even crazier as the smooth bottoms of his shoes gained momentum and volume. Every eye in the vicinity turned to see what was causing the commotion. Sam landed gracefully, at speed, just in front of the checkout counter of a large record shop, cup of coffee in hand, gathering his momentum into a jaunty strut. A store employee gave him a stern and disapproving look and said in an angry teacher's voice, "Sir! I'm going to have to ask you NOT to do that again!"

"OK." He said, grinning with a gentlemanly tip of his cup in the flustered woman's direction.

He would sit at the bar where I worked and "take an angle" on me, pointing the top of his nearly empty glass in my direction, rotating the bottom on its axis, and following me around until I filled it again.

We stood in my kitchen once, drunkenly yelling at each other. Sam said the meanest things to me that I'd heard since I was a child, getting yelled at by my manic and manipulative oldest sister. I responded with all the charm and poise of an angry gorilla in a suit. After an hour, we hugged and apologized earnestly.

A few years later, I opened a small business, and Sam was there to "help" as I moved equipment around. I was swamped for several years, and we spent less time together than before. One week, I called him on a Wednesday and made plans to get together on a Friday. When he didn't show up, I called him, but he didn't answer. His phone had been disconnected. I went by his house to pick him up, but it was dark inside. A few days later, when I hadn't heard from him, I contacted his parents, afraid something might have happened. They told me he was fine but that he'd moved to Minneapolis the previous week. He was literally driving there on Wednesday as we made plans to get together on Friday.

We stayed in touch for a while, both of us struggling with our respective relationships, his in Minnesota and mine in Tennessee. I was planning to move to Austin, TX, and he was moving to Arizona to be with his parents. We met up in Texas while I was interviewing with Willie Nelson's Biofuel company. We spent a few nights single, drunk, and wild once more. On our last day together, he and I argued as I drove him to the airport. I honestly can't remember exactly what we were fighting about, but he got out at the terminal, turned his back, and I never saw him again.

Shortly after that, Sam and his ex-girlfriend started a business in Minneapolis, which was a complete success.

Five years later, I was living in New Orleans. I came home from work one fall evening, and my wife gave me the news - Sam was dead. I got in touch with his business partner and ex-girlfriend. She told me a story of unexpected yet aggressive cancer, startling yet welcome grace, and a passing from the world of the living, which touched his family and friends in ways I could scarcely imagine.

I flew to Minneapolis for his memorial and nearly collapsed at the door when I saw a blown-up photo of my friend standing with a large, happy dog. Sam was sporting the same grin he gave the irate record store clerk. I couldn't speak and had to take a seat to handle the weight of choking tears. I hugged his parents, met his new friends, and marveled at the stories of his success in business. The story of his passing was powerful but is not mine to tell. I'm happy to say that he died in his own bed, in the company of his father, his mother, and his close friends. Sam's body was washed, covered in scented oils, and wrapped with great care by the people who loved him most.

I was honored to be asked by his parents to spread some of his ashes. Most of them had been scattered into the Mississippi River in Minneapolis by his friends and family. They all shared a laugh when the wake of a passing paddlewheel boat pushed the ashes back onto the shore. I was about to move to California from New Orleans, and they asked if I could stop in Joshua Tree National Park on the way. Before I left town, a small box of his remains was shipped to me. In typical Sam fashion, the package was delayed and did not arrive in New Orleans until the day after I left. The next available place on the route to forward them was, incredibly, the airport in Austin, TX.

Five years after he and I parted company for the last time as living beings, we were reunited in almost the exact spot. I wept as I took the small and nearly weightless parcel from a joyless airport employee.

I've cried for you, friend.
On mountains,
In fucking airports!
Once in a shower and many times in a print shop.
Your ashes hit the river, then the shore.
Yet another laugh.
I scattered some in the four cardinal directions on a hill in the
desert.
You would have made fun of me for it,
Just as you would this poem.
As it doesn't rhyme, and
unlike your short life
It doesn't sing.

# Capitan Flip–Flop Will Have the Hepatitis Alphabet Soup, Please

Sunday evenings have always been different, unique in the fictitious continuum of earmarked moments. Even for a guy like me, often working a job that pays no mind to the typical workweek-weekend boundary - Sunday nights are especially calm. For a brief spell in my early twenties, I indulged in a relaxing ritual I looked forward to every week. On balance, it was totally tranquil ... until it wasn't.

I lived about five long blocks from a happening part of midtown Memphis, a short walk from several bars, shops, and restaurants. Working as a bartender at one of those restaurants, life was easy. I made more money than I spent, had more fun than I could handle, and was happily unencumbered by the ugliness of ambition.

The bar I liked most was a combination of a restaurant, pool hall, and music venue. I saw a lot of great music there over the years. On Sundays, it was busy enough to feel exciting but not so busy that a guy couldn't get a table and watch the band. The Sunday band - "Andy Groom's Living Room" - was fantastic. One of my friends was the drummer, and the singer and songwriter was an uncommonly talented guy with a range of influences from jazz, rock, and country to lounge, classical, and world music. They were laid back and dynamic, creating the perfect fried pickle eating soundtrack.

After smoking a few puffs from a joint in my apartment, I'd walk to the bar wearing the uniform of the lazy young man at that time, shuffling the blocks in shorts, a t-shirt, and the most useless of all human footwear, flip-flops.

One warm summer Sunday evening, I arrived stoned enough to feel like sitting down but not so high that I couldn't look the waiter in the eyes. I sat at my favorite booth - near the front door and directly across from the stage. The back of the seat I liked to sit in was against the large glass window in the front of the bar. After eating a basket of fried pickles, I'd stretch out my legs in the booth, with my back to a brick wall and the glass window to my right, listening contentedly to the band as they settled into their set.

I'd quit drinking for about a year, and the bartenders and waiters that knew me would occasionally tease me about it, mostly because I drink water even faster than most people drink beer. One guy called me the thirstiest man in Memphis. I made sure to tip like I was having beers, though, and did my best to make it worthwhile to have a single guy occupy a whole booth for over an hour. If the place got busy, I would move out and let someone else take over the table.

This particular Sunday, the restaurant wasn't too busy. One of those nights when hardly anyone was listening to the band or eating inside. Most of the crowd was hanging around the pool tables, and several tables of drinkers were on the patio out front. The long bar was occupied but not full. It took three bartenders to keep the drinks flowing. The wide-open dance floor between my booth and the stage made it feel like I was getting a private show - one where I could remain invisible to the band - a stoner's heaven.

Stretched out, flapping the soles of my flip-flops against the bottoms of my feet, more or less in time with the beat, and gulping tap water like it had been days since my last sip, I was thinking about getting up after the next tune to visit the john for a much-needed piss break. I missed that opportunity for a few complicated reasons.

First, the next tune was one of my favorites, and I didn't want to miss it. Second was the arrival of an unexpected customer with an outrageously bold agenda.

The bar crowd, mostly people between the ages of 20 and 30, was a mix of stoners, football fan guys, pool-playing girls, musicians, service industry types, and introverted weirdos who just wanted to drink water and eat pickles in the corner. When a guy in his mid-forties walked in wearing the tattered and grimy uniform of the crack cocaine-addled local, it would have been difficult not to notice.

I watched him tick and twitch into the bar. I recognized the shimmering and quivering joints, the awkward gate matching the troubled beating of his heart and the jangling of his nervous system. He lurched forward and sputtered as rapidly declining amounts of foreign chemicals made their way through his system like lizards on a skillet. He was clearly out of shit and needed to score.

I'd like to mention I'm suspicious of those who pass judgment on addicts. And judgment coming from a stoned and pickle-munching creep, observing from an antisocial perch in a corner, is worth an extra helping of skepticism. Judgment aside, as a bartender in that neighborhood, I recognized the risks the guy posed for the establishment, and my experience led me to question his intentions. To be clear, I don't judge anyone for their addictions and don't want to stigmatize drug use. But it's foolish to ignore the close association between crack addicts and crazy shit. Also, I'll be using the term crack-head from here on out. Just know, this is a function of economy of language and not meant to cast aspersions on folks who just like to have a little crack now and then to loosen up for special occasions.

I kept my eyes on him as he headed straight for the toilets; hoping piss was all he was there for. I could empathize with that, really, having been haunted countless times by a desperate need to go in environments where toilets are militantly guarded by a pay-first, piss-later policy. As I mentioned, the same impulse was asserting itself upon my increasingly diffused attention at that very moment. But with the band so perfectly wound up and my favorite tune nearly over, I had no choice but to wait it out. The song ended just before the guy emerged from the john and shambled to the bar. Before I could get up to go, the waitress stopped by my table to refill my water and clear the empty pickle basket.

As soon as she was gone, I saw the guy pull out a few greasy dollars in front of the bartender and point to the brown liquor behind his right shoulder. The moment the bartender turned his back to grab a bottle of whiskey from the shelf behind him, the crackhead grabbed a large glass jar from the bar top, dropped his own greasy bills inside as he snatched it, and bolted for the door.

This jar had at one point held a tightly packed bundle of pickles – possibly the same pickles which had been sliced into long strips, then fried to crispy perfection for yours truly. At that moment, it was holding one-third of the staff's cash tips and being carried out the front door at top-crackhead speed. Like some idiot-hippie antihero, I followed.

Stoned, pickle-stuffed, and flip-flopped, I was still quick. I hit the front door in time to see the guy lower his shoulder like a running back and take out a young woman in his way. She splayed out over one of the patio tables and crashed to the ground in a heap of purse straps, chairs, and spilled drinks. Yet another young woman leapt out into the street in front of him as he ran for the opposite side. She, too, was knocked backward by his ferocious momentum, landing painfully on her back.

Lest I give the wrong impression, I'd like to make clear that I have never considered myself a tough guy. I've only been in one fistfight and was not the winner of that pointless contest. I do have a complex relationship with the idea of justice, fairness, and the disproportionate distribution of fortune, though. I'll explain what I mean by that.

Clearly, this poor guy was suffering, desperate, and in terrible need. I try to look at other human beings with empathy first, even crackheads. Sometimes especially crackheads. There is no mistake another can make that I, given similar life circumstances, am incapable of making — "there but for the grace of god, go I" and all that. I'm fortunate to not be addicted to a powerful and life-wrecking drug, and I regret that life dealt this guy such a terrible hand. I'm fortunate not to be so desperate for money that I would be willing to steal from others by such bold and aggressive means. One could add to the poor man's list of misfortunes, and my own list of unearned gifts, that I'm much larger and faster than the two brave young women so violently handled by this wild and frightened man. I'm also just impulsive enough to fling my lanky ass into the fray.

In other words, I had no intention of hurting him, but I wanted that money back in the hands of the people who had worked so hard for it - I wanted justice. I knew how I would feel if someone stole all the money I'd earned in a shift and hoped that someone closer to the action would intercede on my behalf. What I had difficulty reckoning with was the savagery dealt to the women in the doorway and in the street. The more desperate shit this guy did to escape, the worse it would be for him once he was caught by the much angrier and less peaceful bartenders likely following me. Even as I pursued him, I became less sure about what I was doing. Also, I was becoming increasingly aware of the possible danger this guy could pose to me personally. Did he have a knife, a gun, or maybe hepatitis alphabet soup under his fingernails?

Despite the relative uselessness of flip-flops in a high-speed foot chase, I closed the distance between us, yelling out, "I'm gonna catch you, fucker! Drop the goddamn jar!" I could have reached out and grabbed him, but I really didn't want to.

He ignored me and made a hard right towards a school playground that connected two streets. I was less than a foot away from him and decided to kick his heel to trip him up. Before I did, entirely on his own, he tripped on a broken piece of the sidewalk and pitched forward in a wild, momentum-filled tumble. I never even touched him.

He fumbled the big glass jar, which flew out in front of him, bounced once, then shattered into a million pieces on the sidewalk. I had to leap over his tumbling body and the now atomized jar. Covering the distance between us, a mosaic of sharp glass, greasy-green bills, and shiny coins reflecting the strange light of streetlamps splayed across the pavement with nearly biblical menace. Like the relationship between Sunday evening and Monday morning, there was a whole new quality to our entanglement — one is tranquil and pleasant, the other is all business. Our new reality was a far cry from the odd-ball comfort of the chase. I was facing a sweating, heaving, and worried man. A man who was clearly willing to do anything to keep this money.

A tortured moment passed between us. I looked into his eyes, wet and glistening like glass shards under a streetlamp and quivering like electric jellyfish on ... well, crack, I guess. I wanted no part of his violence. Flip-flops and glass don't mix. Besides, I'm more of a gazelle than a lion. Many cowards have convinced themselves of the same sentiment to stay out of a fight. I appealed to what I hoped was a flicker of reason and not just lamp light in his eyes, "Three angry bartenders are heading this way. You're fucked, man ... I'd run if I were you."

He was totally crazed and dangerous. I was out of my depth, but I'd gone too far to back down. Showing too much weakness could have made things even worse for me. I balled up my stupid fists, bent my knees, and slid my right leg back, hopelessly flip-flopped as it was, relaxing my muscles to keep speed on my side if he decided to lunge for me — hopefully not fingernails first! He was hunched into a ball of furious energy. Dirt and small rocks had collected on his brow where he had landed after his fall. His knuckles and the palms of his hands were dirty and bleeding. He had one knee on the ground, and the other bent like he was about to leap. He didn't say a word. He breathed like an old, worn-out car with water in the fuel. Fortunately, he did not choose violence and instead ripped his vibrating gaze from me and threw it at the cash on the ground. "Come on, man. Don't do it." I said in exasperation.

I could hear heavy footsteps in the distance behind me. One of the bartenders working that night was a big guy and something of a fighter. The guy on the ground in front of me was out of gas. As furious and crazed as he was, he didn't stand a chance against any one of the guys headed our way, and definitely not the big one!

I'd done all I could do. I dropped my hands and came out of my ridiculous stance. "Seriously, man, just get the fuck out of here."

He looked up from the money and saw the colossal bartender in the street pounding the pavement with his massive shoes. The sight of the big guy was enough to make him abandon ship on his crouching-crackhead-hidden-nightmare pose. He spun on a dime and took off in a wild sprint. Seconds later, the crunching of glass and coins made a matchless sound, both lonely and beautiful, as the bartenders flew past me. I didn't want to see what they would do when they caught him. I left the scattered pile of loot to a waitress running up behind me, also ready to lend her fists to the pursuit of justice, if necessary.

The two young women who had been knocked down were sitting at the same table that had broken the fall of the first would-be blocker. They were attending to each other, assuring me they were both OK. A gaggle of rubberneckers spilled out of the bar, hoping to catch a glimpse of the action. The kitchen staff had come out to keep an eye on the place while the whole front of the house was either running down and brutalizing a crackhead, on the phone with the police or sweeping up pickle jar glass and cash.

One of the rubberneckers asked me what happened, 'Uh, I don't know, I just got here.' I pointed down the street over her shoulder and asked, 'What's that?' When she turned to look, I walked back inside.

The band, of course, never missed a beat and played gleefully through the fracas. I was impressed by their professional commitment to the show. A big, red, hard-plastic cup of water was sweating beautifully at my table. I was looking forward to stretching out again and taking a pull from that tall glass of Sunday calm. It would have to wait, though. I needed to pay a visit to the toilet for a double dose of relief - grateful to the hand of fate for sparing me from a flip-flop-fisticuff with a hepatitis monster and thankful I hadn't pissed myself on a surprise late-night sprint.

I'm not sure what lessons I learned from that exchange. For sure, I've come to dislike the flip-flop, as it so perfectly represents the worst of both worlds - wearing footwear and going shoeless. I'd say I learned that I am good at chasing and terrible at catching, but I knew that long before I leapt from my booth to chase after another man's cash.

I took my seat again, chasing away the sour-justice blues with a long sip from the red plastic cup. As the band stretched out several rounds of a mellow chorus, allowing the guitar and piano players to take solos, I noticed the flickering of blue and red lights on the sweat of my water cup. A police cruiser parked aggressively out front, taking up most of the street. The bartenders were standing around, catching their breath, and an officer started taking their statements. In the back of the cruiser, I could see the unlucky thief. His eyes were already swelling shut from multiple punches to the face. He was awake but seemed more at ease than when I first encountered him. It may have been a concussion, leaving him too injured to be freaked out, but I wanted to believe he could simply relax now that he knew where he was headed for the night.

The brutality of the whole thing made me incredibly sad. I wondered to myself, *how many times had this man been arrested? Was anyone, other than a dealer, expecting him anytime soon? Did he have any people in his life who would miss him or bail him out of jail? Was there any hope of relief from the pangs of his physiological need, or would the cops ignore that pain like the gashes and bruises on his body?*

He was heading to a terrible place, in terrible shape, and it broke my heart.

I then thought about my supposed detachment from the workweek/weekend dynamic, realizing that, compared to the miserable and dehumanized man in the back of that car, I was as tied to the rhythm of the week as any working stiff in the world. It was that man, bleeding and oddly calm in the back of the cop car, who was completely free from the expectations of the work-a-day life. His freedom came at a hell of a price.

Had justice been served? Would he have escaped if I hadn't chased after him? Did he deserve what was happening to him? Should I have stayed out of it? Who the hell knows?

The police then took a statement from the two women who had been knocked down. They didn't know each other before the incident, but you could tell they were bonding fast. One held a bag of ice to the back of her head, while the other held a glass of whiskey to her lips. They would be fine. The bartenders would be fine. And I'd be back the following week for pickles and music. The man in the back of the squad car was a long, long way from fine and highly unlikely to return for any reason. But if he had, I'd have been keen to hear his side of the story and maybe share a few notes on how to get a little less out of a Sunday evening.

# Spazuccino

"**H**ey, sweetie, you want a coffee?" The waitress grins at me with her long hair piled up high and pinned tight to her head by a lattice of bobby pins and many years of practice. Like jewelry in a house fire, her eyes reflect the sun coming in through the diner's windows. Something about how I say "Yes, please" causes her grin to blossom into a full-toothed smile. Without a word, she swivels her hips and turns confidently on thick-soled sneakers - sturdy instruments that have traveled countless miles between the kitchen and the tables of this hearty slice of the American dream.

She returns with a serving tray, on top of which sits a white porcelain sugar caddy, which I do not need, a small bowl of plastic creamer containers, which I do, and a mug the size of a newborn elephant's wash tub, filled with steaming black coffee. Everything feels just right. She lays it all neatly in front of me with such care and consideration I feel like a champion congratulated and awarded the gold medal by the Olympic Breakfast committee. "I'll give you a sec with that menu, Hun." She turns to walk away, and as she does, I reach for one of the creamers.

My diner habits are well-formed and rarely vary. With a practiced plucking motion, I bring the creamer to my lips and lightly nick the bottom of the plastic container with my incisors, creating a tiny pinhole. As I do this, the waitress spins around again, holding a spoon. She pauses mid-twirl, and her toothy, late-spring smile withers under an unexpected frost of confusion. We make eye contact, like when a dog gets caught humping a pillow, and I give her a sideways, wide-eyed glance.

She approaches my table like I might take a small bite out of her next. "What in the world are you doin' with that creamer?"

I show her.

With the small hole pointed above the wash tub of coffee, I grip the container's body between my pointer and middle fingers, firmly placing my thumb over the paper tab, which most normal people peel back to pour out the creamer. It's critical for the thumb to maintain even pressure or the paper will burst, sending an embarrassing splash of creamer all over the table. I give it a squeeze with my two fingers resulting in a two-toned blending of magical delight. The coffee is flavored, cooled, and stirred with one simple motion, leaving a frothy, cappuccino-like texture on the drink's surface, rendering a spoon unnecessary.

I take a moment to consider what it might be like if I were the captain of a tiny boat on the steaming lake of coffee. From above, a powerful geyser of white cream blasts from the bottom of an enormous plastic bucket as the energy from a giant's fingers becomes a powerful cream stream, plunging mightily below the surface of Laguna de Cafecito. The roiling waves would be magnificent, as the aroma of roasted coffee, so floral yet heavy with heat and the sweetness of the cream, spray luxuriant foam around my daring vessel.

The waitress looks a little too puzzled. I pray she can't see the madness in my eyes. I think to myself, *remember when we connected over that grin ... we're pals now, right?*

She returns the spoon to the marsupial pouch of her apron, gently cradled and preserved for the next chump who can't fathom such brilliance lighting up his morning cup. Once ablaze with a fiery sparkle, her eyes now feature a mere glassy shimmer as the ripples on Lake Cafecito dance in the same daylight previously captured by her iris. She looks like she wants to speak but is unsure what to say. Through a more muted, late winter version of her grin, she tells me, "I'd guess I've been a waitress for about as long as you've been alive." Peering into the beautiful, well-earned wrinkles encircling her eyes and her grin, I believe her. She pauses to collect her thoughts, then continues. "In all those years, I'll bet I've served about a million cups of coffee. But not once in all that time have I seen anyone do THAT!" Her puzzlement borders on revulsion, but she can't break free, even as the small silver bell in the kitchen window rings out, calling her to deliver the hot food like a god whistling for his dog.

"Who taught you to do that? Please tell me it wasn't your parents?"

I tell her the truth, which seems to bring a sense of satisfaction, if not relief. "I learned it from a guy called Filthy."

The god whistles a bit more forcefully, and the pull is too great to resist any longer. "Sounds about right. I'll be right back. I got more questions!" She spins again on those sturdy heels and collects two arms' worth of hot plates. Each piled high with delectable treasures; hot buttery pancakes, crispy-edged eggs flecked with pepper, gently folded and cheesy omelets topped by green garnishes, and small mountain ranges of toast so crispy I can sense it from ten yards away.

She returns to my table quickly. I hope her next question will have something to do with what I want to eat, but deep down, I know it won't.

She leans against the booth at a comforting and casual angle, suggesting she recognizes we've been through something together. I can almost hear her, years from that moment, recalling — "Remember that time you grossed me out by biting the nasty little bucket of creamer?" But that future moment would have to wait. For now, we have other things to discuss.

"You know, I can't guarantee those creamers are clean. They go from table to table. No telling how many people touch those filthy little things!" This is not a news flash, but a calculated risk I'm willing to take for the thrill of transmogrification - reshaping a beverage from mere coffee to something so magically weird yet delicious and tactile.

"You got a name for that?" It would have been a funny question from anyone else, but not from her — my new and only friend. I had to admit, I had thought of a name but had never shared it. We were old friends now — *Remember that time you made me tell you secrets in the early morning before you would feed me?*

So, I tell her. "I call it the Spazuccino."

She blinks so slowly, I wonder if maybe the coffee here is so good that I'm traveling through time at a different speed. "Yeah, that sounds about right as well." Straightening up, with a fresh appraisal of my mental state, she takes my breakfast order, scribbling what looks like hieroglyphics onto the short-order paper.

As she spins away again, my wishes literally resting in the palm of her hand, I lift the drink to my lips, delighted to have it all to myself. I take a pull of its nutty, warm genius and relax a bit more into the loud vinyl of the seat. I'm not embarrassed, and only a little jealous, when I see the cooks peaking over the window, standing so close to my new-old-only friend as they giggle and point.

# Dead Letter

Hey Dad, how weird is this? Honestly, I'm not sure who I think I'm talking to now, but if you are somehow taking correspondence in the afterlife, which, for your sake and mine, I certainly hope is not the case, I've got a few things on my mind. I've got to tell you, I'm having a hard time remembering a few things. For one, I don't remember what I called you. I'm sure I didn't call you daddy, pop, father, or Allen, but I just can't remember ever saying, Dad. Why is that? Do you remember what I called you?

Also, I can't quite remember what your voice sounded like. I can hear just about any song I want to call up from my memory, even tunes I haven't heard in years and tunes I don't especially like. But your voice eludes me. I don't know if anyone has any recordings of your voice, but I occasionally feel a weird sadness knowing it's totally lost to me. The strangest part is if there were a message from you, directly to me, it would be weirder somehow. Even dead, I'd prefer to hear you talking to someone else.

I'm also having a hard time remembering exactly why it was so weird between us. Since you died, I've had conversations with my brother about your take on our relationship. He told me you were also aware of how awkward and strained it was. Why was that? I obviously never told you how I felt about any of this when you were alive. Did you know I felt like we only ever had one full conversation?

I, unfortunately, can remember trying to talk to you on car rides, and it was weirdly painful for me. I never felt inarticulate or nervous in conversation with adults. One of my favorite people to talk to when I was young was a man who was twenty years older than you. I could speak to him about anything and even make him laugh. But when you and I would talk, I stuttered, couldn't remember words, and generally felt like an idiot. I could tell you didn't like how I dressed, the music I liked, or the hobbies I was into. To be fair to you, I know better than to expect you to enjoy the same things I did. You were an adult, and I was a child. But I can converse and find common ground with all kinds of people whose interests are drastically divergent from mine; I'm sure you did it all the time when you were alive – why couldn't we make it happen?

I know this seems like I'm laying a bunch of shit at your feet, and I guess I am, in a way. But I think it's got to mean something that I'm writing this to you now in a conversational tone that you and I never achieved in person. Only twenty years after your death can I even consider writing this weird letter.

You were very good to me, in your way. I never needed anything that I didn't have. You wanted me to have the best education possible and every advantage you could afford. For those things, I am grateful. After your death, I got some money. Some of it was from insurance policies, and some of it was won in a legal battle with the physicians responsible for your death. I bought a house and started a business. I still have the house; Colleen lives in it with Brendan and her daughter, Ayden. I sold the business and basically ate and drank the rest of the money through travel and impulse. I'm grateful for the money and even more thankful for the lessons I learned with it.

I suppose if this letter has any point to it, it would be to thank you for taking care of me, apologize for not getting to know you, and forgive you for not getting to know me. On balance, I think we did alright. I've certainly met guys who had a much more difficult time with their dads. You never hit me, didn't yell at me or hurt anyone I love, so there's that.

Of course, I haven't told you anything about my life other than I spent all the money I got from your passing, and I started and sold a business with it. What kind of business would a guy like me create? I'm not sure if you would have liked it much, it involved working on diesel engines, alternative fuels, and environmental issues. It was dirty, a little crazy, and got the press's attention. I bought a building in Memphis and filled it with tools and a funny makeshift kitchen. I sold it all in 2007, right before the economy shit the sheets. I was lucky.

Anyhow, there's much more to the story than that. I married Tiffany; you met her a couple of times. It took a while for that to come together, ten years of dating before we tied the knot, but it was the best decision I ever made. We looked after your dog, Sammy, until she died in 2015. Sammy was a lovely creature who traveled with us and improved our lives immeasurably.

Tiff and I have had a pretty good time in life. She's a nurse, and I'm a handyman. Tiff repairs hearts, and I repair houses. She makes good money, and I make do. We rode our bicycles from Florida to California. When we met cyclists traveling the opposite direction, they invariably told us we were going the wrong way, riding against the prevailing winds. More than once, we reminded them they were heading to Florida, which sounded more like the wrong way to me. We also spent two years traveling in a van with our dog from California to Alaska, then Costa Rica. I had a stroke and a weird heart procedure, getting the tiniest glimpse into the fear you must have experienced on a much grander scale, many more times with all your heart troubles. I'm fine now, but it was eye-opening. The long and short of it is, I had a hole in my heart, a small clot came through it, and caused a stroke. The hole was patched, and now I'm much less likely to have that kind of stroke again.

So, yeah, those are a few of the things you've missed in nearly twenty years. Obviously, there is a lot more to the story, but there always is. I know so very little of your story. I've made a point of collecting stories from people, largely because I knew so little of yours and have a lingering regret around that. Thank you for that strange and unintentional gift.

I guess I'll leave you be again. Seriously, if this is somehow making it to you, I'm sorry. Honestly, I hope it isn't because that would mean consciousness survives death, and that is truly my worst nightmare. If this is reaching you, though, I don't know what else to say, other than I'll see you soon enough, I suppose. Maybe it will be easier for us once we're both dead? Good luck out there, and tell whoever's in charge of this show to knock it off; the joke isn't all that funny.

Love you, dad.

# In The Soup

You may notice, when speaking of the dead, we tend to glo-
rify them. This is particularly true when it comes to our
loved ones. The impulse to amplify the character traits of de-
ceased friends and family gave birth to the heroes who popu-
late our myths. Embellishment makes our stories more interesting. I suspect we exaggerate the details of the departed out
of some sense of respect and perhaps to lend meaning to our
own lives before we join them.

Like many of you, I've lost a friend. It was sudden, but
I think anyone who knew him could have seen this coming.
That feels like a harsh thing to say, but unfortunately, harsh-
ness, much like understanding, has its place here. I'd like to tell
you about him now.

I'll do my best to avoid any over-amplification of my dead
friend. And the truth is, his tale and his impact on my life are
adequately powerful in their natural, unadulterated states. I can
say with a clear conscience that my telling of his story is lacking in fantastical detail rather than being overpopulated with it.
The best I can do here is to give you an honest reckoning of
one of the most complicated, intelligent, lovable, and dynamic
men I have ever known - my friend, Alex.

Alexander Major, born in Mississippi in 1947, was what
many people would call a character. It would also be true to
call him a wild man, a thoughtful man, a gifted and well-spoken
entrepreneur, a con artist, an articulate apologist for the green
movement, a snake-oil salesman, a passionate crusader for ter-

minally ill children, a liar, a pilot, a disgraced pilot, a talented musician, an average musician, an ex-con, an innocent man, a terrible friend, and a good friend. He borrowed money he never repaid and made good on loans on which he voluntarily paid interest. He had perennial and various grand visions, including plans to start a biofuel company with no money of his own, and a plan to refurbish and fly the very first private jet ever made around the world with celebrity pilots, raising funds for St. Jude. For all the time I knew Alex, he lived on the backs of those plans as they floated down a river of trusting investors, helpful friends, and good intentions.

Before I knew him, Alex had breathed the rarified air at the top of the mountain of financial success, living in a penthouse in New York while developing a whole city block in Manhattan to be a world-class recording studio with lofts and a media production facility. He also breathed in the dank and wretched air at the absolute depths of sadness after his only child, Jesse, died at the age of 4.

The magnitude of success and failure takes time to build up. Long before he hit the big time, Alex's band, "The Wallabies," were among the very first bands to record with the legendary Jim Dickinson at Ardent Studios in Memphis, TN. In 1969, Alex and the group headed out to San Francisco, despite being discouraged from doing so by Erik Jacobsen, the producer of Norman Greenbaum, The Lovin' Spoonful, Chris Isaak, and others.

After arriving in San Francisco and receiving an earful of "great honesty" from Erik, Alex proceeded to pivot on a dime, fire his band and offer his services as a carpenter to Erik, who was then remodeling a houseboat in Sausalito's famed gate #5. Alex turned out to be a competent builder, and he and Erik remained close for the next 50 years.

Alex stayed in the San Francisco Bay area, at the pinnacle of counterculture and consciousness expansion of the late 1960s. He sold LSD under the oddly common moniker of "Magic Alex." I say oddly common because, as it turns out, there was another "Magic Alex" doing business with the Beatles around the same time. After leaving the Bay Area, Alex got married, had a child, and opened a recording studio called "North Star" as well as a green-produce store called "Earthly Goods" in Boulder, CO. He enjoyed success in his business dealings and had a relatively happy existence until the death of his son.

Alex shared many stories with me over the years, and recounting them fills me with a familiar sadness and guilt. This sadness comes from having a third-person, hindsight perspective of the past, with all the horrible, unavoidable, and unfolding momentum it carried right up to the moment of death for Alex. I feel guilty because I am so absorbed with myself that I do not remember details, like what exactly took his son's life. What I do know is Jesse's death, as you might expect, changed Alex forever.

He spoke of his son but not in recollection of what it was like to spend time with him or what he was like as a child. On the rare occasion when he and I made it to the subject of Jesse, Alex was vague and focused on the effort to raise money for sick children and not the memory of his own son. He did write a very touching song, which he played for me a few times, about the pain of that terrible loss. I never pressed him to tell me more; I have no reference for that sort of agony ... I can only hope I never do.

Alex was genuinely complicated. He didn't talk about deep philosophical subjects often. Instead, he would jump from topic to topic, speaking of building a biofuel project, to creating a music studio on the island of Sardinia, or his exploits in New York in the eighties, then back to his languishing dreams of his charitable round-the-world flight. He was obsessive, not a great listener, and would regularly hijack conversations with details about his wild and unfunded schemes. Eventually, his ideas struck me as just possible enough to not be dismissed entirely, but delusional to the point where I never took anything too seriously; that was not always the case.

I met Alex in 2004 at my shop in Memphis, TN. I had opened a renewable fuel business, using discarded cooking oil to power diesel engines. A little press had helped bolster my business, and things were going well. I was also full of grand and unfunded plans. One evening, while cleaning up some spilled vegetable oil, a bright-eyed man in his late fifties walked through the large roll-top door of my shop - Alex. Confident and unannounced, he launched into action and embedded himself in my life.

After a brief introduction, he began grilling me to see if I knew what I was talking about regarding renewable fuels and the "green movement" in general. Question after question, he tested me. Eventually, he gave me his number and told me to call him in the next few days to discuss a business venture. He came across as a guy with money interested in funding my dreams. As it turned out, he had lots of borrowed money and was considerably more interested in telling me about his dreams – past, present, and future.

We became friends quickly. He inspired me the way a sprained ankle inspires an athlete to train harder. Alex's madness made me want to focus. We cooked together, smoked pot, and talked for hours (he spoke, and I listened). We played music on my front porch, and he met the woman who would later become my wife. He told me I should marry her long before the thought occurred to me.

He told me about his time in prison. At the height of Alex's financial success, he owned and was remodeling an estate in Provence, maintained an apartment in Manhattan, flew a private jet all over the world, and had played a part in developing large cargo planes, retrofitted to help with wildfire suppression. Amid all this, Alex managed the finances of a group of individuals who were bringing "Thai Sticks" into the American market. This is, of course, completely illegal, and by a crazy twist of fate, Alex was implicated in the scheme by a couple of fishermen arguing in a bar about who was paid more to bring the cannabis to shore. A federal agent was listening in on this argument and brought the whole operation tumbling down. After a lengthy and ill-advised legal battle, Alex was eventually convicted and sentenced to many years in prison.

When the writing on the wall was becoming clear, and his eventual sentencing became more and more likely, Alex devised a plan to scope out the prison, which would be his home for years to come. Under the guise of a journalist writing a story about life in American prisons, Alex arranged a tour of the facility with the warden. Throughout the tour, Alex peppered the warden with questions about the daily life of inmates and managed to find out the best place for an incoming prisoner to position himself.

The warden told him that operating the prison's dairy would be the most lucrative, as success was rewarded with gallons of ice cream. In that prison, ice cream was a mighty currency. After reporting to prison, the warden met Alex, remembered him, and took a liking to him. He ended up with a glut of ice cream and found a niche as an inmate with resources.

Alex and I met many years after he was released. His time in prison was something he did not share with people. I discovered it by doing a background search after he hinted at doing business with me. He didn't tell me about it for a few years. I eventually told him I knew about it but didn't care about prison time for a drug bust. I have strong feelings about the futility of prohibiting marijuana while you can buy liquor and baby formula in the same store. Our relationship deepened after that.

I once helped him load his airplane, a Beechcraft King Air, onto a flatbed trailer when he moved from Memphis to Kansas. I felt deeply sad when he and I shared our last meal at an Indian restaurant in Memphis. I loved him and would miss his regular company.

Alex and I would often go for many months without speaking, mostly out of a great reluctance on my part to talk on the phone. Those who know me are likely aware of my disinclination to engage in phone calls. This aversion to being on a call was compounded by the long monologues about improbable and complex projects with which Alex was regularly consumed. Our conversations, when they happened, would last for at least an hour and often ended without ever sharing very much with my friend about my own life. To be sure, Alex's life was often much more interesting than my own.

At no cost to himself, he was flown around the world to speak at conferences about the necessity to develop "bio-jet fuel." He regularly delivered a presentation titled, "Can We Still Fly Jets and Save the World?" Every time I spoke with him, he was in negotiations with some company for donations for his airplane, or a hangar space with on-staff technicians to help rebuild it. He even managed to get new brakes for his car, via a donation, in the-middle-of-nowhere-Utah! He was so incredibly convincing and charming, I believe he could have done anything so long as it didn't require working for someone else.

At one point, when a couple of young guys from New York came down to Memphis to interview me for a documentary film on renewable fuels, I reached out to Alex to see if he could set up an on-camera interview with Morgan Freeman. At the time, Morgan and his partner, Bill Luckett, were planning to build a large biodiesel plant in the heart of the Mississippi Delta. They had also loaned Alex a great deal of money to initiate the "King Air Foundation" (Alex's effort to restore and fly that crazy airplane around the world). For some time, Alex lived above Morgan's blues club, "Ground Zero," in Clarksdale, MS, and considered him a friend. The young filmmakers and I met with Mr. Freeman at his club in Clarksdale. The interview with Morgan made it into the 2006 film, "Greasy Rider."

I met up with Alex again on a trip to Europe after selling my business in 2007. He invited me to join him at the European Business Aviation Convention and Exhibit in Geneva, Switzerland to help him man the only non-profit booth in the show. Despite being shoved to the back of the exhibit hall, Alex made his way confidently around the sprawling exhibit, shaking hands with CEOs, Saudi Princes, billionaires, and worker bees, all with the same enthusiasm and easy charm.

His sister, Babs, had a similar ease with talking to the rich and influential, though it was perhaps less charming. He once took me to a Grammy Awards gala in Memphis, honoring local musicians and creative luminaries. Babs and her husband Jerry were with us. We had a blast and watched as Justin Timberlake was honored by the organization. Babs tipped back the Chablis in earnest. Near the end of the evening, I saw her chatting up a lovely woman whom I recognized as an actress. She had the actress cornered and was talking nonstop when I approached. The conversation was incredible to me. Babs addressed the woman with great enthusiasm and familiarity as if she were in character in one of her films. I reached out, touched the actress on the shoulder, and said, 'Excuse me, would you mind if I borrowed Babs for a moment?' Cameron Diaz turned to look at me, widened her eyes to the size of the dinner rolls we had just been served, and silently mouthed, "THANK YOU!" She politely turned back to a still rambling Babs, shook her hand warmly, and said goodbye.

In 2012, I got a somewhat desperate-sounding email from Alex. I called him right away and heard a voice I almost didn't recognize. Alex's manic high had given way to a despondent low. He had been staying with his longtime friend Erik Jacobsen in the San Francisco Bay area for almost a year. It was time for him to leave, and he didn't know where to go.

I didn't quite understand just how low Alex was. I had no idea depression could change a person's voice. I felt for my friend and told him he could stay with me.

My wife, Tiffany, and I lived in a small, one-bedroom shotgun-style house in New Orleans. We had a long sofa in the front room I offered to him. It was meant to be temporary while Alex figured out what to do next. Unfortunately, he was in no state to be able to do that. It wore on Tiffany. She did not like Alex in any condition. In his depressed state, he was especially irritating to her.

To be fair to Tiffany, she was not alone in disliking him. Some people saw him as a free-loader, self-absorbed, sometimes smug, and quick to take advantage of his friends. I was not blind to those aspects of his character, but I also saw something of myself in him. Alex and I were equally restless. Like him, I am undereducated but remain confident in my capacity to make my way in the world by learning on the fly. I saw my potential future in him. It still frightens me.

I also saw a vulnerable friend who needed support. His depression struck a chord with me, and I wanted to be able to help him through it. Tiffany wanted him off our couch and out of our house. It was stressful. After several months in New Orleans, I bought him a one-way ticket on Southwest Airlines, where he made his way to a friend's place in the improbably named city of Truth or Consequences, New Mexico.

I learned a great deal from that encounter; the limitations of friendship, the impotence of good intentions in the face of deep trauma, and the need for better mental health care in this country. I also learned about the type of person I am and the type I want to be.

I am not religious, but I do take inspiration from the archetypes in religious myths. Jesus had shitty friends but stood by them. Siddhartha spent too much time alone in the woods but made it out with a heroically relaxed attitude. When Lao Tzu got fed up with city life and wandered off into the wilderness, the resulting book he was forced to pen contains wisdom that has stood the test of time. If Muhammad had been a touch more explicit about his successors, life might be a little less interesting in the world ... you get the point. In other words, I saw my relationship with Alex as a chance to practice what I felt was an honest way of life, to follow in the footsteps of the archetypal figures I admire. I failed often. He was not always easy to like, but I loved him anyway. If I only listened to what others said about him, I would have written him off long ago, but to do so would have been a self-betrayal as much as a betrayal of friendship. I'm still conflicted about what sort of friend I was to Alex.

Alex spent several months bathing in the healing waters of Truth or Consequences, where he had daily access to hot springs known to be high in lithium. He eventually resurfaced from his depression and decided to buy a van to live in. It would become his roving office and base of operations. When business associates asked where he was staying, he would tell them he had a room at the "Grand Hotel," a cheeky reference to his Chrysler Grand Caravan.

A few years later, after Tiffany and I moved to Sonoma County, California, I got a call from Alex. He said he would be visiting his friend Erik, only 20 miles south of where we were living. He invited us over for a July 4th barbecue, where we met Erik for the first time.

Erik and I have since become good friends, and he has been kind enough to hire me to work for him over the years. It was interesting to spend time with two men I admired, Erik and Alex (Al, as Erik called him). Watching these two old buddies navigate their 50+ years of friendship was hilarious. Erik could be a little tough on Alex, but it was good to hear someone challenge Alex on his craziness.

I'm unsure if it is my age or that I trend embarrassingly toward the extreme ends of politeness, but I tend not to challenge people unless the bullshit is exceedingly thick. Erik does not have this problem.

Over the next few years, I saw Alex a handful of times. Living out of a vehicle was taking its toll on him. There would have been plenty of room in the back of the van for a mattress, but a wheelchair lift was in-place. When I asked why he didn't remove it, he told me he had plans to donate the vehicle and get another one. That never happened, and he slept in the front seat of that van for years.

Our conversations often landed on his relationship with his ex-girlfriend and her son, Dylan. Alex had developed a very close bond with Dylan. He spoke of Dylan often and in glowing, paternal tones. I met Dylan once, when he was about five years old, and found him to be an adorable and bright little guy. Alex loved that kid dearly.

Alex was eventually exiled from his ex's life and Dylan's. He maintained a fleeting but ongoing relationship with the boy until a teenage Dylan told Alex he didn't want to see him anymore. As devastating as this must have been for him, Alex said that Dylan would grow out of that and make his way back into Alex's life when he was older.

In the same year Dylan told Alex he didn't want to see him any longer, Alex suffered a string of heavy losses. First, his sister, Babs, died of heart failure. Then one of his oldest friends and former bandmates was killed in a car crash. His best friend, Bruce, died a few months later. Bruce owned the place in Truth or Consequences, leaving Alex with one less place to land in times of need. I cannot imagine how deeply saddened he must have been by this cascade of loss.

When Tiffany and I decided to take our van-based journey, Alex had many tips for living out of a vehicle. He was incredibly supportive of our trip and enthusiastic about our podcast, and he even left a thoughtful review on iTunes. The last time I saw him was on my way to Topanga Canyon to meet and interview a famous author. Alex helped calm my nerves and encouraged me with thoughtful consideration.

The last time I spoke with him was a few days before Thanksgiving, 2018. I was visiting Erik and his wife, Lala, at their home in the Bay Area. We called Alex and put the phone on speaker, so we could all talk to him. His tone was utterly despondent. He was in poor health. His back hurt, his teeth were falling out, and he had nowhere to go.

I could not host him, and neither could Erik, and he could no longer live out of his van, as the pain in his back from sleeping in the front seat was causing him significant discomfort. The friend with whom he was staying had asked him to leave. For the first time since either Erik or I had known him, Alex dejectedly told us he could not imagine any of his many schemes ever working. He had been hit by the weight of this realization quite hard. The result was devastating - an impossibly deep depression set in.

Erik offered him a generous advance in exchange for writing his autobiography. Alex didn't have the energy to accept. Even in the throes of depression, he took a moment to tell me, one last time, that he was enjoying our podcast and really liked all the characters we had been meeting on our journey. He trailed off and ended the conversation without his usual "over and out" and simply said, "bye;" sadly, that was the last word I heard him speak.

Alex texted me the following day, asking if we could talk privately. I texted him back the next morning but never heard from him again. I still have a string of unanswered text messages on my phone. My final message to him was somewhat desperate. I told him I was worried about him. I didn't know he had been dead for two days when I sent it.

Alex ended his journey on his own terms. I don't know what was on his mind when he chose to do it, but deciding to kill himself seems to me one of peculiar bravery. I can only imagine, when the weight of depression is so much greater than the weight of the unknown that shrouds one's death, the will to live must be mighty hard to bear. On January 9, 2018, my outlandish, complicated, charming, reverse barometer of a mentor, confidant, and friend ended his life by walking in front of a train.

I am writing these words now in a room often occupied by Alex. That room is in the basement apartment of Erik Jacobsen's home. It is a surprisingly well-lit apartment for having only one wall with windows. The view is delightful from almost any angle. A large and old rose vine hangs above the small side yard, and fragrant vines crawl along the fence which separates Erik's yard from his neighbor's.

I'm sitting here thinking about human potential and the madness of life, preoccupied with the way we dance along the knife's edge, separating serendipity from catastrophe. In the cosmic soup of the conceivable, with ingredients like chance, tragedy, opportunity, fate, and intention, we float in a quantum state. At times, we're like flies in the soup, disgusting the great customer. At other points in the continuum, we bob like tasty little dumplings, toothsome and plump, delighting the big lady with the spoon. If, like me, you take no comfort in the concept of an afterlife or a supernatural deity to judge you, this metaphor may seem empty and unsatisfying. In any case, whether discarded in disgust or consumed with delight, much like soup, the experience of being alive in the world is also quite brief.

I loved that man
Although I told him so,
I'm not certain he knew it.
Rest in peace, Alejandro.
And to you, Stranger
Good luck on *your* journey,
Remember to tell your friends
Often
How much you love them
And do it now

# Just Call Me

A delicate vibration from the small black computer in my pocket reminds me it's also a telephone. I see an unfamiliar number, take a deep breath, and allow myself a tiny grin as I answer.

"Hello?"

"Hi, is this Wilson?"

'No, I'm afraid you've got the wrong number.'

"Oh, well, maybe *you* could help me, this is Tom from the Policemen's Benevolent Association, and I was wondering if we could chat for a moment."

'The police?!? How did you find me? Uh, I mean, am I in some kind of trouble, officer?'

"I'm sorry? Um, no, I'm calling on behalf of the Policemen's Benevolent Association, and I was … "

"Oh, God, please. How much time do I have before you guys get here? I just want to say goodbye to my wife and kids before you kick in the door, oh man … ."

"No, sir, please stop crying, I'm not calling as a police officer. I'm calling on behalf of the … "

"Oh, Jesus, Tom, look, it was an accident, alright! Honestly, man, it was dark, and he was wearing all black and gray, and it was raining, and I really hadn't had that much to drink, and if you ask me, he looked like he was pretty ill anyway, so I don't know, I mean, it may have just been his time, you know what I mean, Tom ... Hello? Tom?"

As a kid, I had some bad habits. Before I learned to play guitar, I'd pick random numbers from the phone book, dial them up, and lay down a crazy script on some poor, unsuspecting person. Sometimes I'd pretend to be a radio DJ, offering tickets to a show or cash prizes if the person on the other end of the call could answer some absurd or impossible trivia questions. 'Name all fifteen planets in our solar system in under ten seconds. Starting ... now!'

On other calls, I'd pretend to be from the phone company, making promises or demands. 'On the count of three, pull as hard as you can on the phone cord for a complimentary *three feet* of cable!'

Other times, I'd act out some wildly idiotic misunderstanding. A successful call might end with something like - "Listen, kid, I told you, Jenny doesn't live here! I mean it, Godamnit! I don't care how much money she owes you. Figure this out, and DON'T CALL BACK AGAIN!"

Later, I got hip to the classified section of the Sunday paper. People would list things for sale and publish their ACTUAL PHONE NUMBERS in the back of the newspaper! That was a goldmine of stupid-premised madness for me.

Most of my randomly selected victims had a hard time buying the fake voice I had to adopt to hide the high-pitched pre-pubescent one which naturally came out of my mouth. Honestly, only the most dim-witted of my victims ever fell for my schtick. Lucky for me, those beautiful dimwits inspire what I now use as a stand-in for prank calls. When pranking the folks in the classified section, my job was much easier.

All I needed to do was play it straight while asking increasingly absurd questions. The goal was never terribly specific. I just wanted to get an honest reaction. If that meant getting them to hang up the phone after the first dumb question, I considered it a small win. If they suffered through my stupidity with charm and grace, politely sending me on my way, it was still a win, but not nearly as satisfying.

My favorite reactions were the ones where my victims would squirm uncomfortably, trying to remain civil with the idiot on the other end of the call. Usually, these were people with something lousy for sale. You could almost hear them salivating, desperate to foist their used wares onto an imbecile like me. I could tell early on where things were headed. I'd crank up the idiocy until, in spectacular fashion, they lost their temper in furious and frustrated fits of rage. The hardest part was keeping my giggling out of the receiver when someone said something like, "No, dumbass, it's a controller for a video game - shaped like a gun, not a real gun! Idiot!" The rhythmic and thick clatter and click of a violently slammed-down telephone: exquisite, savage, beautiful. I miss the hum of the dial tone which followed.

But those days are gone, and I no longer call people just to piss them off. For many years I gave up on my old, immature pastime, painfully aware of how childish and absurd it is to get my kicks by frustrating innocent people over the phone.

In recent years, however, fortune has brought my old habits out of the dusty, catch-all drawer in my brain. My latent and malformed gift has been given a second life by the solicitors, telemarketers, and political campaigners who now have free access to our numbers. I can now legally make prank calls by simply answering the phone!

Seriously, what a gift! Answering these calls is, of course, totally optional. Anyone can tell when an unknown number is dialing. Most people don't answer these calls, and for good reasons. But if you ever find yourself hanging out with me when one of those calls comes in, let me answer for you. Or, better yet, answer it yourself and see where your imagination takes you. It isn't just an unsolicited call you are receiving; it's the universe whispering in your ear, "Permission granted, dear."

I get that a portion of these calls represent someone's job and that everybody must make a living somehow, but every job has risks. Firemen run into burning buildings, chefs slice off their fingertips, doctors get sued by the families of dead patients, and telemarketers must deal with me – the dumbest person they will ever reach. I approach this pursuit free from guilt - these bastards called me, and as far as I'm concerned, they're asking for it!

I've tried many tactics - being unusually aggressive, speaking with a fake accent, or pretending to be distracted by other things in the room. "Damnit, Billy, I said get out of the refrigerator! You could die in there! Sorry, you were saying ... " These methods, while fun, lacked something I couldn't quite put my finger on. Then I remembered my poor victims, back when I played the villain, the good-natured dimwits who took me seriously! But I've found playing a nearly cartoonish fool is the most surefire way to get a reaction. I've been hung up on and angrily abandoned by these would-be solicitors more times than I can count. I've listened carefully, with resounding cheer in my heart, to the crumbling façade of a telemarketer's politic as it falls to pieces under the terrible weight of my ignoramus thickness. I haven't had anyone swear at me yet, but there is hope.

I started off this story with an example of a recent call where I played an affable half-wit. Unfortunately for me, that role is entirely too easy for me to play, and it isn't difficult to create an atmosphere of chaos and confusion. It just unfolds naturally. Regrettably, in that call, Tom kept his cool and calmly hung up before I could really get into it. Maybe on the next one I'll get to explore the true depths of my character.

So, the next time an odd number shows up on your phone, don't just block it or ignore it. Answer and give your creativity a spin. Pick a character and go for it. Obviously, I don't recommend giving out any personal details, and be sure not to get so lost in your role that you accidentally buy a timeshare or donate any money. Remember, not all young pranksters find their way back into the fold - some of them have grown into soulless, vampiric scam artists and assholes. What a shame they never learned to harness their powers for good.

# Why The Long Face?

'I hate everyone just a little less than I hate myself.' It's hard to reconcile this statement coming from my mouth, but it has, and I meant it when I said it. I do not feel that way at the moment, so now is a good time to think about what causes me to embody this grim attitude because that is where depression takes me when it takes me. The first time I heard someone say, "I love myself," it made me wonder - 'Do I love myself?' Even when I'm not languishing in depression's grip, the closest I come to "Self-Love" is complicated at best.

Much has been written about depression. Academics, poets, drunks, weirdos, and writers of every stripe have had quite a bit to say about the phenomenon. Some have written about it indirectly, leaving their prose sticky with a sadness whose origin not everyone will recognize. Others have told us about it directly in plain, clinical terms, while others have done so in starry-eyed, mystical ones; each offering various prescriptive measures for dealing with it. For our purposes now, I'd just like to describe it. You can draw your own conclusions. And to be sure, I don't have the slightest clue about a remedy; time has been the only influence to which my depression has ever responded. Obviously, there's little to do if you're counting on the ticking of a clock to save you.

Let's start with the sensation of depression as I've experienced it. The first time I recognized something was wrong I was about to graduate from high school. Family members from out of town were there, and my girlfriend and I had plans to drive to Florida for some time on the beach with friends. I had my own car, a job, and an apartment in the city with my older sister when I returned from my trip. On the surface, I had absolutely no tangible reason to be sour. The world was my oyster, and I like oysters.

A few days before graduation, I noticed I felt awful. I didn't know why, but a terrible sadness was growing in my chest, along with a strange dislike for the chest in question. I couldn't pin it down. Almost like I had woken up in an enemy's dream and saw myself through the eyes of someone with good reason to dislike me. It was sad, for sure, like a loss, but not of a thing or a person; it was more like I'd lost one of my senses or a limb. Something elemental, essential to the whole, badly needed and deeply missed, was suddenly gone. I've felt similar sensations when looking for a lost dog or coming home to a burglarized house. That desperate moment when "where the hell are you?" kicks in and settles in my stomach like a stone at the bottom of a lake. And that was just the beginning.

I found I was growing irritable. Tiny things were pissing me off. A little sister's annoying behavior, usually a premise for creative teasing, made me want to get out of the house. My sweet girlfriend's voice made me angry. My mom's reasonable questions made me want to yell, and God forbid I dropped something or fumbled with an object; it was enough to make me want to destroy it right there with my bare hands. This was a new sensation for me. I recognized how abnormal it was but didn't know what it meant.

Rage, coated in sadness, was weighed down by an inner nature that despises conflict and longs for peace. I felt tortured and became sadder by the day. I'd never even thought about hating people as a whole and didn't think about myself in terms of love and hate, but without warning, I did, and it was awful. The bottom fell out of my ambitions – broadcast journalism, learning to write, playing music, finding some kind of career, the love I felt for my girlfriend, my desire for travel, my "future" writ large. I watched an Alka-Seltzer slowly dissolve and disappear in a glass of water and felt a little jealous, thinking to myself, *what a gift to be able to disband and vanish.*

It took about a month for my mood to swing around, making a twenty-point turn in the narrow channel of my character. I didn't talk about it with anyone. I just had to make apologies where they were necessary and excuses where apologies didn't fit. I postponed the trip with my girlfriend and took a solo drive to Kansas City, of all places. The solitude and time were both good and bad. Good for the others around me who didn't have to deal with my unpredictable mood, and bad for me in that driving at seventy miles per hour while feeling hopeless can be especially dangerous.

I've dealt with this depression, on and off, for the last twenty-five years. Sometimes it leaves me for years, sometimes it only lasts for a week, and other times it sits with me for months. It doesn't matter where I am, what I'm doing, or how things are going in the outside world.

No matter how often I try to remind myself of the suffering of other beings - children dying of cholera in Yemen or women everywhere going to bed afraid of their husbands - I can't shake the pain in my gut. I feel ashamed of my state of mind, especially considering my good fortune. This only makes shame and self-loathing more pronounced, providing good reason to dislike myself. Tall, fortunate, well-fed, and well-loved white boys shouldn't get the blues. The feedback loop of negative self-reflection is agonizing. The sense of hopelessness, one I can empathize with even when I'm feeling good, is overwhelming.

If you've never faced the cosmic pointlessness of all things, I congratulate you and hope you never do. There is something horrifyingly satiating and troubling about letting the mind settle on the carnage and futility of existence, like staring at a body on a stretcher as you drive by a car crash or digging your fingernails painfully into itchy skin. To feel it in your body, not just your mind, that every human birth, gift, or death is of no more significance than the same milestones for the microbes in the belly of a snake crushed by a hopeless man driving on a backroad, does something for a worried mind which my words will fail to convey. To then feel sad about it, rather than liberated, also amplifies the sense of self-hate as you think to your-self, *If nothing matters, why not have a good time at least?*

We are all fortunate that human beings are helpful by na-ture. Have you ever noticed that everyone in your orbit has a remedy when you have a cold, suggesting your illness comes from a lack of some pill/herb/activity? Have you ever done the same to another person? I know I have and wish I hadn't. This tendency in people does not change when it comes to giving advice about depression. "You just need to get some sun and exercise. Have you tried meditation/Prozac/yoga/ talking to someone?" I know they mean well. The fact that I hate them for it compounds my self-loathing in a complicated and self-fulfilling way. How can you explain to someone just trying to help you that they might as well suggest that you stop a cold by hitting it with a hammer? I once heard a man say, "A headache is not caused by a lack of Aspirin." The same may be true of despair – it's not caused by a lack of great shit.

So far, I've managed not to harm myself or anyone else, at least not physically, in the quarter century of battling this neb-ulous issue. To be clear, I've never even thought about hurting someone else, and my thoughts of self-harm are more along the dissolve and vanish plane than the mutilate and destroy variety. With years of experience, I can feel it coming before the full dose kicks in. I know roughly what to do. Fortunately, my wife also knows how to handle it and gives me a wide berth with plenty of judgment-free space to work it out on my own.

Like a sprained ankle needs **R**est, **I**ce, **C**ompression, and **E**levation (the RICE method), my own brand of depression needs **S**olitude, **H**ands-off-**I**solation, and **T**ime (the SHIT method). This is NOT a recommendation, and I have no solu-tions or advice for anyone suffering from depression. I'm pain-fully aware my case is highly manageable. It's mild, and I am grateful for that. I know it gets much worse for some folks, and for that, I am truly sorry. But, for whatever reason, it's bizarrely comforting to see how indiscriminate depression can be and that I'm not alone in having its attention from time to time. So, if you're reading this and prone to depression, for good or ill, remember - you're not alone.

**Love Thyself?**
I've met people who will say,
With an improbably straight face.
"I'm awesome! Of course, I love myself!"
The first time I heard someone say this,
Unsurprisingly,
It was in California.
After puzzling over it for many days,
I recognized,
The closest I've come
to California-Style Self-Love
Is having a sense
Of non-self-directed-personal-gladness
On the rare occasion
When I manage not to put
All the Popcorn
in my mouth
All at once.
So yeah, congrats.
What's not to love?

# A Moron's Mirror

A carnival barker bays at you from the entrance to a big, dumb tent. "Step right up to the moron mirror, man! Can you face it? Come one, come all! Test your will! Test your resolve! Test your Ph! It won't matter because I'm not really here, and this world is not my home!"

There are few things I like less than being treated like a moron. Well, there are quite a few things I like less than that - hitting my thumb with a hammer, getting my dick caught in a zipper, or searching desperately for something I just had in my hands, to name the first three which came to mind. The list is long, endless, really. But the point is less complicated than I'm making it. Simply put, I dislike being called or treated like a moron. So, why then write a book in which the central character is a moron and also happens to be me? Just because I find it unpleasant doesn't make it untrue. This slice of reality is one we all could chew on a bit more thoughtfully. In other words – I *am* a moron. While I'm not happy about it, I'm resigned to it for the simple fact that I'm in good company. My hope is, by sharing these stories, while hopefully being a little bit entertained, you might have forgiven yourself a bit for being a moron as well; because you most certainly have been one at least once, if not regularly. Remember, even the smartest people in the world, just like the dumbest, have affairs, burn their fingertips, and do at least one dumb thing every day.

I once attempted to purchase an antique mirror from a cranky old man at a yard sale. We met near it to discuss the price. It was early in the day, and his coffee cup still pushed up

293

a healthy steam. He stood to my right, out of the reflection, while I framed myself in full view of my own lanky image. The filigree of the frame shone reluctantly in the morning sun, as if disgusted by the nude daylight; if inanimate objects can convey resentment, this mirror surely was resentful for being exiled from the house.

He sipped his coffee, eyebrows raised, wordlessly waiting for me to tell him what the hell I wanted. Without making eye contact, pensively looking over the mirror's surface like I'd found something seriously wrong with it, I told him, 'I like it, but you gotta come down from your asking price.' With all the joy you might expect from a salted slug, he said, "And why's that?" 'Well, there's an idiot in there.' He barely blinked while not laughing at my hilarious joke and let his eyes land instead on a potential customer handling an ancient vacuum cleaner. Self-deprecating humor, it turns out, is not everyone's flavor. It's also not a great way to get a deal. That mirror is not mine.

I've told you this story just now for the same reasons I've written this book. Some of those reasons are probably obvious, while others might be less so. But ultimately, this book is meant to be more like a funhouse mirror than a one-to-one representation. I'm trying to reflect back to you an image of yourself, although distorted and curved with extra weirdness around the nostrils – metaphorically speaking, of course. While you may never have chosen to do any of the things I've chosen to do throughout my life, I'm guessing you will see something you recognize as needing understanding and forgiveness in yours. Like the way seeing your own torso, elongated or wavy, it is at once recognizable, totally incorrect, and not your fault.

So, I ask you, a bit more gently than the carnival barker, please take a moment to stand in front of this mirror. Maybe you'll get a kick out of the odd shapes and familiar colors without having to invest in them?

A reflection doesn't need much to exist.
It just needs you to be around.

# Acknowledgments

What you have just read would likely not exist if not for a single, sensitive, and thoughtful prompt from my mentor, Susannah Rigg. Thank you, Susannah, for believing in me and for being honest!

The power of the unsolicited email is not to be underestimated. One such email opened up a world of possibility for me when I reached out to Dr. Christopher Ryan. Although he and I are no longer pals, his willingness to be a guest on my podcast, then host me on his, set in motion a series of events that continue to unfold today. Through his generosity and network of curious connections, my life and this book have been enriched immeasurably.

I've got a pal in Canada, Glenn Vanderkloet. Together we produce a fake radio show called Raised By Whoops. Glenn has been a constant source of encouragement, friendship, and inspiration. Thank you, Glenn and your partner Ashley, for reading this book in stages and manuscript form. Here's to many more weird projects and more fake radio!

Thank you, Cathy Barber, for your words of wisdom and reassurance. No "Able-Man" should talk as much as I do! I'm fortunate to call you a friend.

Lala & Erik Jacobsen - you two have been beyond kind and generous to me. Most of this book was written at your house with the fabulous aromas of Lala's cooking in the air. Erik, you inspire me to pursue a creative life and be myself without compromise. I love you both.

My friend and editor Joseph O'Leary, by all rights, you should be writing your own damn book! Thank you for taking the time to read mine again and again. Reader, if you have found this book digestible, you can thank Joe. If you skipped to this paragraph specifically, you're either Joe's mother or you found the book indigestible and came here to see what apologies I offered my editor. In any case, Joe is great, and I'm glad I know him.

To my siblings. If you remember any of this differently, which I imagine you might, consider that memory is unreliable and not to be taken too seriously. Should you have crucial gripes with my telling of our shared history, I encourage you to write your own.

To my mom, I love you and am grateful to be one of yours. Thank you for guiding my ship in the general direction of sweetness and mostly away from the treacherous shoals of dickishness.

To my late father, I apologize if this book reads like a negative Yelp review of your parenting. While I hope the dead are not reading the memoirs of the living, if you are out there taking in new data, I would want you to know that I feel lucky to be your son.

I have many talented and interesting nephews and nieces. Knowing that you guys are in the world and doing good work has made the decision to keep my degenerate seed out of the gene pool much easier. I want to thank my nephew, Brendan Couch-Smith, and his younger brother, Ian. You two are some of the funniest and most creative people I know. Thank you, Brendan, for being the first person to read a draft of this work and for giving a shit. Their little sister, Ayden, said she liked the cover – that means a lot to me!

Dan Piraro, thank you for reading drafts of some of my stories and for your approval of the cover. Yours is the only opinion I can think of that would have made me abandon it.

Marie Bartz, thank you for your design help on the cover!

Lastly, and most importantly, my wife, Tiffany Couch. You have supported, tolerated, encouraged, and loved me for more than half of my life, and I love you more now than ever. Your support of this project is one of many reasons I'm the luckiest moron alive. Oh, and obviously, he doesn't read, but I'd like to thank my dog, Pelé. He has been near me for every last word.

# About the Moron

See Previous 99,700+ words

Born in Memphis, Tennessee in 1979, Andrew Couch is mostly just some guy. In what he refuses to call his career, he has held over forty entirely different occupations and has even enjoyed a few. From washing dishes in an Egyptian-owned catfish restaurant to professionally petting tipsy women in California, Couch has rarely known a dull moment. He seeks fulfillment as a traveler, a chronicler, an observer, and a pal of the weird and easily overlooked. You could call him a champion of the mundane or a conduit between those who like stories and the events which give birth to them, but he'll settle for being called Couch.

Learn more or contact Couch @ www.MoronBook.com

Made in the USA
Coppell, TX
30 August 2023

20984601R00173